Corpus Linguistics for Language Learning Research

Research Methods in Applied Linguistics (RMAL)

ISSN 2590-096X

The *Research Methods in Applied Linguistics* (RMAL) series publishes authoritative general guides and in-depth explorations of central research methodology concerns in the entire field of Applied Linguistics. The hallmark of the series is the contribution to stimulating and advancing professional methodological debates in the domain. Books published in the series (both authored and edited volumes) will be key resources for applied linguists (including established researchers and newcomers to the field) and an invaluable source for research methodology courses.

Main directions for the volumes in the series include (but are not limited to): Comprehensive introductions to research methods in Applied Linguistics (authoritative, introductions to domain-non specific methodologies); In-depth explorations of central methodological considerations and developments in specific areas of Applied Linguistics (authoritative treatments of domain-specific methodologies); Critical analyses that develop, expand, or challenge existing and/or novel methodological frameworks; In-depth reflections on central considerations in employing specific methodologies and/or addressing specific questions and problems in Applied Linguistics research; Authoritative accounts that foster improved understandings of the behind the scenes, inside story of the research process in Applied Linguistics.

For an overview of all books published in this series, please see *benjamins.com/catalog/rmal*

Volume 12

Corpus Linguistics for Language Learning Research
by Pascual Pérez-Paredes, Geraldine Mark and Anne O'Keeffe

Corpus Linguistics for Language Learning Research

Pascual Pérez-Paredes
University of Murcia

Geraldine Mark
MIC, University of Limerick

Anne O'Keeffe
MIC, University of Limerick

John Benjamins Publishing Company

Amsterdam / Philadelphia

TM The paper used in this publication meets the minimum requirements of the American National Standard for Information Sciences – Permanence of Paper for Printed Library Materials, ANSI z39.48-1984.

DOI 10.1075/rmal.12

Cataloging-in-Publication Data available from Library of Congress:
LCCN 2025003865 (PRINT) / 2025003866 (E-BOOK)

ISBN 978 90 272 2027 1 (HB)
ISBN 978 90 272 2018 9 (PB)
ISBN 978 90 272 4487 1 (E-BOOK)

John Benjamins Publishing Company · https://benjamins.com

Table of contents

Acknowledgements   IX

Foreword   XI

Introduction: Aims and structure of the book   1

**PART 1. Corpus Linguistics for language learning research:
Global considerations**

CHAPTER 1. Key concepts   8
1.1   Frequency, contrast, and representativeness   9
1.2   Corpus linguistics: Not just word frequency   12
1.3   Corpus linguistics and language learning research: L2 learning
       and teaching   13
1.4   Summary   14

CHAPTER 2. The basics: Key functions of using a corpus   15
2.1   Corpus functions and tools: Word and phrase lists   15
       2.1.1   Creating word and phrase lists   16
       2.1.2   Comparing word and phrase lists   19
       2.1.3   Comparing word and phrase lists: Normalisation   20
       2.1.4   Lists of multi-word units   21
2.2   Corpus functions and tools: Using concordances   25
2.3   Corpus functions and tools: Keywords   29
2.4   Summary   30

CHAPTER 3. Corpus types and research perspectives   31
3.1   Types of learner corpora   32
       3.1.1   Examples of learner corpora   34
       3.1.2   Corpus metadata   36
3.2   A contrastive perspective   38
       3.2.1   Background   38
       3.2.2   Examples of contrastive studies   40
       3.2.3   Contrastive Interlanguage Analysis (CIA) revisited   41
3.3   Developmental perspective   42
       3.3.1   Background   42
       3.3.2   Examples of developmental studies   42

3.4   Corpus-pedagogy and language learning   45
3.5   Designing and building a learner corpus   46
    3.5.1   Creating a design matrix   48
    3.5.2   Building a corpus: An example of the ACE Corpus   49
    3.5.3   Collection, transcription and annotation   50
3.6   Summary   52

PART 2. Units of analysis in learner language research

CHAPTER 4. Researching word classes using corpora and POS tagging   56
4.1   Early learner corpus research: The International Corpus
    of Learner English   58
4.2   Part-of-speech (POS) tagging, tagsets and learner corpora   61
    4.2.1   Examples of POS tagging   62
    4.2.2   Understanding different tagsets   63
    4.2.3   Trialling POS tagging   64
    4.2.4   Learner errors and tagging errors   68
4.3   Researching word classes   69
    4.3.1   Looking at word classes: Applying a contrastive perspective   70
    4.3.2   Study 1. An analysis of the pronoun *I* in two corpora   74
    4.3.3   Study 2. Pronouns in subject positions and transfer effects   76
4.4   How to POS tag a corpus   80
    4.4.1   Tagging a corpus using *TagAnt*   80
    4.4.2   Tagging a corpus using *Sketch Engine*   82
4.5   Summary   84

CHAPTER 5. Researching phraseology: Collocations   85
5.1   A phraseological approach in learner corpus research   86
5.2   Introducing collocation analysis   88
5.3   Collocation analysis: Representative studies   92
    5.3.1   Durrant & Schmitt (2009): Using frequency and collocation
    strength measures   93
    5.3.2   Kreyer (2021): Studying collocations using a longitudinal
    research design   94
    5.3.3   Wang (2016): Delexical verbs + noun collocations in L1
    and L2 corpora   97
5.4   Summary   99

CHAPTER 6. Researching grammatical patterning   100
6.1   Colligation   101
    6.1.1   Colligation in learner language: Signalling nouns   102

6.1.2   Colligation in EFL textbooks: Exploring priming effects
        in L2 input   106
6.2   Collostructions   107
6.3   Verb-argument constructions in learner language   110
6.4   Summary   114

PART 3.   Researching corpus applications in language learning and teaching

CHAPTER 7.   Researching indirect uses of corpora for language teaching
and learning   116
7.1   Corpora and dictionaries   117
7.2   Corpora and grammars   120
        7.2.1   Study 1: *There is, there's* and *there are: English Grammar Today*
                (Carter et al., 2011)   122
        7.2.2   Study 2 linking adverbs and register: *The Longman Grammar
                of Spoken and Written English* (Biber et al., 1999)   124
        7.2.3   Study 3. Investigating learner patterns within a register:
                Academic writing   127
7.3   Corpus-based tools to analyse learner writing and texts   130
        7.3.1   *Compleat Lexical Tutor*   131
        7.3.2   English Profile frameworks: *English Vocabulary Profile* and *English
                Grammar Profile*   137
        7.3.3   *Text Inspector*   140
        7.3.4   *Tool for the Automatic Analysis of Lexical Sophistication*
                (TAALES)   144
7.4   Exploring the aboutness of texts and corpora: Keyword analysis   145
7.5   Summary   146

CHAPTER 8.   Researching direct uses of corpora for language teaching
and learning   148
8.1   What does DDL look like in practice?   150
8.2   How has DDL been researched?   154
8.3   Research into DDL through meta-analysis and meta-studies   166
8.4   Towards an enhanced research agenda for DDL: Linking with SLA   170
        8.4.1   DDL and its associative links to constructivism   171
        8.4.2   DDL and links to sociocultural theory   172
        8.4.3   DDL and SLA   174
8.5   Summary   178

Coda   180
    Corpus linguistics, SLA studies and learner corpus research:
        Some challenges   180
    Corpora in language learning and teaching   183
    Corpus linguistics and ethical research practice   184
    The future   185

References   187

Index   205

Acknowledgements

This book attempts to bring corpus linguistics (CL) research methods to the study of language learning. Our goal is to showcase the opportunities of CL tools and methods for those interested in examining different language learning contexts, language acquisition and development through real samples of language. Many researchers have gone before us and We also wish to acknowledge the feedback that we have received from Prof. Rosa Manchón as Series Editor. We are also very grateful to Prof. Michael McCarthy for his generous foreword, to Prof. Laurence Anthony and Prof. Mark Davies for providing the sophisticated corpus tools we've used in this book, and to Dr Justin McNamara for permission to use the ACE corpus. We thank Jeremy and Gretchen for their humour. We would also like to thank our families for their love and support: Nani Tornero, Alicia and Arturo Pérez Tornero, Bernard, Rory and Niamh Payne, Ger and Jack Downes.

Foreword

One of the enduring problems with terms such as *language learning, language acquisition* and *language pedagogy* is that they all allow for a wide and ofttimes slippery range of interpretation. For some, language *learning* and language *acquisition* overlap or are even synonymous; for others, they are opposing or at best complementary notions. Language *pedagogy*, for some, is centred on the interaction between teachers and language learners in classrooms; for others it sweeps everything into a ragbag of issues pertaining to materials, methods, motivation, cognitive demands, assessment, technology, teacher education, curriculum design and language planning.

Then there is *corpus linguistics* and its more recent offspring, the study of *learner corpora*. These too are broad churches. Corpus linguistics can cover anything from number-crunching on datasets to give statistical underpinning to descriptive statements, to patient but wearisome poring over concordances and drilling down into individual texts in an attempt to tease out contextual meaning and function in the data. Learner corpora can be snapshots of populations or of individuals, or data collected over time; they may be made up of student writing in informal contexts or as assessment tasks, or spoken data recorded in similar environments. Meanwhile, data-driven learning (DDL) has brought learners into direct contact with corpora and some of the less technologically demanding procedures of corpus linguistics. More recently, artificial intelligence and the large language models that fuel it have entered the territory of language pedagogy in the form of chatbots and automated feedback and assessment. Machine learning has rendered the entirety of human knowledge as a potential corpus, one which feeds the hungry maw of the machine rather than serving as material for human analysts.

Given this vastly diverse disciplinary landscape, who but the bravest, would take on the task of writing a book with the title *Corpus Linguistics for Language Learning Research*? In the hands of a veteran scholar whose purview was not restricted by the exigencies of university research rankings, it might be a calmy executed *magnum opus* nurtured over many years. On the other hand, given the right team of highly experienced scholars, the enterprise might flourish and bear fruit in a timely way, in that unique fashioning of extra insight that close collaboration can capture.

The three scholars who have worked together to produce this book can lay claim to being a perfect team to write the comprehensive and thoroughly detailed text that their collaboration over a number of years has made possible. Pascual Pérez-Paredes, Geraldine Mark and Anne O'Keeffe bring different but overlapping perspectives to bear on the complex relationships between language learners and learning (from synchronic and diachronic perspectives), various types of corpora (learner corpora among them), different techniques of corpus analysis (quantitative and qualitative), technology in language learning (e.g. DDL, mobile learning) and very practical questions of language teaching.

Navigating a disciplinary landscape where, for many years, it seemed that second language acquisition (SLA) researchers and corpus linguists spent little time talking to one another might seem to be a territory fraught with massive challenges — inhabited by dragons perhaps. However, the authors of this book manage to show, in a non-mystifying way, that recent developments in SLA theory, in particular usage-based theories of acquisition, can speak directly to corpus linguists and allow for empirically supported observations of the emergent interlanguages of learners, both in terms of large populations studied at a fixed moment in time or in fine-grained records of the trajectories of individual learners observed over time. Both SLA and learner corpora studies benefit enormously from such conceptual proximity. This recent example of cross-disciplinarity takes us a long way from the days of morpheme acquisition experiments, claims about universal orders of acquisition, early contrastive analysis (based on comparing languages rather than how learners use them) and bland statements about interlanguage lacking robust empirical support. Equally, developments in spoken corpus compilation and the analysis of variety and variation, made possible by greater access to spoken data, have meant that learner corpora studies have been able to move away from simple error analysis, deficit notions such as underuse, or proximity/distance from native-speaker targets towards a more sensitive and socio-pragmatic understanding of how learners approach and use the L2.

Research by the authors of this book into grammatical acquisition is a good case in point: The emergence of certain grammatical items in the output of learners as they progress through graded systems such as the CEFR tells us little on its own. What is far more illuminating is the evolution of pragmatic competence that the increasingly complex choice of grammatical items reveals in the learners. This is no small issue. The CEFR has struggled for years with the problem of sufficient discrimination between the upper levels of the system to make them practically useful. A corpus-analytical approach that brings pragmatic competence into the picture can make a major contribution to such unresolved dilemmas.

The real value of the present book, however, rests not only in its clear grasp of SLA theory, corpus linguistics and language pedagogy which the many years of experience racked up by the authors bring to the table. It is also, and perhaps more importantly, marked by their ability to link the disparate disciplinary perspectives in a coherent, reader-friendly and immensely practical textbook which is designed not for corpus linguistics (a population well-served by introductory texts and practical manuals) but for the very people who might best benefit from the insights generated by the interweaving of SLA theories and learner corpora studies, graduate students of Applied Linguistics struggling to conceptualise some kind of unity in their chosen discipline, along with language teachers who similarly seek common threads across the paradigms of their profession.

When I began, in the early 1980s, to be interested in the possible benefits of corpus linguistics to English language teaching, learner corpora were in their infancy and SLA investigators and corpus linguists dwelt in separate stratospheres. It is to the huge credit of Pérez-Paredes, Mark and O'Keeffe that they can demonstrate that this need not be the case and that both disciplinary groups have a lot to say to each other. Would that I had had this book in my hands in 1984; I would have saved myself years of entanglement in a jungle of theories, terms, techniques and ideas.

Michael McCarthy
Cambridge, October 2024

Michael McCarthy is Emeritus Professor of Applied Linguistics in the School of English, University of Nottingham, UK. He holds/has held Visiting Professorships at the University of Limerick, Ireland, Newcastle University, UK, and Penn State University, USA. He is an Honorary Professor of the University of Valencia, Spain. He has been involved in the study and teaching of English for more than 50 years. For the last 30 years, he has worked with large, computerised corpora of English texts, investigating them to establish how the vocabulary and grammar of English are really used at the present time and how they are evolving and changing. His research has focused on everyday spoken English.

He is author of 58 books and 120 academic papers dealing with research and teaching of the English language, especially as a second or foreign language. He has taught in the UK, the Netherlands, Spain, Sweden and Malaysia. He currently teaches EAP part-time at Cambridge University. He is a Fellow of the Royal Society of Arts.

Introduction
Aims and structure of the book

This is a book about how we can increase our understanding of language learning by using corpus linguistics (CL) methods. It is about how we empirically use large bodies of language data (known as corpora, or the singular, corpus) to gain insights into language learning, both as a product and a process. The book seeks to introduce readers to corpus linguistics data, tools and methods, and to the exciting possibilities that these data, tools and methods offer for the study of language learning.

This book has been written for graduate students and researchers in areas such as Applied Linguistics, Second Language Acquisition (SLA), Teaching English to Speakers of Other Languages (TESOL) and language teaching in general who are new to CL and who seek to gain a deeper understanding of how CL can inform their research. To this end we have adopted an approach that will allow readers to progressively acquire the basic concepts for the autonomous analysis of language corpora in language learning research contexts. To contextualise the use of CL, in places we offer a historical overview, sometimes a critique of the development of practices in corpus linguistics that need to be understood as part of the emergence and evolution of the discipline across the last four decades. If the reader is already familiar with corpus linguistics, or has received formal training in this area, they might already have an understanding of some of the topics covered in the book. However, they may discover applications and insights that can inform further uses of corpus linguistics methods in relation to language learning.

This book looks at how use of CL can inform language learning perspectives such as contrastive analysis (CA) of learner language, learners' L2 acquisition, as well as corpus-informed pedagogy. These perspectives are, in turn, informed by a range of concepts that are central to the use of corpus methods, which will be dealt with in Chapter 1.

We use the term *corpus methods* to refer to the methods that, originally pertaining to the field of computational linguistics, have become widely used by corpus linguists to extract and analyse corpus data (McEnery & Hardie, 2011). In the context of the present book, we follow Gries (2022) and Pérez-Paredes and Curry (2025), who distinguish between central and peripheral corpus methods. Central corpus methods are integrated into the most commonly utilised corpus analysis tools, such as *AntConc* (Anthony, 2024) and *Sketch Engine* (Kilgarriff et al., 2014). According to Gries (2022), central methods are corpus-specific statistical techniques that involve quantitative analyses through statistical testing. Some of these central methods are frequency analysis, concordance analysis, collocation analysis, colligations analysis and keyword analysis. In contrast, when we refer to peripheral corpus methods we mean advanced statistical methods not typically available in standard corpus analysis software, such as regression and exploratory techniques (Gries, 2022). These advanced methods are frequently disseminated among researchers as reusable R scripts or Python scripts for application in various studies (Desagulier, 2017). Although the emphasis is on central methods, peripheral methods are also discussed in some of the chapters. In the book, we similarly demonstrate how tools facilitating quantitative analyses provide a springboard for close engagement with corpus data through qualitative approaches.

Corpora and corpus applications are not new, of course, but they have never been more available and accessible. Years of insights have already accrued on language learning, primarily as a product or output, based on corpus research, as we shall discuss in this book, and this has widely informed language learning, classroom and reference materials development, and language testing materials, among other areas. Additionally we have increased our understanding of how learners use certain features of language, in differing contexts, and how a range of variables (e.g. first language, proficiency level, task type) might be impacting on this use, for example by comparing large bodies of data, one with another. (Gilquin et al., 2008; Osborne, 2015; Tono et al., 2012). We can say the research that has helped to increase our understanding of language as a product is situated primarily in traditional CL theory and praxis (Sinclair, 1991; Granger, 1996, 2015, 2024),

However, there has not been a similar concomitant growth in the use of corpus linguistic tools to investigate the *process* of language learning and language development, which frames its inquiry within SLA theories and agendas, seeking to understand *how* second or foreign languages are learnt by young adults or adults that have already mastered at least one mother tongue (The Douglas Fir Group, 2016). Mitchell (2021) suggests that, although L1 corpora and learner corpora can have direct pegadogical applications, it is also true that there is a "theory-related gap [...] between ISLA researchers and those who adopt corpus-based practices in the language classroom" (Mitchell, 2021, p.257). As McEnery et al. (2019) pointed out, CL provides many opportunities for the study of second language development, including access to large databases of spoken and written language forms; an openness in terms of sharing and replicating results that can reduce effort in data collection, and a scale of analysis that gives robustness and confidence when looking at language patterns across many speakers and contexts.

Learner corpora have been largely examined through tasks that represent pedagogical tasks "in the context of the language learning classroom" (Gilquin, 2015, p.10). However, McEnery et al. (2019) have argued that the research output in learner corpus research (LCR) has focused on language output that "can tell us relatively little … about the processes behind language learning and production" (McEnery et al., 2019, p.76).

A widely-accepted top-down approach in corpus-based learner language research involves the selection and examination of the contexts of use of a set of linguistic features. For example. Gablasova et al. (2017) have explored the use the pragmatic marker *I think*, adjectival phrases modified by an adverb as a syntactic feature (ADV+ADJ), simple past tenses as a morphological feature or the passive construction as a syntactic/stylistic feature in corpora. These researchers show evidence of how both L1 and L2 corpora provide information about the range of interspeaker variation and how this may inform *how* language is acquired by individual speakers or groups of speakers (Gablasova et al., 2017). As we shall discuss throughout the book, there are many great further examples of work in this area that focus on learner language output that we can build on, but our main motivation in writing this book is that we too feel there is so much more that CL can bring to our understanding of language learning, especially when used more strategically through an enhanced theoretical lens. Therefore, in this book, we aim to provide examples, knowhow, skills and insights that can facilitate the use of corpora and CL tools in deepening current understandings of language learning in a second language context and equip readers with the skills to build on current insights.

This book explains the key considerations around the collection of data. It underlines the importance of rigorous corpus design and the notion of representativeness of data. It demonstrates how learner output, both spoken and written, first needs to be carefully curated if it is to be useable as a corpus (or as part of one). In order to prepare learner data for CL methods, for example, there are also important processes required for tagging and annotating the data. Essentially, just because a group of students have produced a body of texts, in spoken or written form, does not automatically make them a corpus. The rigour of building a corpus and making a corpus representative will be discussed in Chapters 1 and 3. We cover several crucial standards and procedures that a researcher needs to be aware of when preparing a dataset of learner output so as to form a corpus on which CL approaches and methods can be applied. Once a corpus is formed, the analysis needs to be mindful of the core processes and quantitative measures that are used in CL approaches.

In terms of terminology related to the language learner and learning, we have tried to avoid the use of terms such as *native speaker* and *non-native speaker*. Previous research in learner corpus research has extensively used these to refer to users of a given language. We prefer, whenever possible, to use *L1* and *L2 users* or, in the case of the latter, L2 *learners*. However, we are aware that the term *learner* is often misleading as most of the engagement with corpus data implies individuals who may or may not be, strictly speaking, language learners at the time of the data collection, i.e. engaged in any formal language instruction. The term is problematic and our use in the context of the book does not imply any kind of imposition on the status of the individual in question or a value judgement on the quality or level of their L2.

The term *learner language* has come to be used by the CL community to designate an area that explores a body of learners' texts through the compilation of corpora as well as the use of corpus research methods. It is therefore a broad term that, depending on the researchers, may stand either for textual evidence of learners' output (written or spoken), or for learner corpora and learner corpus research in general. The widespread use of *learner language* is utilised in this book to engage with research that has examined language outputs. More often than not because of the nature of data collection, the language outputs tend to come from instructed learning contexts, some of which are produced by learners under the contrastive interlanguage analysis (CIA) framework (Granger, 2015, 2024). See Chapter 3 for a more detailed account of CIA.

The use of the term *language learning* in this book is a broad one. We take an inclusive perspective that acknowledges the variety and the complexities of many converging areas of research such as SLA, CL, Learner Corpus Research (LCR) and corpus-based language teaching when outlining what constitutes language learning. Our perspective encompasses language learners, teachers and researchers worldwide, and extends to various research communities in areas such as second language acquisition (SLA), learner corpus research (LCR), language teaching or the development of materials for the language classroom.

Following this Introduction, this book is divided into three parts comprising eight chapters. Part 1, Corpus Linguistics for Language Learning Research, includes Chapters 1, 2 and 3. Chapter 1 provides a short, basic introduction to key concepts of frequency, contrast and representativeness, all of which are central in applying a CL approach to language learning research. Chapter 2 looks at the key functions of corpora and corpus tools, such as wordlists, key words, n-grams and concordances, all of which contribute to the basic knowledge required to use corpus linguistics methods. Chapter 3 looks at types of learner data and at the differing research perspectives that are central to the contributions of CL to language learning research.

In Part 2, Chapters 4, 5 and 6, Units of Analysis in Language Learning Research, we explore how different corpus methods and techniques (such as frequency analysis, collocation and collustruction analyses, POS tagging, examination of concordance lines, among others) have been used in league with corpora to advance our understanding of learner language. Chapter 4 surveys some of the research that has examined parts of speech in L2 and describes in detail how POS tagging can be used by researchers. Chapter 5 showcases how different phraseological units can be analysed through collocation analysis and Chapter 6 discusses methods to analyse grammatical patterning through colligation, collostructions and constructions in L2.

In Part 3, Researching Corpus Applications in Language Teaching, Chapters 7 and 8 discuss indirect and direct applications of corpora for language teaching. These two chapters reflect the fact that the impact on language teaching plays an integral role in we way we conceptualise the use of corpora for language learning. Some of the methods and practices that have been used by corpus linguists to inform L2 materials design and pedagogies are covered in Chapter 7, while Chapter 8 explores research on other applications of CL in the classroom such as data-driven learning (DDL).

Throughout the following chapters, we have adopted a hands-on perspective that seeks to guide the readers in their process to understand the scope of corpus linguistics in language learning research and the specific methods and tools needed to carry out their own research.

We hope that, by the end of the book, readers will have acquired a good understanding of *how-to-use* corpus methods and *what* they can do for their research.

Throughout the book we have recommended relevant further reading. Readers will find these in each chapter under the heading *Recommended reading*. They will also find this icon $\mathcal{O}$ which highlights some key elements for consideration under the heading *Focus*.

PART 1

Corpus linguistics
for language learning research
Global considerations

CHAPTER 1

Key concepts

This chapter offers an introduction to key concepts in corpus linguistics, including frequency, contrast and representativeness. While the concepts will be widely discussed in the book, the present chapter provides a background to some of the defining characteristics behind the research methods considered.

Corpus linguistics involves the study of real spoken or written language samples using specialised software. The term 'corpus linguistics' was not coined until the early 1980s (Aarts & Meijs, 1984; McEnery et al., 2006) but the notion of looking at a corpus of texts dates to the 13th century when biblical scholars combed line-by-line and page-by-page through the Christian Bible to manually index its words (see O'Keeffe & McCarthy, 2022). This endeavour arose out of a practical need to specify, for other biblical scholars, in alphabetical arrangement, the words contained in the bible, along with citations of where and in what passages they occurred (McCarthy & O'Keeffe, 2010). Nowadays, the toil of 500 monks can equate to nanoseconds of computing when searching and indexing electronic texts. In the last decade alone, at the time of writing, corpus interfaces such as *Sketch Engine* (Kilgarriff et al., 2014) and the *English-Corpora.org* (formerly known as *BYU Corpora,* curated by Mark Davies) store multi-billion-word corpora. For instance, *Sketch Engine* contains over 500 corpora across 95 languages (Kilgarriff et al., 2014). As we write this book, the newest 2023 version of the Sketch Engine Spanish web corpus provides 29 billion words across 19 varieties of Spanish and 20 annotated topics from games to science. The *English-Corpora.org* interface contains multi-million and multi-billion-word corpora of contemporary and historical English, as well as specialised collections such as The TV Corpus (325 million words); The Movie Corpus (200 million words); the Corpus of American Soap Operas (100 million words). As O'Keeffe and McCarthy (2022) point out, in the last decade, the limitations on corpus size have been obviated by the capacity to store vast amounts of data in the Cloud but it has also seen the honing of artificial intelligence tools to automatically gather data according to defined curation parameters, thus leading to big data collections that can be rapidly assembled and expanded over time. It has never been easier for a researcher to access corpora, usually free of charge. A researcher who is interested in using corpora to investigate language learning will find many useful resources available to them. It is reassuring to remember that while there are now several corpus tools available, the core functionality which we discuss in subsequent chapters is generally similar.

1.1   Frequency, contrast, and representativeness

CL is both a field with a huge potential to describe and understand linguistic phenomena and a research methodological approach that uses comparison as its cornerstone. CL examines textual evidence in collections of texts to gain insight into the linguistic variation found in corpora representative of different types of texts, tasks, or speakers. Let us examine how the three concepts of frequency, contrast and representativeness cooperate in linguistic analyses of language use. A defining feature of CL methodology is its empirical foundation, using extensive collections of naturally occurring language data to study patterns and uses across diverse contexts. This approach values statistical analysis and frequency data, which allows for insights into language use that are more representative and comprehensive than anecdotal examples alone. The methodology often emphasizes objectivity by quantifying linguistic data, although it acknowledges the role of interpretative subjectivity, especially in areas like discourse studies or translation research (Pérez-Paredes & Curry, 2024, 2025).

Core to CL is the study of how the *frequencies* of selected linguistic features, dispersion of such frequencies and co-occurrence of such frequencies cooperate to help us understand language use (see Chapter 2). According to Stubbs (2007), CL is based on two empirical principles: (1) the observer must not influence what is observed; (2) repeated events are significant. Frequency data helps linguists make inferences about typical or unusual patterns and how language structures and vocabulary are distributed across contexts (Pérez-Paredes & Curry, 2024; Szudarski, 2017). *Contrast* and *comparison* of observed frequencies are at the heart of our understanding of how variation operates in language by assuming that different registers (e.g. telephone conversation, university lectures) perform different functions across a variety of situations. This comparative approach enhances understanding of how language varies based on factors like the L1 of the speaker, L2 proficiency, or medium, making it a powerful tool for studying language use, evolution, style, or, among others, discourse. Frequency enables comparisons between texts or language samples, facilitating the analysis of linguistic variation and helping linguists identify significant or recurring features of language use, which might be linked to social, educational, or, among others, psychological phenomena.

Research has shown that distinctive distributions of frequencies of linguistic features (e.g. present tense, third person singular pronoun, relative clauses, nominalizations) explain the singular functions of registers (Biber, 1988, 2019; Biber & Conrad, 2009). For example, in the context of a university, e-mails serve a different purpose than, for instance, the set readings of a given subject. The frequencies and the distribution of linguistic features across these texts and registers are, in turn, affected by situational communication characteristics such as the role of the speakers or the medium of communication. Figure 1.1 shows a *comparison* of the frequency per 1,000 words of some of the most common word classes across three registers in university settings: conversations, e-mails and academic prose.

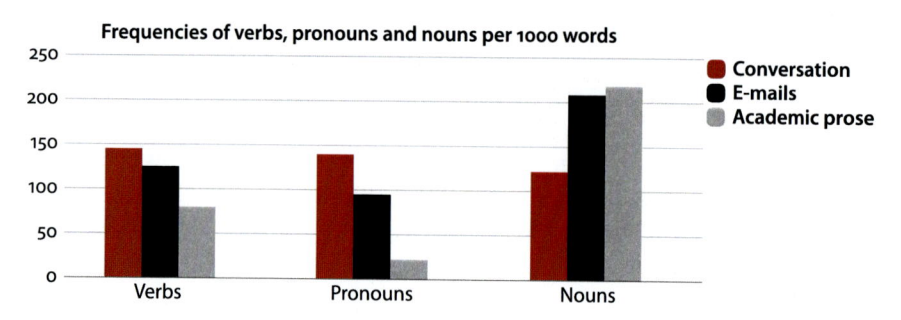

Figure 1.1 Frequency of word classes in 3 registers from Biber and Conrad (2009, p.182)

Figure 1.1 shows that, while verbs are moderately common in conversation and e-mails, they are not comparatively frequent in academic prose (80,000 verbs per 1 million words). In CL research, the frequency of a linguistic item is a first port for further analysis. Given the frequency of verbs in Figure 1.1, it can be hypothesised that in e-mails we would find a high presence of clauses, whereas densely packed writing would include elaborated noun phrases, with frequent attributive adjectives and prepositional phrases. The frequency with which linguistic items occur shapes our engagement with communication and language. Exposure and engagement with frequencies determine how humans form and develop language-related categories out of experience. Frequency matters because, for many researchers in CL, it is the organising principle of language use. Bybee (2007) has noted that humans are sensitive to both prototypical linguistic structures as well as to individual patterns. This combination of foci explains how humans are able to both generalise and come up with 'original' language, and remember and reuse prefabricated, off-the-shelf language chunks.

Frequency is consequently a useful concept that mediates our understanding of how language variation operates across a range of variables. In CL, frequency comparisons have been used in the study of language use across the lexical, syntactic, morphological, and pragmatic levels. In its application to learner language (see introduction), Gablasova et al. (2017) have highlighted that information about the frequency of the occurrence or co-occurrence of a unit or sets of units in learner language (from words to formulaic sequences) can help us uncover linguistic patterns that point to underlying factors in second language acquisition (SLA). According to these authors, the frequency of selected linguistic features can reveal the state of L2 users' interlanguage and is a first step in the study of what motivates the use (or avoidance) of these features in their language (Gablasova et al., p. 135).

While the frequency of a word or a phrase may be relevant in CL, the distribution of the observed frequencies in a corpus is crucial. Deshors and Gries (2020) have noted that L2 corpus researchers rely on the distributional hypothesis, that is, the notion that the distribution of words and constructions on their own reveals something about their functions and/or processing characteristics and, potentially, the minds of the speakers whose language production is studied. In language teaching, frequency data facilitates the use of authentic language examples in teaching materials, which can help learners engage with the language as it is actually used, rather than relying solely on textbook examples (Curry et al., 2025).

The unwavering role of frequency in CL is not necessarily considered relevant in other areas of language learning research. This is largely due to two reasons. First, historically most language learning research has not necessarily been interested in the sole examination of naturally occurring language data to derive insight into the nature of language learning. Second, the use of language data in SLA has not necessarily entailed the use of corpora. Dörnyei's (2007) classification of the types of data in applied linguistics research includes no discussion of corpus data. This initial lack of attention to corpora may have contributed to some of the invisibility of corpus linguistics methods in mainstream SLA in the past. However, the tide may be turning. Researchers such as Mackey and Gass (2022) acknowledge that learner corpora are increasingly popular in SLA research and chapters on learner corpora such as Paquot and Tracy-Ventura's (2023) are included in recent guides to SLA research (Mackey & Gass, 2023).

A third relevant concept in CL is the notion of *representativeness*, which has been a central topic in the design of corpora, predominantly in the field of linguistics (O'Keeffe & McCarthy, 2022; Sinclair, 1991). Hunston (2022) has suggested that representative corpora such as the British National Corpus (BNC) can be used to "establish norms of frequency and usage against which individual texts can be measured" (Hunston, 2022, p. 14). This is an excellent instance of the assumed epistemology which also infuses L2 corpus research: objectivist epistemology (Gray, 2018). This view holds that there is an objective reality out there. Research therefore sets out to discover this objective truth. CL has devoted much attention to developing methods to ensure that the texts that make up a corpus are *representative* of the linguistic variety under analysis. So, what does the frequency of a word or a formulaic sequence tell us about the language of a given group of speakers or individual speakers? If a corpus is representative of a given variety of use, the frequencies of the linguistic items or phenomena under analysis may reveal how a group of users (e.g. speakers of a given language) or specific texts (e.g. tourist leaflets as in Baker (2006)) use such discrete features in attested uses of the language. In learner corpus research, the combination of the above-mentioned concepts has provided improved descriptions of learner language (Granger, 2002). Particularly, CIA methodology (Granger, 1994, 1996, 2002, 2015) has used corpora in the past to compare, on the one hand, learner language (L2) with native speaker language (L1) and, on the other, learner language corpora of speakers of different L1s (see the introduction for terminology in this book). In sum, frequency, contrast and representativeness are the fundamental principles of CL research.

1.2   Corpus linguistics: Not just word frequency

It is important to underline that CL is not just counting words in texts. Frequencies provide ways into the data. They give us starting points for further analysis, whether that be through other statistical routes or through detailed, qualitative manual analysis facilitated through use of corpus tools (as we will illustrate throughout this book). Hunston (2022) has suggested that CL research has become more sophisticated thanks to the use of statistics that do not only relate to words and phrases (i.e., frequency, keywords, collocations, see Chapter 2), but also to categories such as groups of texts themselves. An example of the attention paid to the analysis of linguistics categories is multidimensional analysis (MD), a multivariate statistical technique, highly influential in CL particularly in North American CL, that, using data reduction approaches such as factor analysis, can discover dimensions of use in corpora that can be interpreted using functional linguistics (Biber, 1988, 2019). In short, MD can reveal how the frequencies and distributions of many linguistic features co-select themselves across different registers. Dimensions in MD represent quantitative, continuous parameters of variation (Biber, 2019b) where factor loadings are coefficients found in a factor structure matrix, in our case, a dimension of language use. Dimension 1 in Biber (1988), for example, explains the differences between oral and written discourse. Positive features include contractions, the use of pronouns, verbs or, among others, time and place adverbials. Negative features include the use of nouns, word length, type/token ration, the use of prepositional phrases or passive verb phrases. This dimension classifies oral registers such as conversation or service encounters and written registers such as research papers or textbooks on different ends of a continuum. The study of the distribution of a set of linguistic features can shed light on the nature of, for example, conversations if, rather than describing them in isolation, we compare conversation corpus findings with findings from a different register/corpus, such as academic language. Biber (2019) has referred to this approach as the text-linguistic register framework. It is characterised by describing text categories for both situational and lexico-grammatical characteristics, and it is based on the claim that situational characteristics have a systematic functional relationship to lexico-grammatical characteristics, and the claim that those lexico-grammatical characteristics can be described in a continuous quantitative space of variation.

In this book we will discuss some of the most widely used statistics in CL research, including both nonfactorial research designs (Brezina, 2021) as well as a some of the emerging multivariate designs in corpus-linguistics-informed analysis of language learning (Hilpert & Blasi, 2021; Schäfer, 2021). The latter favour a more complex understanding of L2 use in corpora and are increasingly relevant to SLA researchers as they factor in variables that have attracted the attention of SLA and applied linguists.

1.3 Corpus linguistics and language learning research: L2 learning and teaching

In language learning research corpora are used as proxies of usage, that is, as providers of evidence of communication, spoken or written (Pérez-Paredes & Mark, 2022). Most of the methods discussed in this book will facilitate the use of two types of research designs that favour the collection and examination of such evidence. Cross-sectional research designs rely on the collection and analyses of L1 or L2 corpora. This kind of research design facilitates comparison of data collected at a single point in time across a range of variables (e.g. comparing use of a linguistic feature across different L1 backgrounds). The second research design, longitudinal designs, specify different collection times of L1 or L2 corpora with a view to generate insights into language gains or variation of use across time (e.g. comparing proficiency levels) (See Chapter 3 for a detailed description). Patently, the learner language data that was used in early learner corpora research was, according to Tracy-Ventura and Paquot (2021), primarily in written mode, cross-sectional and mainly focused on advanced learners' output. Myles (2005) has argued that these first learner corpora were useful in documenting differences between L2 and L1 users' language.

Some studies, however, combine both cross-sectional and longitudinal designs. Vyatkina (2012), for example, looked at the development of linguistic complexity in the writing of beginning learners of German both as a group and as individuals over four semesters. To do this, she put together and annotated a longitudinal learner corpus. Complexity was analysed at two intersections: between cross-sectional trendlines and the individual development paths of 2 focal learners, and between different complexity variables. Note that in this research the learner corpus data is contributed by two individuals whose writings were collected across 19 time points. For Vyatkina (2012), the longitudinal data analysis shows the variability in developmental pathways of individual learners against the backdrop of the cross-sectional developmental trend. In her research, the frequencies of automatically annotated parts of speech (POS) were used as proxy measures for syntactic complexity.

The application of corpus methods, however, goes beyond the study of learner language outputs. Corpus linguistics methods contribute to language learning pedagogies that are informed by the analysis of corpora. In this sense, corpus linguistics has shown that the insights gained from the analysis of authentic language use in corpora can inform the L2 publishing industry and language teachers worldwide. These analyses make use of some of the methods in Chapters 4, 5 and 6. It is in this wider context that encompass L2 learning and L2 pedagogy where we situate our analysis of the affordances of corpus linguistics. Corpus data can shape language resources, offering insights for syllabus design and textbook development. CL tools and methods help educators understand authentic language usage, allowing them to incorporate real-life examples and usage patterns into teaching materials. By integrating corpus findings, language educators can create more targeted and effective learning materials that reflect actual language use. Hands-on interaction with corpora can help language learners examine authentic language samples, enhancing their understanding of context-specific usage and grammar. CL not only supports material based on authentic language use but also empowers students to engage directly with real-world language, making learning more dynamic and relevant. Chapters 7 and 8 will show that methods that facilitate such approaches.

1.4   Summary

This chapter has introduced core concepts in corpus linguistics, like frequency, contrast, and representativeness. Corpus linguistics is the study of real spoken or written language through corpora analysed with specialised software. Although the term emerged in the 1980s, studying language patterns in texts dates back centuries, with modern advances allowing instant analysis of billions of words. Key concepts in CL include frequency (how often language features appear), contrast (comparing language across contexts), and representativeness (ensuring corpora reflect diverse language use). These tools help linguists explore linguistic variation. CL methods also enhance language learning by offering real-life language examples, which can improve teaching materials and allow students to analyse authentic language. The chapter lays the foundation for using CL to understand language patterns and support language education.

CHAPTER 2

The basics
Key functions of using a corpus

Recommended reading 2.1

Anthony, L. (2022b). **What can software do? In A. O'Keeffe, & M. J. McCarthy (Eds.),**
Routledge handbook of corpus linguistics (2nd ed., pp. 103–125). **Routledge.**

This chapter, written by the creator of AntConc, surveys the strengths and weaknesses of ready-built online and offline tools and compares them to custom-built do-it-yourself (DIY) tools. The chapter walks the reader through the typical functions of corpus software using AntConc screenshots to exemplify these. The functions include word and keyword frequencies, clusters, n-grams, lexical-bundle patterns, and Key-Word-In-Context (KWIC) concordances. The chapter also looks at how corpus tools can be used in more sophisticated ways to examine language patterns, cohesion, register variation, discourse structure, and pragmatic phenomenon.

Recommended reading 2.2

Sinclair, J. McH. (2003). *Reading concordances.* **Pearson.**

The book introduces corpus work to students and researchers interested in interrogating a corpus in order to find evidence that is relevant to a linguistic enquiry. The book is divided into sections that include a series of mini-tasks consisting of questions and instructions to retrieve linguistically relevant information from the data, concordances and how they can be used to build up evidence and, finally, very useful responses to the mini-tasks.

In Chapter 1 we looked at some key principles of corpus linguistics and we considered the opportunities that it offers for the study of second language acquisition. In this chapter we will discuss the key functions of corpus tools. It is reassuring to remember that while there are now several corpus tools available, they all have similar core functionality. We will now look at these typical functions one-by-one: word (and multi-word unit) frequency lists, concordancing, and key word functions.

2.1 Corpus functions and tools: Word and phrase lists

As noted in Chapter 1, *frequency* is one of the key principles of CL. The frequency of occurrence a word or multi-word unit in a corpus can tell us much about its profile and its use. In the context of LCR, we can also look at the variables behind usage including both language users' variables (first language, level of proficiency, age, gender, level of education, etc.), or language use task-related variables (including mode of production — spoken or written, or issues of genre and register involved in the task). When we talk about 'variables', we mean the different qualities or characteristics that lie behind the data within the context of data that is stored in a given corpus. The variables that are available for a given corpus are not standardised and this can be challenging when working with more than one corpus. For example, some learner corpora may provide proficiency information in terms of the year of study of the learner who produced a given spoken or written data sample to the corpus while other corpora may offer information on the proficiency using the CEFR.

2.1.1   Creating word and phrase lists

Generating a word or multi-word list is the very first step in examining a corpus. This will simply provide a list, ordered by frequency ranking, from the most frequent to the least frequent words in the whole corpus.

Let us look, for instance, at the written work of one English as a Second Language (ESL) student collected in an adult education ESL context in Ireland. We will apply corpus tools to generate word and phrase lists from this small dataset and we will compare these with another larger corpus. The collection of five samples of writing from one student does not constitute a corpus in the strictest sense of being widely representative, but it does form an electronic database that represents all of the writing of this one learner in a term of 12 weeks. By way of background on this learner, the student is a male, from the Democratic Republic of Congo, aged 50, who has been living and working in Ireland for 6 years. His level is B2 on the *Common European Framework of Reference for Languages* (CEFR)[1] (Upper Intermediate). His first language is French. The dataset comprises five texts that he has written on the following topics (amounting to 1,796 words in total). These were collected at two-week intervals during the term. These data are a sub-set from McNamara (2020) which looked at formulaic vocabulary development in two class cohorts at A2 and C1 levels:

To make a frequency list based on this mini-corpus, we first need to load the files to the software. In this chapter, we will use *AntConc* (Anthony, 2022a). Tutorials on using *AntConc* are available online.

---

1. The Common European Framework of Reference for Languages (CEFR) (Council of Europe 2001) is a widely used benchmark for language competence levels. It comprises six levels: A1 (Beginners); A2 (Elementary); B1 (Intermediate); B2 (Upper Intermediate); C1 (Advanced); and C2 (Proficiency). The Framework offers generic descriptors, or "can do" statements for each level.

Table 2.1 Titles of written tasks collected over one school term

Text	Title of written work	No. of words
1	The Smoking Ban in Ireland	479
2	One world, one language	261
3	Language: could automatic translation replace human language skills?	362
4	Prevention medicine versus reactive medicine	275
5	Book review of The Curious Incident of the Dog in the Night-Time (Mark Haddon)	419
Total		1796

These are the steps to loading files to a corpus to *AntConc*:

1. If you want to load files to *AntConc*, they need to be saved in *plain text* format (.txt) rather than in word or pdf format. [2] This is the case for most corpus software. Using plain text files is considered a good practice in CL even when pdf or docx files can be read by the software.
2. Click on *file* in the *AntConc* menu. Choose *Open Corpus Manager...* and check *Raw Files* (see Figure 2.1) and click Add File(s) and upload the .txt file(s) that you wish to examine. You may wish to give this corpus a name while uploading it.

By selecting the *word* function (at the top, see Figure 2.2) and clicking *start* (bottom centre), the word frequency list is generated instantly in order of frequency of occurrence across the mini-corpus. As Figure 2.2 illustrates, *the* is the most frequent word with 113 occurrences and *a* is the second most frequent with 59 occurrences and so on.

Other useful information about the frequency of the words is their *range*. We can see that the top 10 most frequent words have a range of 5. This means these words are in all 5 texts whereas the 11th most frequent word *smoking* has a range of 2 because it only occurs in 2 of the 5 texts. Looking more closely at the top 20 most frequent words in Figure 2.2, we can make a few initial observations:

---

2. To convert a word file to a text file, simply save the file as a *plain text* file in the *Save as* drop-down menu (at the bottom of the window, there is a drop-down for file type). You will then get a warning *Saving as a text file will case all formatting, pictures and objects in your file to be lost.* Click *OK* and your file will be in plain text (.txt) format and ready to load to the software. In the case of Apple devices, you may need to choose UTF-8 format as an additional step.

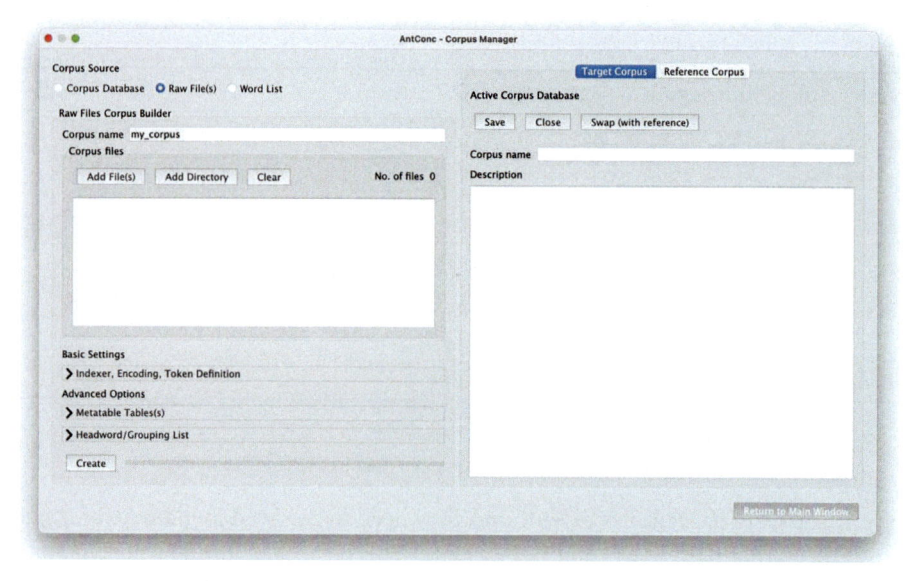

Figure 2.1 Screenshot of *AntConc 4* (loading files)

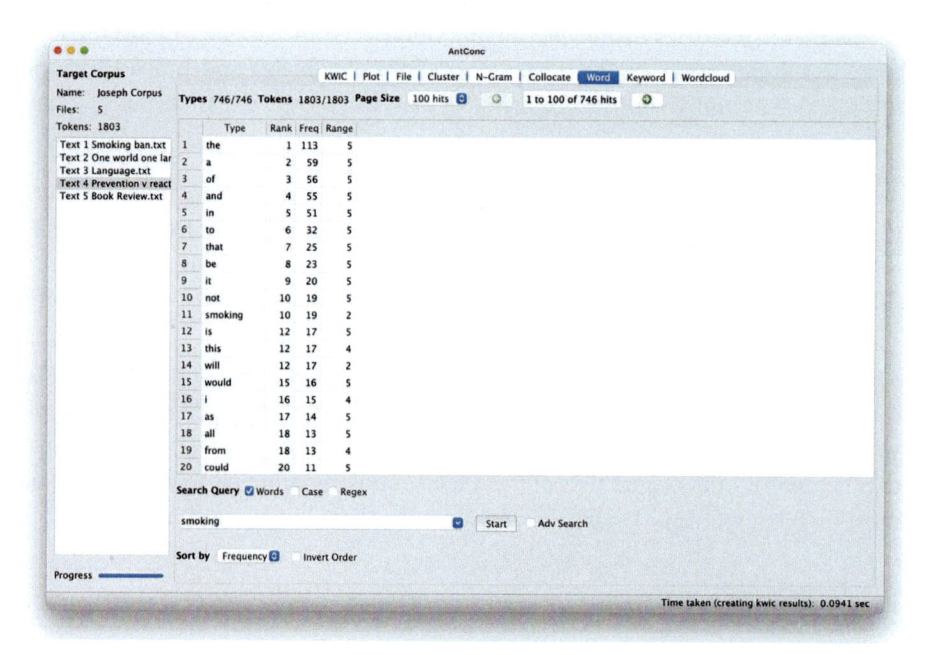

Figure 2.2 Screenshot of word list top 20 most frequent words in *AntConc 4* based on five files containing ESL writing (1,796 words)

- the word *the* occurs around twice as often as the next most frequent words *a, of, and* and *in*;
- the words in the top 20 are mostly grammatical words (75%).
- there are only five unambiguous content words (25%) in the top 20 (*smoking, will, would, could*). Some uses of *is* may be as a main verb but examination in context is needed to ascertain this.

2.1.2   Comparing word and phrase lists

As we discussed in Chapter 1, comparison is one of the key principles of CL. When we look at a frequency list, we always need to compare it to some baseline because without a baseline, our observations are difficult to interpret. For example, it would be useful to know whether *the* is the most frequent word in other corpora.

Corpora such as the British National Corpus (BNC), which aim to represent a variety of a language, are useful points of comparison as they offer a baseline or norm (that is, the BNC can be taken to represent British English in general). The BNC is a corpus of 100 million words of written (90%) and spoken (10%) collected in the early 1990s (Burnard, 1995). It was designed to offer a representative sample of British English. Table 2.2 shows a comparison of the top 20 most frequent words from the BNC (spoken and written components) compared with those in our mini-corpus of writing from an ESL student.

From Table 2.2, we can see, in broad terms, that:

- *the* is the most frequent word in the mini-corpus and in the BNC and, in both, it occurs roughly twice as often as the next most frequent word.
- the order of the most frequent words, apart from *the* differs.
- the BNC top 20 spoken and written lists comprise almost entirely of functional (grammatical) items (and in the BNC Spoken list, we can see the vocalisation *erm* featuring as the 18th most common item).
- the frequencies of the BNC are many times greater than the ESL mini-corpus.

However, all the results in Table 2.2 are *raw*. This means that they are of little use comparatively because we are not comparing like-with-like. For example, we cannot tell whether the ESL student's frequency of use of articles *the* and *a* (113 and 59 times, respectively, out of 1,796 words) is relatively more or less frequent than the norm as represented by the BNC frequency (5,739,934 and 2,913,193 times out of 100,000,000 words, respectively). To address this issue of comparability, we need to *normalise* the frequency results.

Table 2.2 Word frequency lists compared: ESL texts vs BNC Written and Spoken

Rank order	ESL mini-corpus		BNC Written		BNC Spoken		All BNC Written & Spoken	
	Word	Freq.	Word	Freq.	Word	Freq.	Word	Freq.
1	the	113	the	5529513	the	210421	the	5739934
2	a	59	of	2820005	and	121822	of	2913193
3	of	56	to	2321161	to	114287	and	2438445
4	and	55	and	2316623	I	106583	to	2435448
5	in	51	a	1942423	that	104285	a	2034829
6	to	32	in	1772037	you	101132	in	1840393
7	that	25	that	877366	of	93188	that	981651
8	be	23	is	858945	it	92494	is	906927
9	it	20	for	795808	a	92406	it	881422
10	not	19	it	788928	s	71192	for	827489
11	smoking	19	was	769842	in	68356	was	802982
12	is	17	on	640685	we	56552	s	697204
13	this	17	s	626012	er	55200	on	675096
14	will	17	as	600548	is	47982	I	667192
15	would	16	with	600055	t	38360	as	623251
16	I	15	be	580193	they	37773	with	621414
17	as	14	I	560609	on	34411	be	609545
18	all	13	he	554028	erm	34366	he	571916
19	from	13	by	486809	was	33140	by	496597
20	could	11	at	464278	for	31681	you	495596

2.1.3   Comparing word and phrase lists: Normalisation

To make results from different corpora comparable, we need to bring the results to a common base. The base could be out of 100, 1000, 10,000 or 1,000,000, etc. This process is called *normalisation*. As McEnery and Hardie (2012) note, normalisation answers the question, "how often might we assume we will see the word per X words of running text?" (2012, p. 49). In our case, for example, we could ask, 'how often might we assume we will see the word *smoking* per one million words of running text?' Some software packages will automatically normalise results. Alternatively, frequency results can be exported to *Microsoft Excel* and normalisation can be done within this file. To normalise results manually, there is a simple formula:

$$\text{Normalised frequency} = \frac{\text{raw frequency}}{\text{total number of words in the corpus}} \text{ X normalisation base}$$

For example, if we want to scale the raw frequencies in the mini-corpus and the BNC to a base of one million words, we need to:

1. In the case of the mini-corpus: divide the frequency for word X by the total number of words in the mini-corpus (1,796) and multiply it by 1,000,000.
2. In the case of the BNC: divide the frequency for word X by the total number of words in the BNC (100,000,000) and multiply it by 1,000,000. (Or, by way of shortcut, because the BNC comprises 100,000,000, we can just divide by 100).

For example, the word *the* occurs 113 times in the ESL writing tasks in a total of 1,796 words. If we scale that up to frequency per million words, we divide it by the total number of words in the mini-corpus (1,796) and multiply it by 1,000,000. This will give us a 'per million word' (PMW) result of 62,673 words. Table 2.3 shows us the top 20 results of mini-corpus of ESL writing tasks in PMWs in comparison with the frequency of that item in the BNC (PMW). This allows for further observations that might lead to interesting insights from the data (see column 5 in Table 2.3).

2.1.4 Lists of multi-word units

It is important to remember that analysis of frequency should not be limited to single word items. Multi-word units (MWUs) are of particular importance in general but, as we shall discuss in this book (see Chapter 5 for collocations or Chapter 6 for different types of patterns such as colligation and collostructions), they are of great significance in the study of learner language because they can indicate syntactic development in learners' use of language across levels of proficiency. MWUs are referred to by various terminology (sometimes with slightly differencing definitions). These include *inter alia*: formulas, formulaic units, formulaic sequences, routines, fixed expressions, prefabricated patterns (prefabs), clusters, chunks, concgrams, strings, N-grams and lexical bundles/lexical phrases (see Gray, 2022; Gray & Biber, 2015; Greaves & Warren, 2022, for coverage of differing terminology, methodologies and research findings).

Even with a small set of learner language, we can use corpus software to explore the patterns of MWU that are used most frequently.

Table 2.3 Top 20 words in ESL texts compared with BNC (with normalised to per million word frequencies), with observations

Rank order in ESL writing	Word	Frequency in ESL writing PMW	Frequency in BNC PMWs	Observations
1	the	62918	57399	Overall, there seems to be more articles used in the ESL texts
2	a	32851	20348	
3	of	31180	29132	*of* is used with similar frequency though slightly higher in ESL texts
4	and	30624	24384	ESL texts use coordinating conjunction *and* more
5	in	28396	18404	*in* is used 20+% more in ESL texts
6	to	17817	24354	*to* is used 16% less in ESL texts
7	that	13920	9816	ESL texts use *that* more
8	be	12806	6095	ESL texts use *be* circa 50% more
9	it	11136	8814	*it* is used 10+% more in ESL texts
10	not	10579	3959	*not* is used 45+% more in ESL texts
11	smoking	10579	2847	*smoking* is used around 99% more in ESL texts
12	is	9465	9069	Usage of *is* is similar in frequency
13	this	9465	4161	*this* is used more the 50% more in ESL texts
14	will	9465	2362	*will* is used 3 times more frequently in ESL texts
15	would	8909	2142	*would* is used 4 times more frequently in ESL texts
16	I	8352	6672	*I* is used 10+% more in ESL texts
17	as	7795	6232	*as* is used 10+% more in ESL texts
18	all	7238	2508	*all* is used almost 3 times more in ESL texts
19	from	7238	4053	*from* is used almost twice as much in ESL texts
20	could	6125	1329	*could* is used 4.5 times as often in ESL texts

Figure 2.3 shows the 2-word combinations, their frequency and their range across the five texts. These results are generated through *AntConc* using the N-gram function (set at 2-words).

We can see that the ESL learner's writing shows a number of recurring two-word combinations, many of which are grammatical and operate as 'frames' for other structures (e.g., the pattern *in the* can frame a noun within prepositional phrase). We see that as the strings of multi-words get longer, the instances become fewer. This is normal and it is unlikely to find many multi-word units longer than six (see O'Keeffe et al., 2007).

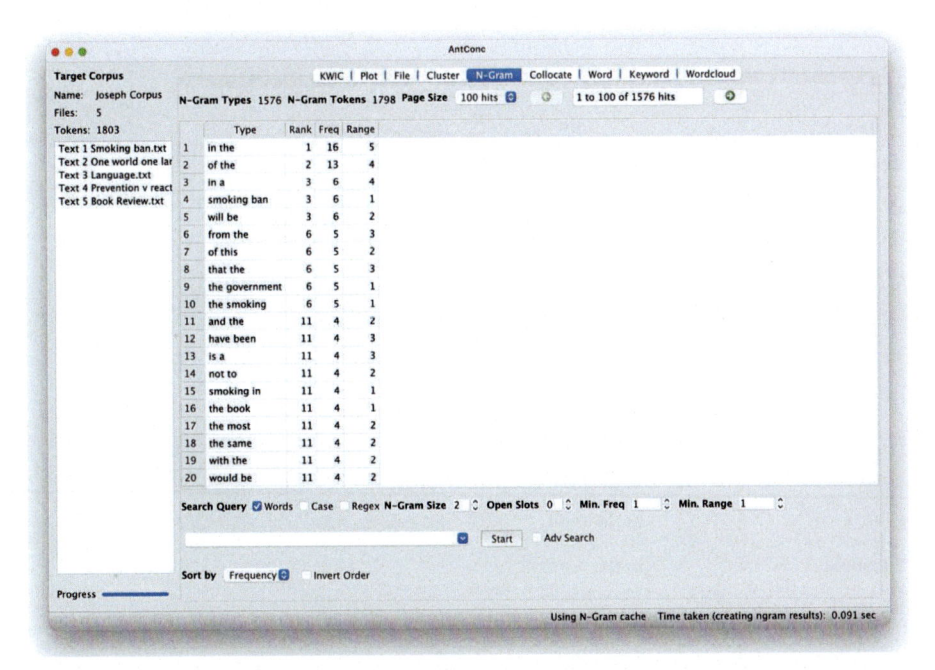

Figure 2.3 Two-word units that occur more than twice in the ESL texts, using *AntConc* N-gram function

There are several points of note arising from the findings in Table 2.4. Some of the multi-word units are influenced by the writing task(s) (see Table 2.1) (*smoking ban; learning a language, the book*). When designing a learner corpus, the tasks that generate the data are a very important consideration. When MWUs are analysed, wordings from the task rubric may be used by students in their writing.

Some of the multi-word units occur only twice. This is because the dataset is very small. This is also reflected in the range or dispersion of these items also where often they are only found in one or two of the texts. For example, *the smoking ban* occurs three times but only in one text. When looking at a larger

Table 2.4 The most frequent multi-word units in the ESL student's writing

Type	Freq	Range	Type	Freq	Range	Type	Freq	Range
in the	16	5	one of the	3	2	the Republic of Ireland	3	1
of the	13	4	Republic of Ireland	3	1	at the same time	2	2
in a	6	4	smoking in the	3	1	in the public places	2	1
smoking ban	6	1	the fact that	3	2	in the Republic of	2	1
will be	6	2	the public places	3	1	on the other hand	2	2
from the	5	3	the republic of	3	1	one of the most	2	2
of this	5	2	the smoking ban	3	1	smoking in the public	2	1
that the	5	3	a translation software	2	1	the government of the	2	1
the government	5	1	all kinds of	2	2			
the smoking	5	1	all over the	2	2			
and the	4	2	at the same	2	2			
have been	4	3	example of this	2	1			
is a	4	3	government of the	2	1			
not to	4	2	in the past	2	2			
smoking in	4	1	in the public	2	1			
the book	4	1	in the republic	2	1			
the most	4	2	is not a	2	1			
the same	4	2	learning a language	2	2			
with the	4	2	not to be	2	2			
would be	4	2	of learning a	2	2			

dataset, you may wish to set the threshold for minimum frequency of an N-gram in *AntConc* to a higher number, for example, five occurrences.

While frequency is usually the starting point in corpus analysis, corpus-oriented approaches go well beyond frequencies as we shall illustrate. To find out more about items that appear on a frequency list, the software can instantly generate a list of all of the occurrences of the word or phrase. These are called *concordances,* as we shall discuss next.

2.2   Corpus functions and tools: Using concordances

A concordance "is an index to the places in a text where particular words and phrases occur." (Sinclair, 2003, p.173), In a concordance, the search word that you enter will appear in the middle of the search screen. This is referred to as the *node* (see Figure 2.4 where *is* is the node).

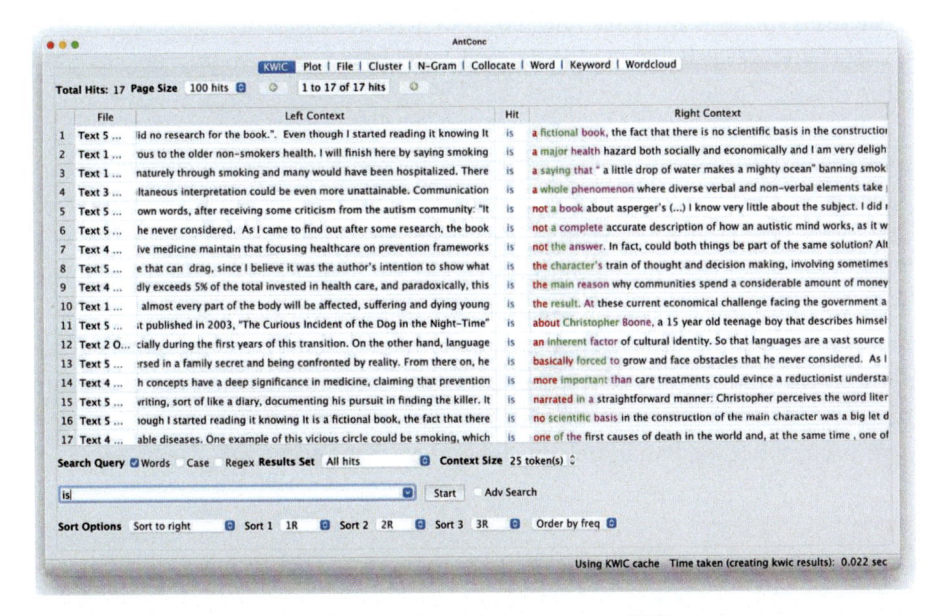

Figure 2.4 Concordance of all instances *is* in mini-corpus of ESL writing texts using *AntConc*

Looking at words on screens of concordance lines is often a follow up in the process of corpus investigation where the word (or phrase) frequency list (see above) is the starting point. In order to look in greater depth at the pattern(s) of use, the meaning(s) and the context(s) of any item on a frequency list, the concordance function is useful because it generates all of the instances of that item in the corpus, in running order (i.e., starting with text 1, then text 2 and so on). For instance, returning to the top 20 items in Figure 2.2, we were unsure as to whether *is* was operating as both an auxiliary or a main verb and we cannot tell from the frequency list. A concordance of *is* will immediately help us, as Figure 2.4 illustrates. From this we can see that there were only 17 occurrences of *is* in the mini-corpus and we can see all of them in one screen. We can say that only 2 out of 19 instances (10.5%) of *is* are auxiliary verbs and 17 out of 19 (89.5%) are main verb uses. Chapter 4 will look at the use of Part of Speech (POS) tags in detail.

POS tagsets can provide morphosyntactic annotation that can be used to automatisethe process of filtering out different uses of the same word (e.g., auxiliary verb vs lexical verb).

An important caveat concerning concordance lines is that although they retrieve the *node* (the search word), they do not interpret it in any way. It is the responsibility of the researcher to use the software to determine the patterns that are salient and to construct hypotheses as to why these patterns occur. This is an inductive process sometimes referred to as a form-to-function process (Aijmer, 2015). Therefore, as Baker (2006) states "a concordance analysis is ... only as good as its analyst" (p.89).

We will now exemplify some of the typical phases that a researcher might undertake in the process of hypothesis formation with frequency lists and concordance lines. Working from the frequency list in Table 2.3, we can see that the word *smoking* is used in the ESL writing texts 10,579 times per million words (PMW). When compared with the use of this word in the BNC (2,847 times PMW), it is used 3.7 times more frequently than in our BNC baseline. We can see that this merits investigation through concordancing. Figure 2.5 shows all the 19 uses of the word in the mini-corpus of learner writing. We can immediately see that more than 30% of these relate to the *smoking ban* (which was one of the writing tasks — Text 1: The Smoking Ban in Ireland, Table 2.1).

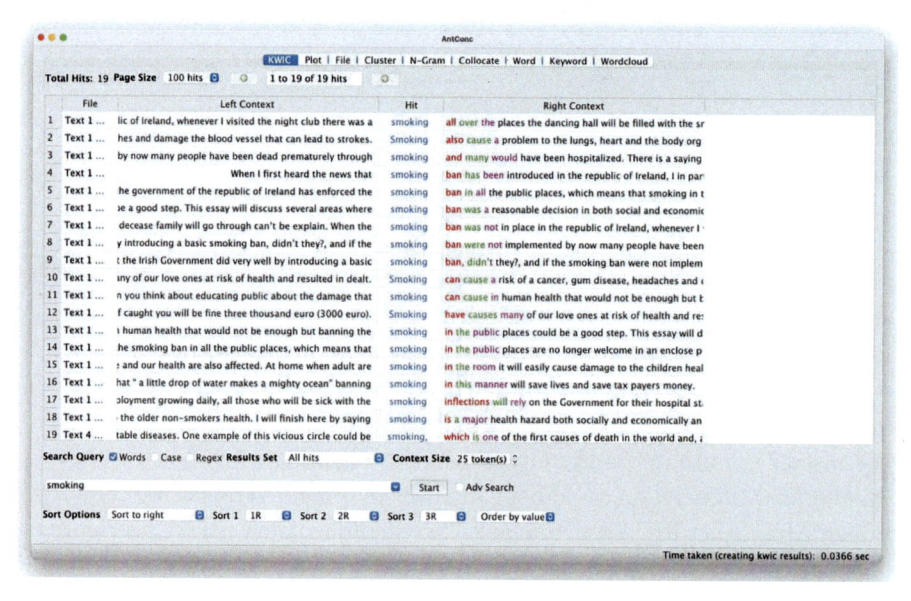

Figure 2.5 Concordance of the word *smoking* in the ESL texts, using *AntConc*

As this is a very small dataset, we can clearly see from the file names that all but one occurrences of *smoking* is in text 1. If the corpus were larger, we could use a dispersion plot function which is available in most corpus software. Figure 2.6 shows the dispersion plot using *AntConc*.

As Figure 2.6 shows, we can see, using this function, that the word *smoking* occurs in just two of the four texts and, in fact, 18 of the 19 occurrences are found, not surprisingly, in Text 1 *The Smoking Ban in Ireland*.

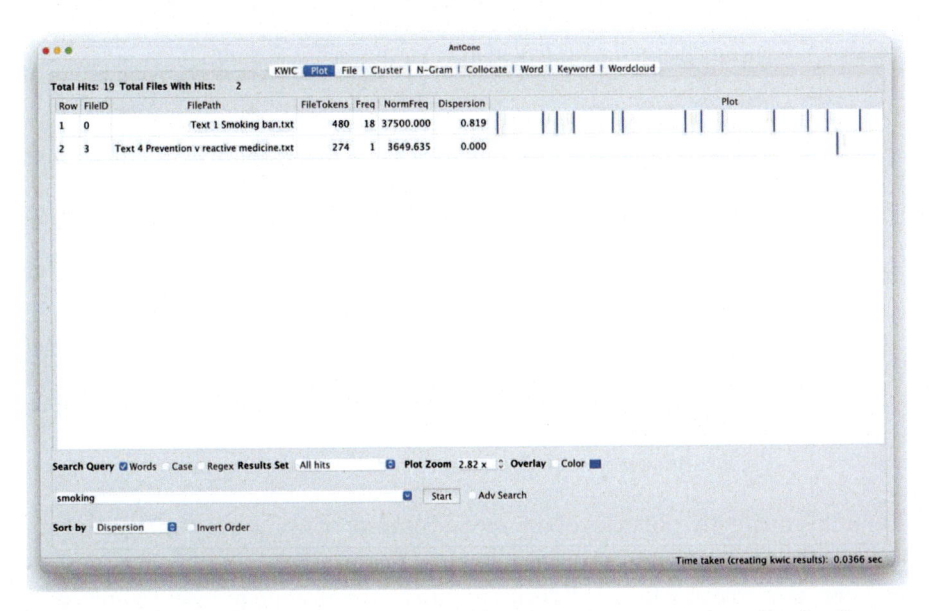

Figure 2.6 Concordance plot of the word smoking in ESL writing texts, using AntConc concordance plot function

This simple and obvious example with the word *smoking* underscores another important consideration when working with corpus results, namely *dispersion*. Just because a word appears to be used frequently in a word list, we cannot assume that it is used with equal distribution across all the texts in the corpus. Its use may be generated by just one text in the corpus. The notion of dispersion in corpus linguistics is related to the concept of dispersion in statistics and it refers to the evenness (or not) with which an element is distributed throughout a corpus.

Let us take another example, the multi-word unit *the fact that* occurs three times in the learner's writing (Table 2.4). The concordance of this phrase is illustrated in Figure 2.7.

We can click on any of these three lines to go to the source file so as to see the full context of use. Figure 2.7 shows the three instances with more context:

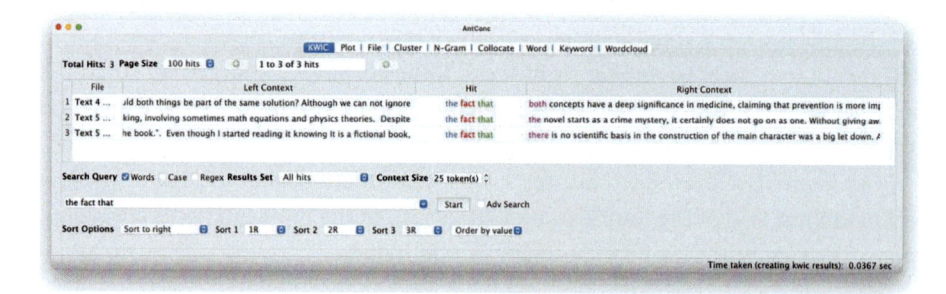

Figure 2.7 Concordance of *the fact that* in mini-corpus of ESL writing

Although we can not ignore *the fact that* both concepts have a deep significance in medicine, claiming that prevention is more important than care treatments could evince a reductionist understanding of medical science.

[Text 4: Prevention medicine versus reactive medicine]

Despite *the fact that* the novel starts as a crime mystery, it certainly does not go on as one.

[Text 4: Book review of The Curious Incident of the Dog in the Night-Time]

... *the fact that* there is no scientific basis in the construction of the main character was a big let down.

[Text 5: Book review of The Curious Incident of the Dog in the Night-Time]

From this qualitative analysis of the actual contexts of use of *the fact that,* we can see that the phrase is used as a subordinator (first example) and that it also plays an important role as a focusing device within complex noun phrases (second and third example).

When looking at concordances, it is noticeable that patterns of words emerge, sometimes fixed in multi-word units and sometimes in patterns of words that occur near each other. Looking at Figure 2.5, we can see *smoking + ban* as an obvious example but when we look more closely, we can see that the word *cause* seems to occur often near *smoking*. This notion of exploring how words tend to co-occur together or near each other can be explored more systematically through most software applications and it is something that is of considerable interest when investigating learner language. The term *collocation* refers to this concept (Firth, 1957a, b). Firth observed that meanings are often created by the associations of words rather than by words in isolation. As Greaves and Warren (2022) report, based on an abundant corpus evidence, corpus linguists concluded that words are often found to have a preference for what words they combine with. For example, one can say *people go mad, insane, bald or blind*, but not *people turn mad, insane, bald or blind* (O'Keeffe et al., 2007). For learners of a language, the kind of vocabulary knowledge can be challenging to acquire.

In sum, concordances are core to CL analyses. They bring depth of understanding to word frequency lists because they inform us about how words combine in patterns and possibly occur in specific texts or contexts. It is important not to lose sight of this. When corpus analysis involves concordances, it involves looking beyond frequencies to the actual texts and, in the context of this book, this means actual learner language. We will now look at a lesser-used but none-the-less important function of most corpus software: the ability to generate keywords.

2.3   Corpus functions and tools: Keywords

Keywords in a text are not the most frequent words but rather are the most unusually frequent or infrequent words, comparatively. In other words, when you compare the word list of your corpus (the 'target corpus') with a baseline corpus (the 'reference corpus'), the words that are used with unusually high frequency in the target corpus are identified as the *key* words. Using the mini-corpus of ESL texts as a target corpus and the BNC as the reference corpus, Table 2.5 shows us the top 20 keywords across the five texts. Corpus software uses a formula to calculate key words and a positive result (marked +) means that a word is key whereas a negative result (marked with –) denotes words that are unusually infrequent.

Table 2.5 Top 20 keywords in the ESL mini-corpus generated with BNC written and spoken as reference corpus

Rank order of keyness	Frequency in the target corpus	Keyness score	Word	Rank order of keyness	Frequency in the target corpus	Keyness score	Word
1	19	+183.06	smoking	11	2	+28.33	autism
2	7	+52.64	ban	12	4	+26.81	medicine
3	10	+46.78	language	13	4	+25.29	languages
4	5	+41.43	prevention	14	5	+23.76	learning
5	2	+34.29	incapability	15	4	+23.12	republic
6	4	+31.61	translation	16	1	+21.64	Asperger
7	4	+31.09	technologies	17	1	+21.64	homewrecker
8	8	+30.13	health	18	2	+21.41	slang
9	4	+29.98	Christopher	19	5	+20.49	cause
10	2	+28.46	math	20	6	+19.74	book

Note that different software may calculate keywords in slightly different ways statistically and that choosing different reference corpora can also mean differing results. For example, if we use both the written and spoken components of the BNC as a reference corpus, we get slightly different results than if we use only the spoken component (compare Tables 2.5 and 2.6).

Table 2.6 Top 20 keywords in the ESL mini-corpus with BNC spoken only as reference corpus

Rank order of keyness	Word	Rank order of keyness	Word
1	incapability	11	Asperger
2	autism	12	evince
3	seduce	13	unadventurous
4	translation	14	HSA
5	Uruguayan	15	Hippocratic
6	reductionist	16	incomprehension
7	technologies	17	capricious
8	homewrecker	18	xenophobia
9	intrapersonal	19	unattainable
10	Haddon	20	interventionist

The keyword function may also be of interest from a pedagogical perspective in that it can assist teachers or test writers in choosing appropriate texts relative to a particular class or proficiency level. We will now look at some more tools and applications that can help us analyse learner language.

2.4   Summary

In this chapter, we have surveyed the core functions of corpus software: word and multi-word frequency lists; concordances and keywords. Throughout the book, these basic functions will be used and we will introduce some others. Word lists, concordances and keywords will be part of any corpus software tool or interface. They may look a little different but there is usually ample help material to support the user. In Chapter 3, we will look at the different types of learner corpus data that are available and at the differing research perspectives that one can take.

CHAPTER 3

Corpus types and research perspectives

Recommended reading 3.1

O'Keeffe, A., McCarthy, M. J., & Carter, R. (2007). *From corpus to classroom: Language use and language teaching.* Cambridge University Press.

From corpus to classroom offers a comprehensive view of how corpus linguistics can be understood and applied in the context of language pedagogy. Chapter 11 specifically offers a perspective on the use of corpora in teacher education and development through collections of classroom interactions.

Recommended reading 3.2

Bell, P., & Payant, C. (2021). Designing learner corpora: Collection, transcription, and annotation. In N. Tracy-Ventura & M. Paquot (Eds.), *The Routledge handbook of second language acquisition and corpora* (pp. 53–67). Routledge.

This chapter in the *Routledge handbook of SLA and corpora* looks at the variables that need to be discussed when designing, collecting, and transcribing corpora. It considers the need to carefully gather complete data about participants, especially concerning their language experience, languages used or studied, namely, L1(s) home language(s), instructed learning of additional language(s), or living-abroad experiences. It looks at careful corpus design and construction and emphasises the need to ensure balanced representation to include texts across genres.

Recommended reading 3.3

Pérez-Paredes, P. (2020). *Corpus linguistics for education: A guide for research.* Routledge.

Chapter 5 in this volume looks specifically at the approaches to transcription and annotation in interview data. It demonstrates that decisions about transcription and annotation are down to the researcher and shows how this is led by the research questions.

In Chapter 2 we looked at corpus tools and their applications. In this chapter we look at types of corpora and research designs. We consider how different research perspectives make use of different types of corpora to inform research on language learning. We also discuss the key considerations for designing and building corpora.

3.1   Types of learner corpora

Learner corpora are gathered to reflect L2 use and, depending on the corpus design, can be used on the one hand to examine language output or product, and on the other to gain insights into the process of language learning. They are collections or databases of language from different L2 users, grouped according to a whole range of student- and task-related variables, for example L1 background, education, proficiency level, age, gender, exam, task types and the context used for the data collection. These variables can be captured alongside the language data, as metadata (see 3.1.2 below), and are used to inform analysis.

Typically, the majority of learner corpora are representations of language use in instructed L2 contexts. They represent the output from the types of (predominantly written) language tasks that are found in educational institutions (such as mainstream schools, universities and specialist language schools) as well as from assessments of language proficiency. In reality, most of the language output in learner corpora is the result of controlled tasks, representing degrees of naturalness, on a scale, from open-ended writing tasks to spontaneous interview questions. While they represent collections of language that are naturally found in the classroom, they are rarely, if ever, representative of language usage 'in the wild'. It is for this reason that some learner corpora are sometimes referred to as databases. Corpora of written language dominate since written language is easier to collect and transcribe. Collecting and transcribing spoken language is a far more laborious task (O'Keeffe et al., 2007; Knight & Adolphs, 2022) as we shall discuss in 3.5 below.

Learner corpora vary considerably in terms of what they represent. The suitability of a learner corpus for a particular research design or for a theoretical research perspective will depend on how it has been put together and what it represents. Learner corpora can be categorised across a range of dimensions. We will come back to corpus design and creation in more detail in 3.5 below, but when thinking about types of corpora and their use, it is useful to think about the dimensions that are central to corpus design and creation shown in Table 3.1.

Different types of corpora lend themselves to different research perspectives. We can think about three broad types of corpora that differ in the way they were collected: (1) cross-sectional (2) longitudinal and (3) pseudo-longitudinal corpora. Cross-sectional corpora are characterised by the collection and analyses of data from a single point in time, whereas longitudinal and pseudo-longitudinal corpora, specify different collection times of data with a view to generate insights into language gains or variation of use across time or proficiency level, typically to look at development.

Table 3.1 Key considerations for learner corpus design

Data collection time:	When is the data collected? E.g., at one point in time, at different points in time?
Mode:	Is the data written or spoken? Is it hybrid?
Task:	What tasks are used to collect the data? E.g., essay, interview, monologue, exam task
Learners:	What characterises the learners? How are they sampled? E.g., L1 background, age, proficiency level, gender?

Focus 3.1 Learner corpus types

🔍 **Learner corpus types**

The main types of learner corpus designs are:

Cross-sectional: data gathered at a single point in time, from different learners. For example, cross-sectional corpora may contain spoken and/or written data from learners from different L1 backgrounds, all performing the same task(s), or learners from different proficiency levels, from the same L1 background. This is the most common type of corpus, and it lends itself to comparison across dimensions, e.g., between L1 backgrounds.

Longitudinal: data gathered from the same learners at different points in time. For example, longitudinal corpora may contain spoken and/or written data from the same learners at the beginning, middle or end of a course, or they may contain data from the same learners over a span of years.

Pseudo-longitudinal: data gathered from different learners at different points in time. Pseudo-longitudinal data may contain spoken/written data from different learners, with different L1 backgrounds, and at different proficiency levels, doing different tasks, at multiple points in time. Cross-sectional data are easier to collect, but do not facilitate analysis of change over time; longitudinal data can be analysed for development across time or proficiency but are more difficult to collect and maintain; because of this pseudo-longitudinal data are typically used as a proxy for truly longitudinal data.

We first take a look at a sample of available learner corpora before moving on to how different perspectives engage with corpora.

3.1.1   Examples of learner corpora

At the time of writing, the Centre for English Corpus Linguistics, Université Catholique de Louvain, Belgium, has curated a list of 209 different corpora from around the world[4] (Centre for English Corpus Linguistics, 2023). While the majority of them comprise English language data, the listing shows learner corpora across many other languages, including: Arabic, Catalan, Chinese, Czech, Dutch, Estonian, Farsi, French, Finnish, Gaelic, German, Hungarian, Icelandic, Italian, Korean, Latvian, Lithuanian, Norwegian, Polish, Portuguese, Romanian, Russian, Slovene, Spanish, and Swedish. Table 3.2 exemplifies some of the types of corpora that are available for the study of language learners.

Focus 3.2 Examples of learner corpora

🔎 **Examples of learner corpora**

Notice how the corpora in Table 3.2 differ in their features. For example, most comprise written data, some are drawn from exam writing tasks, some are from essays. Few are from lower levels of proficiency. Some are millions of words, others are thousands. Some are constructed using specific tasks, others are open-ended. Many of these corpora have been designed as general collections, others are designed to gather specialised data.

Table 3.2 A sample of learner corpora

International Corpus of Learner English (ICLE)
https://uclouvain.be/en/research-institutes/ilc/cecl/icle.html

---

Contains argumentative essays written by upper intermediate to advanced learners of English from several L1 backgrounds; version 3 allows for the regular inclusion of new subcorpora, highlighting the fundamentally dynamic nature of the ICLE project.
Key elements: L2 English, 25 L1 backgrounds, written, cross-sectional, high level proficiency, 5.5 million words of writing.

Louvain International Database of Spoken English Interlanguage (LINDSEI)
https://uclouvain.be/en/research-institutes/ilc/cecl/lindsei.html

---

The spoken counterpart to ICLE, produced by advanced learners of English from 25 different L1 backgrounds, using three interview tasks.
Key elements: L2 English, 11 different L1 backgrounds, spoken, cross-sectional, 1 million+ words.

Trinity Lancaster Corpus (TLC)
https://www.trinitycollege.com/about-us/research/Trinity-corpus

---

A 3.5 million-word corpus of learner (and examiner) speech which can be used in a wide range of research contexts including SLA, language testing, L2 pedagogy and materials development, etc. See Gablasova et al. (2019) for further details.

---

4. See https://uclouvain.be/en/research-institutes/ilc/cecl/learner-corpora-around-the-world .html (Accessed 14 April 2025)

Table 3.2 *(continued)*

Key elements: L2 English, 9 different linguistic and cultural backgrounds, spoken, pseudo-longitudinal, 3 proficiency levels B1 to C2.

The Cambridge Learner Corpus (CLC)
https://www.cambridge.org/corpus

55 million-word corpus of Cambridge exam data (32 million words error coded), from diverse L1 backgrounds, with rich metadata, including age, gender, education, nationality, exam task, year of exam.

Key elements: Written L2 English, exam data, 148 L1 backgrounds, pseudo-longitudinal, 6 proficiency levels A1 to C2.

The Open Cambridge Learner Corpus
https://www.sketchengine.eu/cambridge-learner-corpus/#toggle-id-1

A 2.9 million-word balanced subset of Cambridge Learner Corpus of over 10,000 student responses taken from 3 CEFR levels (B2, C1 and C2) of the Cambridge suite of exams from 60 countries speaking 7 different first languages.

Key elements: Written L2 English, exam data, 7 L1 backgrounds, pseudo-longitudinal, 3 proficiency levels B2 to C2.

The LONGDALE (LONGitudinal Database of Learner English) project
https://uclouvain.be/en/research-institutes/ilc/cecl/longdale.html

Contains a **wide range of data types**, from fairly uncontrolled spoken or written data such as argumentative essays, narratives or informal interviews to more guided types in the form of summaries or picture descriptions, as well as experimental data such as grammaticality judgement tests, collected over a period of at least **three years** at least once a year.

Key elements: spoken and written L2 English; range of text types/task types; longitudinal; intermediate to advanced.

The International Corpus Network of Asian Learners of English (ICNALE)
https://language.sakura.ne.jp/icnale/

A 3.5 million-word corpus of 10,000 topic-controlled speeches and essays produced by L2 English college students in 10 countries in Asia, and L1 speakers. Four text types: Spoken Monologue, Spoken Dialogue, Written Essays, and Edited Essays. Metadata include learner attributes, e.g., age, gender, proficiency as well as motivation to learn and learning background.

Key elements: spoken and written L2 English; Asian context.

Corpus and Repository of Writing (Crow)
https://writecrow.org

A 17-million-word corpus of written academic English from high intermediate/advanced (TOEFL overall score 80–105) learners, from 24 L1 backgrounds (predominantly Chinese and Arabic); a range of genres and text types (e.g., narrative, literature review, argument, proposal).

Key elements: written L2 English, 24 L1s, collected over 2-year period.

The EF-Cambridge Open Language Database (EFCAMDAT) https://corpus.mml.cam.ac.uk/efcamdat2

A 83 million-word corpus from 1 million written assignments submitted to *Education First* by 174,000 learners, across a wide range of levels (CEFR stages A1-C2)

Key elements: written English; 10 L1s, 16 levels (benchmarked to CEFR and TOEFL).

Table 3.2 *(continued)*

Corpus Escrito del Español como L2 (CEDEL2)
http://cedel2.learnercorpora.com/#section6

This corpus allows the investigation of how students learn Spanish. A comparative corpus of L1 Spanish –
L2 English, called WriCLE (Written Corpus of Learner English) was also created.
Key elements: L2 Spanish, L1 English, written, average age 20s; 512,873 words, cross-sectional.

Longitudinal Corpus of Chinese Learners of Italian (LOCCLI)
https://www.unistrapg.it/cqpweb/doc_corpora/LOCCLI_documentation.pdf

350 essays written by 175 Chinese learners of Italian, who attended Italian language courses in Perugia for
6–8 months, and it was collected in 2016. Data was collected in two different points in time, from the
same learners.
Key elements: L2 Chinese, L1 Italian, 175 learners; longitudinal.

Guangwai-Lancaster Chinese Learner Corpus (GLCLC)
http://cass.lancs.ac.uk/wp-content/uploads/2016/05/Poster_GLC-small.pdf

A balanced sample that covers three proficiency levels: beginner, intermediate and advanced, providing a
unique insight into L2 Chinese lexical and grammatical development.
Key elements: L2 Chinese; written and spoken, different proficiency levels, longitudinal, 80 countries
represented, over 1 million.

Arabic Learner Corpus
https://www.arabiclearnercorpus.com/

A 282,732-word collection of written and spoken materials from learners of Arabic; includes, 1585
materials (written and spoken), produced by 942 students from 67 nationalities, and 66 different L1
backgrounds.
Key elements: L2 Arabic, written and spoken, 66 L1s.

The Estonian Interlanguage Corpus of Tallinn University (EIC) https://evkk.tlu.ee/vers1//?language
=en

a 1 million-word collection of written texts from exam tasks language course assignments, and texts
written by secondary school students participating at the olympiad of Estonian as L2. The subcorpora also
include writings of Russian both by native speakers and Estonian-speaking L2 learners, and a reference
corpus of argumentative newspaper articles.
Key elements: L2 Estonian, 8 L1 backgrounds, 6 levels A1 to C2.

3.1.2   Corpus metadata

Largely available learner corpora are often designed to facilitate as many research
queries as possible into the future. Therefore, it can sometimes be challenging to
narrow down data from general corpora to meet the needs of research guided by
specific research questions. The best place to start is to look at the 'metadata' that
is available for each corpora. Metadata refers to the information about each file in
the data and this can vary from corpus to corpus (see Focus 3.3).

Focus 3.3 Metadata

🔎 Metadata

The metadata which is collected alongside language production gives detailed background information about the learners, the learning contexts of the language collected, and the type of data being collected. Metadata can include information about the learners' age, education, gender, L1, other languages spoken, contexts of use, tasks, proficiency level, etc. Metadata plays a crucial role in informing the analysis of the data. For example, it allows the researcher to consider background contextual information and control for variables or relate findings to particular characteristics or learning contexts. It can also be useful in replication studies.

Researchers often create their own corpora to address a specific research question. Larger general corpora will be useful as a point of comparison, as we discussed in Chapter 2. Being able to filter corpus searches using the metadata is very useful for the purposes of comparing variables. For example, using the Open Cambridge Learner Corpus (see Table 3.3), we can search for the collocations of the verb *get* that L1 French speakers use most frequently at B2 and C2 levels in English (based on the exam they took):

Table 3.3 Top 10 Collocates of *get* in B2 and C2 learners whose first language is French in the Open Cambridge Learner Corpus

	B2	C2
1	off	rid
2	bored	involved
3	lost	married
4	work	worse
5	back	away
6	used	off
7	information	out
8	experience	into
9	there	enough
10	well	better

We can then compare these results to the collocations of the verb *get* that L1 Chinese speakers use most frequently at B2 and C2 levels in English (based on the exam they took) from the same corpus (Table 3.4):

Table 3.4 Top 10 Collocates of *get* in B2 and C2 learners whose first language is Chinese in the Open Cambridge Learner Corpus

	B2	C2
1	off	rid
2	discount	married
3	married	hold
4	ready	paid
5	into	into
6	back	back
7	away	used
8	some	better
9	used	up
10	on	some

From this simple analysis we can see a least four points of comparison, across proficiency levels and across L1 backgrounds, contrasting:

- the French B2 data with the French C2 data
- the Chinese B2 data with Chinese C2 data
- the French B2 data with the Chinese B2 data
- the French C2 data with the Chinese C2 data

For this particular example, because of the available metadata in the Open CLC (see Table 3.2), comparisons can also be made across age, gender, nationality, length of time studying English, exam taken, and the year the exam was taken. Learner corpora can offer a rich source of information for language teaching professionals about how learners from different backgrounds use language in different contexts. Consequently, from the early days of LCR, learner corpora were inextricably linked to and driven by language pedagogy, and viewed through a contrastive lens.

3.2   A contrastive perspective

3.2.1   Background

Contrastive Interlanguage Analysis (CIA) is a research perspective which is still widespread in learner corpus research. Granger (1996) found in CIA a way to "establish comparisons [...] between native and learner varieties of one and the same language" (Granger, 1996, p.43). CIA uses a contrastive analytical framework, encompassing two types of contrast which were originally conceived to meet the objectives of LCR: firstly, comparison of a language being learned (L2) with a learner's first language (L2:L1); secondly, comparison of varieties of learner language from different L1 backgrounds with each other (L2:L2). Using cross-sectional corpora, this framework allowed for a cross-sectional comparison of frequencies of linguistic features across different corpora or subcorpora, the results of which are typically reported in terms of quantitative differences of 'underuse' and 'overuse', and qualitative differences of 'misuse' (or 'error') (Callies, 2015). The analysis of misuse relies on corpora which have been tagged for error. (See below and Chapter 4 for further discussion of this terminology.)

The creation of the International Corpus of Learner English (ICLE) (see Table 3.2) became central to this approach. The ICLE is a corpus comprising a collection of written essays from upper intermediate and advanced learners (Granger, 2003). The first version of the ICLE was released on CD-ROM in 2002 (Granger, Dagneaux, & Meunier, 2002) and contained 2 million words from 11 L1 backgrounds, including Chinese, Finnish, German, Russian, Swedish. The current, third iteration, ICLEv3 (Granger et al., 2020), contains over 5.5 million words, from 25 L1 backgrounds and is hosted on a web-based interface, facilitating flexible access and creation of new subcorpora highlighting the fundamentally dynamic nature of the ICLE project (https://uclouvain.be/en/research -institutes/ilc/cecl/icle.html) (See also Chapter 4 for further discussion on the ICLE). Alongside the ICLE, a comparable L1 corpus of writing, the Louvain Corpus of Native English Essays (LOCNESS), was developed with a collection of essays from A-level students in the UK, and university students in the UK and US, totalling 324,304 words. The ICLE and LOCNESS together provided a means for both L1:L2 and L2:L2 comparisons of written data.

Five years after the creation of the ICLE, a spoken counterpart, the LINDSEI project (Gilquin, De Cock, & Granger, 2010) (see Table 3.2) was launched, along with an L1 partner the Louvain Corpus of Native English Conversation (LOC-NEC). Both these corpora follow the same structure, with 50 interviews comprising three separate tasks of varying degrees of control and naturalness, (a monologue on a set topic, a free discussion with a (typically L1) interviewer, and a picture description). These two corpora were compiled and transcribed using the same conventions, to allow for direct comparison. There are 12 subcorpora in the LINDSEI, each from different L1 backgrounds, representing over 550 interviews. All of the tasks are linked to a profile which gives metadata about the interviewee, interviewer and task, and 23 variables have been encoded for each interview, allowing for a fine-grained analysis of the data. There have been over 100 studies documented on the LINDSEI and the LINDSEI bibliography alone https://uclouvain.be/en/research-institutes/ilc/cecl/lindsei-bibliography.html, illustrates how the data can be analysed on its own or in comparison with other corpora to investigate various aspects of learner language, ranging from, for example, lexis (De Cock, 2003), word classes (Pérez-Paredes, 2010), structure (Gilquin, 2018), phraseology, pragmatics (Aijmer, 2004). See also Chapters 4, 5 and 6 for further research using the LINDSEI.

The overriding purpose of contrastive analysis is to discover whether the similarities and differences observed were typical of a particular group or context or whether they could be generalised across groups. CIA (Granger, 1994, 1996, 2003, 2015) combines corpus-based analysis with cross-sectional data and quantitative methods in order to provide insights into learner language. Sometimes, researchers have devised a pedagogical aim and establish comparisons that can be of interest for remedial teaching or other initiatives that use L1 speech as a baseline for comparison.

3.2.2 Examples of contrastive studies

As we will see in Chapters 4, 5 and 6, LCR can offer observations on use of individual words, word classes, phrases, collocations, register, collustruction, and lexico-grammatical patterning. In this section we will survey some of the thousands of studies that have taken a contrastive view of learner data. Aijmer (2004), for example, used both first language and learner language to look at the problems students have when they communicate in the second or target language and, in particular, when learners make use of pragmatic markers. Altenberg and Tapper (1998) contrasted the use of conjuncts in essays written by advanced Swedish learners of English and by English native speakers. They found that Swedish learners underused resultative concluding or inferential conjuncts and contrastive conjuncts in comparison with L1 users. They found that other conjuncts (*still, for instance*) are, however, overused by learners. The authors used the ICLE and the LOCNESS corpora to model learner and L1 languages in their study, two of the most-widely used corpora in the analysis of written language. The notion of a model is crucial to understand the range of research questions that can be explored through the use of CIA and, in different ways, how data are modelled allows for different research questions and designs. For example, some researchers focus predominantly on representativeness aspects. Thus, Tognini-Bonelli maintains that by comparing instances of learner language with normative model corpora, the language of learners can be explored in a much more profound way than the previous work on error analysis was able to do (2010). However, other efforts have a different take on the role of 'model corpora' and, quite evidently, on the lack of a predominant focus on learner language errors. Aijmer (2011) examined how the LINDSEI Swedish advanced speakers of English and LOCNEC English speakers used *well* as a pragmatic marker and found out that frequency of use was not an issue within Swedish learners. Her analysis, however, revealed that the underlying pragmatic reasons for these uses were significantly different. This finding suggests that overall frequency of use alone can only reveal some of the aspects that may potentially play a role in the how adverbs interact with speaking tasks.

3.2.3 Contrastive Interlanguage Analysis (CIA) revisited

The research in the paragraphs above and in subsequent chapters are just but a few selected instances of what we may label as the CIA approach. A new CIA model, revisited by Granger in 2015, acknowledges the role of variation in interlanguage studies and makes it more explicit. Granger (2015) presents a finedgrained analysis on the implications of using CIA that can be summarised in 3 areas: (1) The term under/over use should not be interpreted in a prescriptive or norm-conforming way, it is rather descriptive or statistical; (2) 'native-speaker' language does not necessarily imply the assumption that inner varieties of L1 speakers (UK, US, Australia, etc. in the case of English) should be promoted or adopted by L2 speakers or endorsed by researchers; (3) learner languages can be investigated in their own right. All in all, Granger (2015) maintains that researchers should try to keep theory and method separate and, if anything, understand that CIA is primarily a research method to gain insight into learner language.

Despite the usefulness of early LCR descriptions, researchers are embracing new ways to analyse learner language and are moving away from over-/underuse descriptions towards what Deshors and Gries (2020) term more context-sensitive ways of studying quantitatively the complexity of native language versus interlanguage comparisons. This analytical shift, according to Deshors and Gries (2020), has led scholars to adopt more sophisticated statistical approaches such as cluster analysis, correspondence analysis, and logistic regression modelling. This development, they say, reflects an important effort within the LCR community to harness, rather than move away from, the full potential of the LCR frameworks and their benefits as theoretical concepts by adopting state-of-the-art methodological approaches and statistical techniques.

3.3   Developmental perspective

3.3.1   Background

Increasingly, recent research using learner corpora is broadening its focus beyond the contrastive paradigm to address second language development research questions. Key drivers for this include the *push* of the availability of more dense learner corpora of different types via online platforms and the *pull* of the demand from SLA researchers to expand beyond experimental evidence of acquisition by using large-scale samples of learner language. Among this welcome emerging body of work, we see the growing impact of usage-based theories of language learning, particularly led by the work of Nick Ellis and his associates (Ellis et al., 2016) as well as research into the development of grammatical complexity through a register studies lens (Biber et al., 2020). Where contrastive cross-sectional studies of learner English have resulted in a wealth of description of learner language dominated by product and *performance*, at discrete points in time (Callies, 2015), longitudinal work across time and/or proficiency levels as a proxy for time, is in pursuit of descriptions of learner language *development* (Thewissen, 2013; Ellis, 2017, McEnery et al., 2019).

3.3.2   Examples of developmental studies

Using the 55-million-word Cambridge Learner Corpus (CLC) (Table 3.1), Hawkins and Filipović (2012), and Hawkins and Buttery (2010) identified a series of 'criterial features', properties that were seen to characterise and point to L2 proficiency, at each of the levels of the CEFR as evidenced in the CLC. Their aim was initially to discover these properties at the level of lexis and grammar in order to identify a set of linguistic features which provide the necessary specificity to CEFR's functional descriptors for each of the proficiency level (Hawkins & Buttery, 2009). These features are framed in positive or negative terms compared to their exemplification in L1 usage; where a feature corresponds with L1 usage (in the BNC) it is said to be a positive linguistic property and where it does not it is said to be a negative linguistic property. Different distributions of positive and negative properties distinguish different levels of proficiency. Negative linguistic properties demonstrate error types at a given level and these were seen to decrease as proficiency increased, particularly from B2 to C1 levels, which indicated development between these levels.

O'Keeffe and Mark (2017) also used the CLC to profile learner use of multiple grammatical features, traditionally covered in English language teaching classroom contexts, across six proficiency levels. In this pseudo-longitudinal study, they observed development as an expanding repertoire of lexis and functions and pragmatic competence. As proficiency increased, learners put syntactic patterns to multiple uses, using an increasing lexical range, alongside displaying a greater awareness of the collocational and colligational limitations of a given pattern, as well as an understanding of specialised pragmatic meanings (see Chapter 6).

Murakami and Alexopoulou (2016) used the CLC to evaluate the long-held view that there is a universal order of acquisition for English morphemes (Brown, 1973; Dulay & Burt, 1973). They used a subcorpus of the CLC, from seven L1 groups across five proficiency levels, and explored the development of six most frequently studied morphemes, from morpheme studies, (articles, past tense -*ed*, plural -*s*, possessive '*s*, progressive -*ing*, and third-person -*s*). Their findings demonstrated the role that large-scale corpora in LCR can play in examining SLA hypotheses. They concluded that there was a strong L1 influence in the accuracy of the morphemes, which affected different morphemes in different ways, and refuted the universal order of acquisition theory.

Alexopoulou, Geertzen, Korhonen, and Meurers (2015) took a Natural Language Processing (NLP) approach to following the development of relative clauses, as an exemplar to demonstrate how large datasets can be used to study developmental trajectories across proficiency levels, playing a key empirical role in SLA research. They used the 33-million-word EFCAMDAT, another large pseudo-longitudinal corpus. Their findings indicate L1 effects and show how different types of relative clauses increase with proficiency. At 55 million words and 33 million words respectively, the CLC and EFCAMDAT are considered relatively large in LCR. These studies demonstrate Granger's assertion that learner corpora of naturally-occurring language can facilitate studies that can claim greater representativeness (Granger, 2009, p. 16) than previous SLA studies that relied on an experimental approach involving tasks such as acceptability judgements and gap-fills, with a small number of participants.

Thewissen (2013) provides an important 'crossover' study in which she looked longitudinally and contrastively at sample lexical and grammatical items, moving away from year of study as her cross-sectional point (in favour of the CEFR) and tracking learner development across four proficiency levels (B1, B2, C1, C2) specifically in relation to accuracy. She tracked the developmental pathways of error types in an error-tagged sample of the ICLE (comprising 223 learner essays from three L1 backgrounds — French, Spanish and German, amounting to 150,000 tokens) and observed strong progress (in terms of error decrease) between B1 and B2 levels. She observed a plateauing of progress in relation to errors between B2 and C2 levels which she posits may "hide qualitative development" (Thewissen, 2013, p. 87).

In another study also tracking errors, Meunier and Littré (2013) adopted an experimental approach alongside analysis of the Longitudinal Database of Learner English (LONGDALE) (Table 3.1) to study tense and aspect development in 38 L1 French students, with written contributions of one argument essay per year across three years, noting a decrease in errors over the three years.

Using another small-scale longitudinal dataset, Vyatkina (2013) tracked the developmental complexity of syntactic structures (e.g., coordinate and complex nominal structures per clause) in the same two (German L1) beginner learners, over four semesters. Combining POS tagging with manual checking and annotation, and concordance software, she identified points where target structures emerged in the data. Important to note here is that the developmental profiles of the two learners observed were different, with one learner showing a greater development than the other.

In two studies using the Spanish component of the International Corpus of Crosslinguistic Interlanguage (ICCI) (Tono, 2012; Tono & Díez-Bedmar, 2014) comprising 17,034 tokens, Pérez-Paredes and Díez-Bedmar (2019) and Díez-Bedmar and Pérez-Paredes (2020) also use a combination of methods to measure syntactic complexity, across a range of age groups (grades 8 to 12). In the 2019 study they combine POS keyword analysis with automatic statistical complexity analysis software (TAASSC) (Kyle, 2016) to look at noun phrase complexity and syntactic sophistication through analysis of verb-argument construction (VACs). The 2020 study concentrates on the noun phrase, combining manual analysis with a TAASSC approach (Kyle, 2016). Both studies reveal the affordances offered by different research methods and point to the analysis of complexity of the noun phrase as being of great interest in terms of identifying development milestones in language acquisition (Pérez-Paredes & Díez-Bedmar, 2019). Their findings also include the importance of countable nouns, prepositional phrases, verbs and general adverbs in defining the transition from lower to higher secondary school learning.

In line with this focus on phrasal complexity, Biber and Gray (2011, 2016) offer an innovative framework which highlights the phrase and compressed phrasal structure as an equally important indication of grammatical complexity and development as clausal structure and dependence (Biber et al., 2020). Alongside the phrasal complexity they point to the role of register and register awareness in the developmental process. The compressed phrasal structure takes centre stage in development as learners become more aware of its importance in writing.

Biber et al. (2011, 2020) offer five hypothesised stages of development which indicate a general trend towards a decreased use in dependent clause complexity and an increased use of phrasal complexity (from finite complement clauses to pre and post modified noun phrases). They argue that studies of development should encompass analysis of register, a focus on individual grammatical complexity features, including compressed phrasal structures as well as clause dependency (Biber et al., 2020, 2021). They call for descriptions of writing development that include frequently used devices that mark the phrasal compressions such as premodification of nouns with attributive adjectives, and prepositional phrases as post-modifiers (e.g., *increase in inflation rates*). Several studies have borne this out, among which Staples et al. (2016), using the BAWE corpus (Heuboeck et al., 2008) found that complement clauses, relative clauses and adverbial clauses decreased in university academic writing while noun phrase modification increased. They point out the lack of the types of verb-based embedded clauses which are traditionally associated with 'advanced' writing. Many of these studies, as much of the research into structural complexity, tend to be dominated by learners at the higher end of the proficiency and with academic language production as the focus.

3.4   Corpus-pedagogy and language learning

Corpora are not only used to research L1 or L2 usage as we have seen above. There is a considerable body of research (Boulton & Cobb, 2017; Pérez-Paredes, 2022; Boulton & Vyatkina, 2021; Boulton, 2021) that has examined the use of both L1 and L2 corpora in ISLA. Corpus-based pedagogy has been used in the teaching and learning of languages for general and specific purposes (Cotos, 2017), as we will discuss in detail in Chapter 8. Corpus-based pedagogy exploits the potential of linguistic corpora and their applications in instructed contexts, an approach which has been popular in ESP courses. Yoon and Hirvela (2004) used corpora and CL research methods to develop their students' use of vocabulary and writing skills, including increasing confidence when writing in their L2. Gaskell and Cobb (2004) used concordancing (see Chapter 2) in a lower-intermediate L2 English writing course. Around 40% of the students said using concordance lines helped them improve their writing. A much-cited instance is Lee and Swales (2006), who taught PhD students to put together a corpus of their own writing as well as a discipline specific corpus and query it for language awareness and writing. To do this, the learners used *WordSmith Tools* (Scott, 2008), a professional CL research tool. The learners were instructed to compare their own writing and that of established writers in their fields. The authors claim that using discipline-specific written discourses made learners more engaged with the texts and the whole discovery-learning process. For Lee and Swales using L1 corpora in ESP empowers learners in two ways:

> We believe the corpus approach is decentering because: (i) it allows non-native speakers a chance to make their own discoveries about what is done in the language, instead of relying on native-speaker intuitions or grammar/style books;

> (ii) it typically involves texts from a variety of different writers/speakers [...]
> instead of just one native-speaker teacher standing at the front of the classroom.
>
> (Lee & Swales, 2016, p. 71)

Data-driven learning (DDL) can be considered as the best instantiation of direct corpus-based pedagogy, which we will discuss in detail in Chapter 8.

3.5   Designing and building a learner corpus

Most learner corpora were not built with language acquisition hypotheses in mind, they were built to capture learner language as a variety, and as a result we end up with what Granger describes as all-purpose learner corpus rather than purpose-built (Granger, 2021). This approach has allowed the compilation of large corpora but has not always meant that the data meets the needs of the enquiry. As McEnery et al. (2019) point out, learner corpora are numerous and growing but their variety is limited, and despite Granger's description it is impossible for one corpus to meet all purposes. Early learner corpora have been criticised for inadequate background documentation (Myles, 2021), though more recently through detailed corpus metadata, and the ability to filter corpora along a range of learner- and task-variables (e.g., L1 background, age, gender, task, proficiency, task/exam question type, exam type) researchers have more control and can target specific SLA hypotheses (e.g., Römer, 2019). As O'Keeffe et al. (2007) note, the data we choose to work with needs to be the one which is most appropriate for given research needs. This may mean building one's own.

As we have seen, learner corpora, large and small, are not just any old collections of learner language. They have been compiled following well documented guidelines of principled and representative collection (Atkins et al., 1992; Biber et al., 1998). In this section we give an overview of some of the basic design principles that need to be taken into account when building a corpus. Broadly, the design and building process follows a few basic steps:

- Design and planning
- Data and metadata collection
- Data transcription
- Annotation

The first step is to consider your research questions and create a design matrix which will then guide the collection of data. Similarly, as in all types of research, it is essential to consider critical ethical issues, in this case ethical considerations related to the collection of learner data. Following general principles, Ädel (2021) has stressed the need for approval from an institutional ethics review board before a learner corpus project can even begin. She has suggested that, even if institutional approval is not officially required in an institution, consent needs to be sought from the informants in order to collect, store and use the data for research purposes (ibid). A consent form needs to signed by each informant, as it is the norm for research ethics:

> Asking for permission to use material for a corpus is often done by means of a consent form, which is signed by each informant, or by the legal guardians in the case of children [...] A consent form should clearly state what the data will be used for so that an informed decision can be made. It needs to be clear that the decision to give consent is completely voluntary. It is important how the consent form is worded, so it is useful to consider forms used in similar corpus projects for comparison.   (Ädel, 2021, p. 9)

A further ethical step that is essential in building a corpus is to anonymise the data. This means either replacing identifying proper nouns with codes or with invented replacements. If a sample of learner writing uses names of people, places or events, any of these could potentially identify them. For example, *My name is Rafa and I live in Madrid with my mother and father. After school I study English at The English Academy of Madrid ...* The identifying references to people and place can either be changed either to codes or to invented replacements:

Option 1   My name is [anon_name_01] and I live in [anon_place_01] with my mother and father. After school I study at [anon_place_02]

Option 2   My name is Eric and I live in Rioja with my mother and father. After school I study at Student Campus English School

Option 1   is the norm and allows for consistent use of codes. So if *Madrid* or *The English Academy of Madrid* are mentioned again, they will keep the codes *[anon_place_01]* and *[anon_place_02]*.

As is the case in all research, collecting data from children needs special attention as they are a vulnerable population. As Stoll and Schikowski (2021) note in the context of researching child language:

> Besides obtaining ethics clearance from institutional reviewing boards and/or funding agencies, researchers need to have sufficient knowledge of the socio cultural context and take the time to explain to the participating families in detail what the research implies. In communities speaking under documented languages, involving the community itself may be an additional concern and data protection is of special importance since these communities are often tightly knit.
> (Stoll & Schikowski, 2021, pp. 318–19)

3.5.1   Creating a design matrix

In designing the corpus, we need to consider what variables are essential or relevant to our research. It is useful to think about how the answers to the following questions inform our research design:

–   What type of data do I need to collect? Do I wish to collect a specific genre? What are my criteria for inclusion?
–   Where will I find this data?
–   How much data do I need to collect?
–   Do I need data collected at a single point or over multiple points in time?
–   Do I need data that is gathered over one single point in time, different points in time with the same participants, or different participants?
–   Is my data from a homogenous group or a heterogeneous group? How will I ensure a balanced representation from groups? How will I ensure I understand the variability in the data?
–   How will I ensure that it is representative? (e.g. if my research question relates to Elementary level learners, have I got an adequate representation of learners at this level across a range of task types, etc.)
–   What variables do I need to gather about participants? e.g., age, L1 linguistic proficiency, gender, institutional/learning context, linguistic background (how long have they been studying English? Have they been on a study-abroad period?), etc.
–   What kinds of task do I need to include? What variables do I need to take into account with regard to task? Can I account for the variables and effect of the topic/task on the data?
–   If the data is spoken, do I also need to collect video files?
–   If the data is spoken, is it monologic or dialogic? For example, does the presence of other participants affect the data? Can I account for any effects this might have?
–   What is the feasibility of collecting my data? Is it legal or ethical? Do I have any time constraints?
–   Does the type of analysis I am undertaking have an impact on any of these variables?
–   Does the choice of platform I am intending to use to compile and analyse the data have any impact on the design? For example, if I am collecting multimodal data such as video recordings, to look at verbal and non-verbal behaviour, will standard video communication platforms such as *MS Teams* or *Zoom* suffice to capture gesture and gaze or will other resources such as additional cameras and eye-tracking facilities be required?

Clearly not all of the points listed above will be relevant to all data types or analyses but scoping as much background detail as possible about variables relating to for example environment, context, task and participants, and recording it from the outset will contribute to a fine-grained analysis. Burnard points out that metadata is essential since without it the researcher is left with "disconnected words of unknowable provenance or authenticity" (Burnard, 2005, p.31)

3.5.2 Building a corpus: An example of the ACE Corpus

In this section we look at a specific example of the design and creation of a small, specialised corpus, the ACE (Adult Corpus of English) (McNamara, 2020). This 170,000-word spoken and written corpus was built specifically to answer the following general research question and specific sub-questions:

To what degree can adult learners of ESL use multi-word lexical items (multi-word verbs, delexical verbs, collocations and idiomatic/figurative language) in their speaking and writing?

a. What is the difference between the lexical competence of the A2 level student and the C1 level student?

b. Which level (A2 or C1) use the majority of multi-word units and language strings in their speaking and writing?

c. Is there a progression from more high-frequency transparent strings towards low frequency opaque strings?

The focus of this micro-study was the use of lexical bundles or strings by ESL students at a higher education centre in Ireland, studying for the Further Education and Training Awards Council (FETAC). The overall aim was to ascertain if students at both ends of the language learning proficiency spectrum (A2 and C1) used multi-word items in their speaking and writing. The sub-questions required specific demands of the data: (a) requires data from two proficiency levels, (b) requires both spoken and written data from the same learners, and (c) requires longitudinal data. The overall question requires data from a range of tasks.

We return to the considerations discussed in Table 3.1 to establish a suitable corpus design framework for this study, which is illustrated in Table 3.5.

Table 3.5 Design framework for the ACE corpus (McNamara, 2020)

Data collection time	Longitudinal; over 12 weeks (one academic term)
Mode	Written: 20,000 words (114 samples of writing)
	Spoken: 150,000 words (3 hours each week x 2 weeks)
Task	Spoken: classroom interactions between teachers and students, oral presentations and examinations based on the FETAC syllabus
	Written: assignments, homework and grammar tasks based on the FETAC syllabus, representing a range of ten different formats and genres, including a job application and CV, a narrative based on a picture, a letter giving advice.
Learners	24 participants; background data captured about proficiency level, gender, L1, nationality, occupation, hobbies, length of time studying English

3.5.3   Collection, transcription and annotation

Once the design of the corpus has been decided, the next step is to begin to collect the data and the collection process will vary depending on the type of corpus. To build a corpus we need digital files, typically text files (.txt). The gathering of digitally-created written data in the form of text files or word files is a much more straightforward task than typewritten or hand-written data, which require electronic transcription. These days digitally-created texts are the norm but handwritten or typewritten texts are easily transcribed using more and more sophisticated optical character recognition tools. Transcribing spoken data takes longer. One hour of spoken data can take up to ten to fifteen hours to transcribe (Reppen, 2010; O'Keeffe & McCarthy 2022). However, the spread and increase of automated transcription services may ease the time needed to come up with a first transcription draft. As automated speech recognition of L2 speech is not as advanced as that for L1 spoken language, researchers will almost certainly need to revise the transcriptions manually. Whether done manually or using automated transcription tools, transcription requires careful and detailed consideration about the level of detail to be included.

Focus 3.3 Transcription and automated speech recognition

🔎 **Transcription and automated speech recognition (ASR)**

Whereas in the past it was very common for researchers to transcribe spoken data manually, at the time of writing this book an increasing range of sophisticated tools are available, both free to the user and via subscription services. A simple web search using the term 'speech to text tools' results in an array of software options, with varying features, many of which are suitable for transcription of spoken data. Microsoft Office 365 offers an in-built function to transcribe audio files that, at least with L1 language, provides accurate transcriptions. In the last two years, AI has revolutionised the automatic generation of transcriptions.

In the case of the ACE corpus (McNamara, 2020) described in 3.5.2, the written data was hand-written by the participants and the researcher typed them all up, including errors, to create a digital format. The spoken data was transcribed from the audio data and annotated using a set of conventions which had been applied in the construction of the Nottingham Corpus of Discourse in English (CANCODE) (McCarthy, 1998; Carter & McCarthy, 2004) an L1 English corpus of everyday conversational English. This involved making decisions ranging from use of punctuation and capitalisation to how to represent interruptions, overlaps and incomplete words. As well as the speech representation, each of the target features identified for the study were then manually tagged, for example, in this case all of the multi-word items (multi-word verbs, delexical verbs, collocations and idiomatic/figurative language).

Focus 3.4 Gathering written data: A return to pen and paper?

🔎 **Gathering written data: a return to pen and paper?**

Discussions about the use of assistive technology and AI have become increasingly relevant when considering learner writing (Bailey & Lee 2020; Fitriana & Nurazni, 2022). There is range of tools available to learners during the writing process and this has obvious implications in gathering authentic learner writing. While digital collection of written data is easier for the researcher it does not guarantee an accurate representation of learner language. In the future, hand-written texts produced in controlled conditions, such as the classroom, may be the only way to truly capture the unaided writing of an L2 writer.

The extract below shows an example of the annotation used in the ACE corpus. Each participant is assigned a speaker tag (e.g. <$3>), the Teacher is identified using T, extralinguistic data is tagged using a <$E> tag around a description of the feature (e.g. <$E>laughs<$E>, <$E>points to phone<$E>), and the items in focus are tagged using bold face (e.g. **yoke**) for subsequent manual analysis ; pauses are represented with three dots '...':

In this extract Student <\$3> from the C1 level cohort is explaining a slang Irish word that she has heard:

Student <\$3>: I mean I find it very useful...it can be used for anything anything at all...**yoke**

Student <\$22>: but what does it means?

Student <\$3>: anything...I can say pass me that **yoke** <\$E>points to phone<SE> can I have one of those yokes <\$E>points at chair<\$E> <\$E>laughs<\$E>

Student <\$22>: so we no need learn English just one word

T: <\$E>laughs<\$E> but you won't be understood anywhere outside of possibly Ireland.

Knight et al. (2024) note a lack of agreed standardisation in transcription, thought point to common shared practices and documented transcription guidelines that can be used as excellent starting points (Carter & McCarthy, 2004; Love, 2020). There also exists a consortium, the Text Encoding Initiative (TEI) whose pursuit is to develop and standardise gold detailed standard guidelines and practices for working with machine readable texts (https://tei-c.org). An online archive of resources for the collection of multi-modal data (analysing verbal and non-verbal behaviour) is available through the Interactional Variation Online project (https://ivohub.com/resources/). These resources offer a state-of-the-art description of data collection, transcription and annotation processes, particularly for multi-modal data.

Detailed guidelines are not always needed or relevant for all learner corpus research, which in general favours a broad transcription approach in which orthographic features are enriched with prosodic elements, such as pauses, as exemplified in the extract above. Pérez-Paredes (2020) details this kind of broad approach which was taken for the LINDSEI corpus, (2020). King et al. (2019) put this lack of standardisation down to the fact that transcription approaches tend to be "project-driven, and accordingly, unique in different ways" (2019, p. 194).

In summary, it will be the project focus and the research questions which inform the conventions adopted. A rule of thumb is to transcribe the features that the researchers are interested in, for example if turn-taking is not a focus then there is no need to transcribe overlaps or interruptions.

3.6   Summary

In this chapter we have looked at types of learner corpora. We noted that learner corpora have to be carefully designed so that end-users can address a range of research questions into the future. The robustness of a corpus is linked to careful design and representativeness. The availability of adequate metadata is highlighted: this relates to (1) each learner who has contributed a spoken or written text (age, L1; gender; nationality; year of study; level of proficiency; etc.); and (2) the task(s) which were used to elicit these data (text type; exam question, task, year, level; etc.). If a corpus is missing key information about the data, a research in the future will be limited in terms of the variables that they can explore. Key considerations in building a corpus were also discussed in terms of practicalities such as tagging and annotation, as well as the importance of ethics and data management and compliance (e.g. the need for consent or to anonymise identifying information in the data). The chapter also includes some of the ever-growing list of learner corpora that are available (though some may be require permission or have access restrictions). The contrastive perspective in LCR has a long tradition and this is explained and exemplified in this chapter. The developmental perspective in LCR was also covered here, pointing to important links to SLA. Additionally, we discuss the pedagogic and language learning perspective can also be taken in LCR. We now move from looking at types of corpora, broad perspectives on how they have been research and how to build them to looking at corpus methods and approaches to analysing them.

PART 2

Units of analysis
in learner language research

CHAPTER 4

Researching word classes using corpora and POS tagging

Recommended reading 4.1

Newman, J. & Cox, C. (2020). Corpus Annotation. In M. Paquot & S. T. Gries (Eds.), *A Practical handbook of corpus linguistics* (pp. 25–48). Springer.

In this chapter, the authors provide a comprehensive view of POS tagging and related computational processes such as lemmatization, syntactic parsing and other types of annotation.

Recommended reading 4.2

Pérez-Paredes, P. (2020). *Corpus linguistics for education: A guide for research.* Routledge.

Chapter 3 in this volume looks specifically at corpus design and the role of POS tagging within corpus design. Chapter 7 deals with complex searches in spoken language and demonstrates the practical use of POS tags and tag sequences when using CQL query tools.

Recommended reading 4.3

Gries, S. T. (2017). *Quantitative corpus linguistics with R: A practical introduction* (2nd ed.). Routledge.

An excellent resource for researchers working with R scripts. It offers opportunities to reflect on how POS tags are displayed and treated in R and how they contribute to a corpus-based research project.

Chapter 2 described the basic use of key functions of corpus tools at a word and phrase level, for example through the use of word and phrase lists, multi-word units, keywords and concordances. This chapter looks at the corpus tools and approaches that have been employed to explore the use of word classes (i.e., nouns, verbs, adverbs, etc.) in learner language research. Grasping the impact of word class analysis on learner corpus research is a necessary step to become familiar with the wider range of corpus methods that make use of part of speech (POS) tagging. Methods that explore lexical units other than word classes will be discussed in the next two chapters: collocations in Chapter 5, and colligation and collostructions in Chapter 6.

In the past, if researchers wanted to investigate word classes within corpus data, they would manually identify and tag words with their word class or part of speech. Nowadays, with advances in technology and the development of ever more sophistication of corpus software, automatic POS speech tagging tends to be a standard feature. It is now very likely that every single corpus analysed in language learning research has been part-of-the-speech tagged, but what does this mean? When data is loaded into corpus software, the software working in the background automatically identifies the word class of each word and tags it accordingly. Why should researchers pay attention to an apparently trivial automated process? The reason why this process is relevant is that part of speech tagging needs further consideration and analysis in language learning research as, despite being an automatic process, an in-depth understanding of its nature is essential when analysing language.

Focus 4.1 Tagging

🔍 Tagging

In corpus linguistics, the term tagging is frequently used to denote that a corpus has been subjected to automatic morphological analysis. In POS tagging every word is assigned a tag that shows their explicit labelling as nouns, verbs, etc.

The collection of tags that are used is called a tagset. Tagsets can be very basic, for example N for Noun, V for Verb, P for Pronoun, or more typically they can be more detailed, for example, indicating different types of pronouns, or differentiating between singular and plural nouns, or countable nouns. Different types of corpus software make use of different tagsets (see Focus 4.4). Other types of tagging in corpus linguistics include semantic tagging (i.e., the tagging of word senses) or rhetorical move tagging (i.e. the rhetorical moves in a research article, for example using Swales' (1990) framework). Manual annotation of corpus data is often referred either as tagging or annotation.

In the following sections, we provide an overview of learner corpus studies that compare the frequency of linguistic features through word class analysis across L1 and L2 corpora, particularly in the International Corpus of Learner English (ICLE). Sections 4.2 and 4.3 look at part of speech tagging and word classes, respectively. We begin by summarising early learner corpus research and describing the ICLE which we then use to illustrate POS tagging and research into word classes.

4.1   Early learner corpus research: The International Corpus of Learner English

The first applications of corpus methods to language learning date back to the 1990s with the compilation and widespread use of the ICLE (Granger, 1993). In fact, most of the early research using contrastive interlanguage analysis (CIA) used this L2 corpus. This early learner language research primarily focused on L2 English, making use of cross-sectional research designs, and examining a wide range of lexical units (Granger, 1996, 2015) (see Chapter 2). Importantly, CIA assumed the native speaker perspective, and, accordingly, as Callies (2015) noted was "based on an underlying pedagogical perspective that considers native speakers' language as a kind of benchmark against which differences and features of learner language are evaluated and characterised as native-like or, rather, non-native-like" (p. 49). While learner corpus researchers maintain that using native speaker data offers a normative perspective in foreign language teaching (Callies, 2015), understanding L2 usage as mere attempts to reproduce or approximate L1 norms has been heavily criticised by SLA researchers (e.g. Myles, 2021; Ortega, 2013) (see Chapter 3).

According to Granger (1996), learner corpora allow for the comparison of both native speaker and learner language. The emphasis in Granger's (1996) version of CIA is on *variety*, understood as different types of genres or registers. CIA affords comparisons between native language and interlanguage varieties (L1:L2), on the one hand, and between different interlanguage varieties (L2:L2), on the other. Granger (1996) argues that for applied linguists to implement robust research methods, they need to make sure that there are, at least, some variables that need to be controlled, including the type of learner (i.e., foreign language learner vs. second language learner), stage of learning (i.e. intermediate language learner) and text type (i.e. argumentative essay).

The ICLE is probably the best example of a cross-sectional corpus (see Chapter 3). ICLEv3 (Granger et al., 2020), the most recent version of ICLE, includes L1 speakers already present in the 2009 ICLEv2 (Bulgarian, Chinese, Czech, Dutch, Finnish, French, German, Italian, Japanese, Norwegian, Polish, Russian, Spanish, Swedish, Turkish, Tswana), plus speakers of Brazilian Portuguese, Greek, Hungarian, Persian (Iran), Korean, Lithuanian, Macedonian, Pakistani and Serbian L1s. ICLEv3 offers some 5.7 million words of L2 English.

The first version of the ICLE was made publicly available in 2002 and contained some 2.5 million words produced by learners from 11 different L1 backgrounds (as specified above). Table 4.1 shows the first 100 words from a random essay from the French L1 group. This is an argumentative essay of 561 words.

Table 4.1 A sample from the French L1 subset of ICLE

A sample from the International Corpus of Learner English (ICLE)
ICLE-FR-ULB-0030.1 The most striking features of our modern world is the idea of progress which is particularly linked with the industrial revolution throughout the 19th century. This never-ending need for investigation of new fields, for discoveries, for improvement of our standard of living as well as the accumulation of knowledge are the sources of our blindness to our war-torn, decaying planet. Man has enriched his life by creating physical mobility (through the motor-car, the aeroplane, the train and other means of mechanical transport), telecommunications (TV, radio, telephone), and mechanization, but all this at the cost of an imbalance between man and nature.

This sample exemplifies the kind of student output that was collected in the ICLE. The learners represented in ICLE were 3rd and 4th year undergraduate students of English. The vast majority of texts (94%) in ICLEv3 are argumentative essays. According to Granger et al. (2020), argumentative essays were chosen as a target genre given that they allow researchers to explore a wide range of discourse, lexical, and grammatical features of learner written language. As we will see below, every essay is annotated with relevant metadata. Some of the metadata collected with the essays include information about the learners themselves, such as the conditions under which the essay was written, parents' mother tongues, languages of instruction and years of stay in English speaking countries. Figure 4.2 shows the actual form designed for data collection in ICLEv2.

This type of learner profile information is common in LCR. When putting together their own corpus, SLA researchers can potentially design the metadata collection protocols that best suit their research aims. However, when relying on existing corpora, the metadata that is distributed cannot be enlarged or complemented with further information. Paquot et al. (2023) have recently argued that it is necessary to consider the inclusion of a range of core metadata information in every learner corpus. Their initial proposal includes some 22 core fields such as contact email, version, publisher, handle or character encoding.

As for the proficiency of the learners, the ICLE collection design criteria do not restrict learners' participation based on accredited performance levels. However, it is thought that most ICLE learners are, on average, upper-intermediate or advanced learners of English. An analysis of a sample of the essays (Granger et al., 2020) showed that not every L1 group offers the same L2 English performance profile. For example, while 80% of the Bulgarian L1 essays were rated as C1, only 60% of the L1 German learners were rated as C1. However, 35% of the latter were rated as C2, while only 10% in the Bulgarian data were C2. As for performance levels below C1, the category of B2 or below used by the raters fails to capture the

LEARNER PROFILE
LEARNER PROFILE

:==:
Text code : (do not fill in)

Essay :

Title :
Approximate length required :   −500 words 0   +500 words
                0
Conditions :   timed   0   untimed
                                  0
Examination :   yes   0
        no   0
Reference tools :   yes   0   no
        0

What reference tools ?
            Bilingual dictionary :
            English monolingual dictionary :
            Grammar :
            Other(s) :
:==:
Surname :   First names :
Age :   Male   0   Female
                0

Nationality :
Native language :
Father's mother tongue :
Mother's mother tongue :
Language(s) spoken at home : (if more than one, please give the average % use of each)

Education :

Primary school - medium of instruction :
Secondary school - medium of instruction :

Current studies :
Current year of study :
Institution :
Medium of instruction :
            English only 0
            Other language (s) (specify) 0
            Both   0
:==:
Years of English at school :
Years of English at university :

Stay in an English-speaking country :
Where ?
When ?   How long ?

:==:
Other foreign languages in decreasing order of proficiency :

:==:

                I hereby give permission for my essay to be used for research
purposes .

Date : ....   Signature : ...

Figure 4.2 Metadata form and consent form for ICLEv2[5]

---

5. URL: http://cdn.uclouvain.be/public/Exports%20reddot/cecl/documents/LEARNER
_PROFILE.txt

actual performance level of the learners. A case in point is Chinese and Tswana L1 groups, whose essays were rated at B2 or below in 95% and 90% of the cases, respectively.

Comparisons with ICLE data often use The Louvain Corpus of Native English Essays (LOCNESS)[6] (Granger, 1998) (see Table 3.1), a comparable corpus of L1 English essays made up of British pupils' A level essays (60,209 words), British university students' essays (95,695 words) and American university students' essays (168,400 words). In the following sections, we examine how the ICLE and the LOCNESS have been used by researchers in the past, using POS tags, to research learner language use. However, it is useful that we discuss first how POS tags and taggers are used in CL research and how they are instrumental in gaining insight into learner language.

In the following section we offer an introduction to the relevance of POS tagging in learner language research and some considerations to think about when using part of speech tags in learner language research.

4.2   Part-of-speech (POS) tagging, tagsets and learner corpora

As noted above, nowadays corpus data is typically automatically tagged for part-of-speech (POS). POS tags are automatically attached to each word during the corpus construction stage. They provide information about morphosyntactic properties of a given text. As well as the word or phrase at surface level, there is additional layer of morphosyntactic information sitting below a word, at a word class or part of speech level, to which researchers have access. Different corpus software make use of different tagsets, depending on who has developed the tools and how they have been developed (see Focus 4.1). It is important to note that POS tagging might not always be 100% accurate, typically containing an average of 2–3% errors in the annotated data (McEnery & Hardie, 2012) and because of the nature of the data learner language is likely to yield larger percentages of POS-tagging errors. For example, the Constituent Likelihood Automatic Word-tagging System (CLAWS) tagger, widely used for English, has been reported to annotate POS tags accurately in 97% of the output (Fligelstone et al., 1997). De Haan (2000) found that Dutch learner data displayed 95% of accuracy, meaning that 95% of the words were POS-tagged correctly, learner errors affect tagger accuracy by contributing to tag errors (Van Rooy & Schäfer, 2002), particularly spelling errors.

---

6. LOCNESS can be obtained in the following URL: https://www.learnercorpusassociation .org/resources/tools/locness-corpus/

Thanks to POS tags, L2 use can be automatically profiled (Granger & Rayson, 1998). Salient features of learner language can be measured by analysing the frequency of major word categories (nouns, verbs, adjectives, determiners, pronouns, etc.) as well as the lexical exponents of those categories (e.g. *dream, cancel, important*).

In their research, Granger and Rayson (1998) used the French subcorpus of the ICLE and the LOCNESS. They part-of-speech tagged the corpora and compared the frequency of the POS tags in both corpora. Both corpora were used as proxies for L2 English and L1 English, respectively, or using the terms that have become more widely used in LCR, non-native speaker language (NNS) and native-speaker language (NS). This way, patterns of overuse and underuse in the NNS corpus with reference to the NS corpus could be discovered. Granger and Rayson used CLAWS 4, a tagset developed by the University Centre for Computer Corpus Research on Language (UCREL) at Lancaster University.

4.2.1   Examples of POS tagging

In this section we illustrate the POS tags applied to the first sentence from the ICLE text in Table 4.1 using the CLAWS 7 tagset. The first output is in horizontal view, where POS tags are appended to the words using the underscore as a separator:

> The_AT most_RGT striking_JJ features_NN2 of_IO our_APPGE modern_JJ world_NN1 is_VBZ the_AT idea_NN1 of_IO progress_NN1 which_DDQ is_VBZ particularly_RR linked_VVN with_IW the_AT industrial_JJ revolution_NN1 throughout_II the_AT 19th_MD century_NNT1

In contrast this output shows the text in vertical display:

0000003 010 The	93 AT
0000003 020 most	97 RGT
0000003 030 striking	97 JJ
0000003 040 features	03 [NN2/100] VVZ@/o
0000003 050 of	93 IO
0000003 060 our	93 APPGE
0000003 070 modern	93 [JJ/100] NN1%/o
0000003 080 world	93 NN1
0000003 090 is	93 VBZ
0000003 100 the	93 AT
0000003 110 idea	03 NN1
0000003 120 of	93 IO

0000003 130 progress   03 [NN1/100] VV0@/0

0000003 140 which   93 DDQ

0000003 150 is   93 VBZ

0000003 160 particularly 03 RR

0000003 170 linked   03 [VVN/95] JJ/4 VVD@/1

0000003 180 with   93 IW

0000003 190 the   93 AT

0000003 200 industrial 93 JJ

0000003 210 revolution 03 NN1

0000003 220 throughout 93 [II/100] RL@/0

0000003 230 the   93 AT

0000003 240 19th   14 MD

0000003 250 century   93 NNT1

0000003 251.   03.

The vertical display facilitates reading how the POS tags match the words in the original input text. It is interesting to note how the tagger we used to tag this sentence[7] tells us how words were disambiguated. Take for example the word *features* in the fourth line of vertical text. The tagger offers two tag candidates: plural common noun (NN2) and third-person -s form of lexical verb (VVZ) [NN2/100] VVZ@/0 The tagger software shows that *features,* in the context of this sentence, is a noun and the likelihood that this is so is 100%. Now take *linked*. The tagger annotates this word as a past participle of a lexical verb (VVN), and the likelihood that this is so 95%, although, according to the tagger rules, there is a 4% likelihood that this could be an adjective (JJ) and 1% that this is a simple past form (VVD).

4.2.2   Understanding different tagsets

Researchers are advised to study the available tagset(s) before outlining very specific research questions as different taggers and tagsets vary in the way they tokenise, count, and annotate words and POS tags. For example, different taggers will examine words differently because they count words using different criteria. *Tokenisation* is the process of reading textual data and breaking them down into units that can be further analysed. In most corpus linguistics pipelines, this means that the software needs to find first the words that will be tagged later. This is not a trivial task, as the way textual data are tokenised will affect how frequencies are computed. For example, regarding contractions (don't, *ain't*, et.) a decision has to be taken as to whether they should be seen as one word or more than one (see

---

7. URL: http://ucrel-api.lancaster.ac.uk/claws/free.html

Baisa (2016), for a thorough treatment of language models and their computational treatment).

Researchers need to be aware how a POS tagset can affect the analysis and interpretation of the data. It is advised that researchers become familiar with, at least, the tagset used and explore the depth of the annotation which is provided (see Figure 4.5). For example, CLAWS 7 makes use of some 160 tags, while the FreeLing[8] (Carreras et al., 2004) tagset for English offers a much more reduced variety of tags. And not only that. FreeLing is widely used by the natural language processing (NLP) community in a range of applications where POS tagging in required across many languages. *Sketch Engine*, for example, makes use of FreeLing tagsets for languages such as Catalan, French, Italian Portuguese, Russian, Spanish or, among others, Welsh. FreeLing annotation outputs follow the EAGLES standard (Atwell, 1996) and offer several positions or slots that are occupied by categories and values. A plural common noun in English such as *cars* is annotated as NNS (category + type + number), while a proper noun in Spanish such as *Francia* is tagged as NP00G00 (category + type + class). "0s" stand for empty slots where annotation was not implemented. Table 4.2 offers a comparison of FreeLing POS tagging in English and Spanish.

Table 4.2 FreeLing noun annotation in English and Spanish

English

0	1	2	3	4	5	6
Category	Type	Number	0	0	0	0

Spanish

0	1	2	3	4	5	6
Category	Type	Gen	Number	Class (person, location, organization, other)	Subclass	Degree (evaluative)

4.2.3   Trialling POS tagging

It is essential that researchers run a pilot study where they test the accuracy and the depth of the annotation (that is, the number and implications for analysis of the tags included in the tagset) provided by their software or tagging service. For example, the new Corpus Escrito del Español L2 (L2 Spanish Written Corpus)

---

8. FreeLing manual: https://freeling-user-manual.readthedocs.io/en/latest/toc/

(CEDEL2) (Lozano, 2022) has been tagged using Freeling. The author notes that Freeling "sometimes misclassifies words (particularly learners' novel words) into an incorrect word category" (p. 979). This kind of insight needs to feed back into the construction of the corpus and how the language is queried. If the tagging is unsatisfactory, then researchers need to take action and find practical ways to improve the output provided by the tagger. This is vital in the case of Learner language, where researchers need to know if the tagger of their choice performs adequately with L2 data (i.e., 95% accuracy or above). In fact, researchers are advised to understand how their input data affects the tagging process (see 4.2.3 for tagging of learner errors).

In practical terms, this means that researchers are advised to explore the boundaries of every POS tag that is relevant in the context of their project — this may involve the entire tagset. For example, let us take the tag *DT*. As suggested, it is always a good idea to run a preliminary, pilot analysis of the data. In this context, researchers can explore the number of word forms that are tagged DT. In the following example, we use the Open Cambridge Learner Corpus (CLC) Uncoded (Focus 4.2). This learner corpus was tagged using the English TreeTagger tagset with modifications.[9]

Focus 4.2 The Open Cambridge Learner Corpus

🔎 **Open Cambridge Learner Corpus**

The Open Cambridge Learner Corpus is a subset of the Cambridge Learner Corpus that has not been error-coded. It contains 2.9 million words of around 10,000 student responses from the Cambridge English Language Assessment suite of exams (First Certificate in English (FCE), Cambridge Advanced English (CAE) and Cambridge Proficiency English (CPE)). The students in this open distribution of the CLC display seven L1 backgrounds (Chinese, French, Greek, Italian, Portuguese, European Spanish and Latin American Spanish). It can be accessed on the *Sketch Engine* website: www.sketchengine.eu

---

If a corpus is already tagged, it is essential that the tagset is carefully explored. Figure 4.3 shows how to find out more about a POS tag in *Sketch Engine* using the CQL query type. In Figure 4.3, we are asking for all instances of the POS tag DT (Determiner).

Once in the concordance window (Figure 4.3), researchers can obtain the frequency of the forms that have been tagged DT by clicking on the frequency option (Figure 4.4).

---

9. URL: https://www.sketchengine.eu/english-treetagger-pipeline-2/

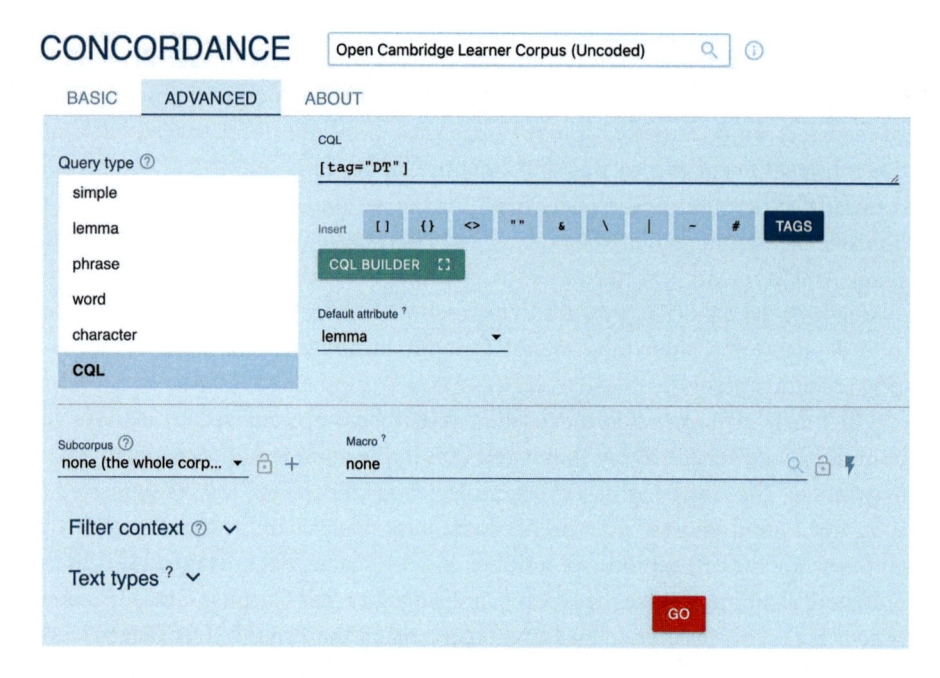

Figure 4.3 Exploring the POS tag DT in *Sketch Engine*

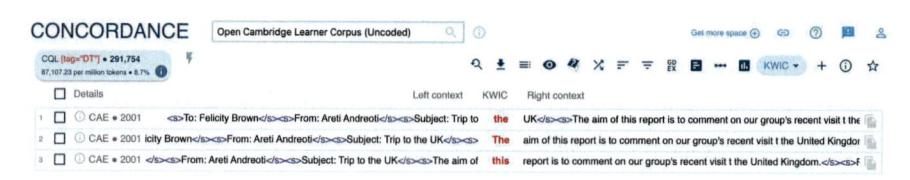

Figure 4.4 Concordance window in *Sketch Engine*. Frequency option in the highlighted square

The forms instantiate the POS tag and will be the basis for future analyses. Figure 4.5 shows the range of words tagged as DT. The five most frequent words are, in decreasing order of frequency, *the, a, this, The,* and *some.* As the reader can see, alternative spellings are treated as separate forms. Infrequent formats such as capital letter THIS, SOME or THAT should also require some attention, i.e., are these intended transcriptions or should they be revised? The absolute frequency as well as the normalised frequency (see Chapter 2) is provided for every single word form in the DT tag.

With this information in their hands, the researchers are in a better position to understand the range of word forms that are tagged as DT in the corpus and can fully appreciate differences with other tagsets and taggers. For example, taking the text from Table 4.1 TreeTagger POS tagged *The most striking features* as

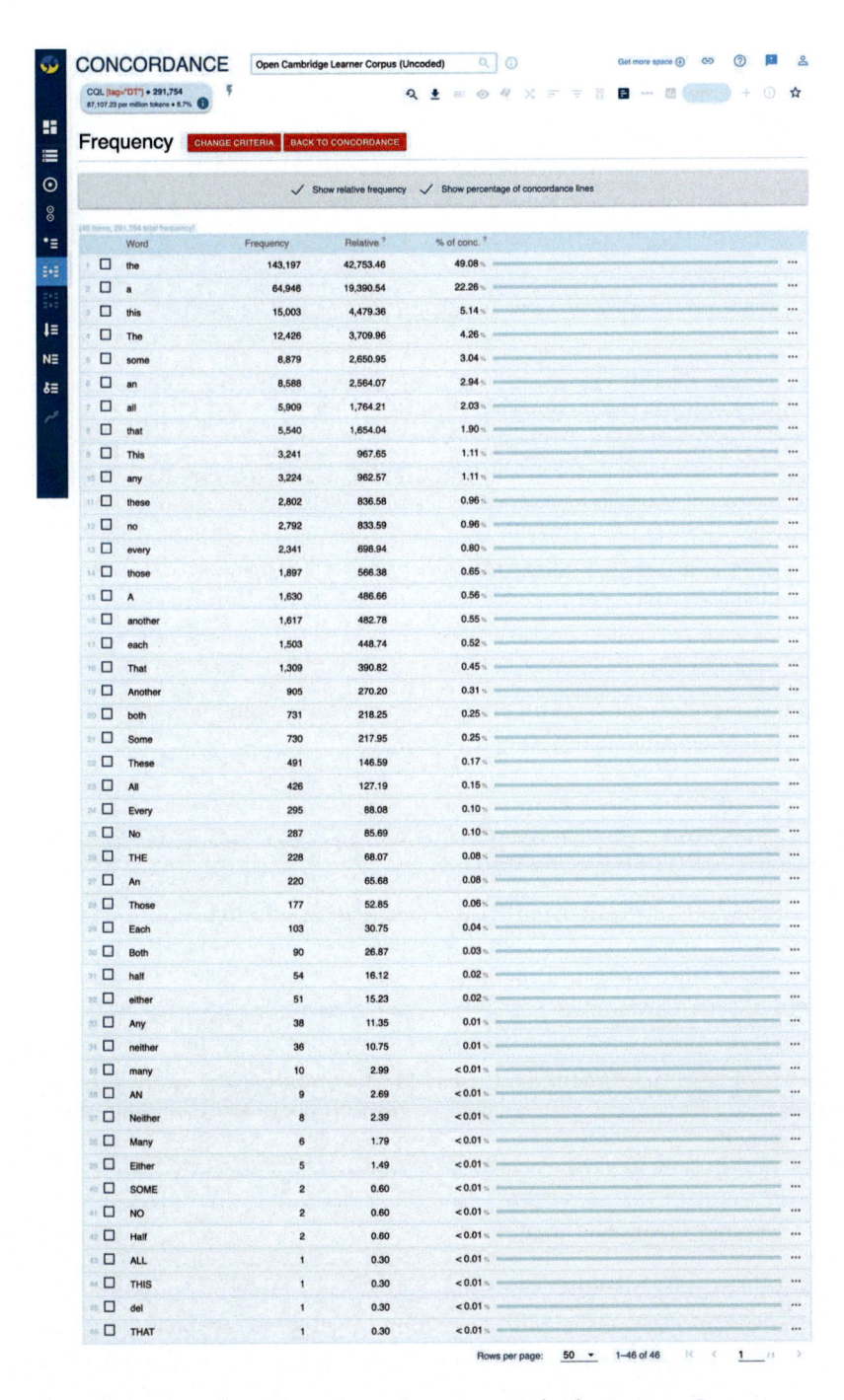

Figure 4.5 Exploring the POS tag DT in the Open Cambridge Learner Corpus in *Sketch Engine*

DT RBS JJ NNS, while the output of CLAWS7 is AT RGT JJ NN2. In the example provided, *the* is seen as both a determiner and an article, while *most* is tagged as a superlative adverb and a superlative degree adverb, respectively. While the tags represent small distinctions, the differences exist and it is necessary that researchers approach their tagged data critically. See Focus 4.3 for an example where different taggers tag the same word differently.

Focus 4.3 AT or DT? CLAWS 7 and TreeTagger treatment of determiners

🔍 **AT or DT?**

Taggers use different tags to name the same morphological items, for example *the* has been tagged either as AT (CLAWS 7) or DT (TreeTagger). Beyond naming conventions researchers need to understand the implications these tags will have on their own analysis. First, they will affect how the frequency of different units is calculated. Second, different labels may overlap grammatical categories. In CLAWS 7, *some* and *any* are tagged as DD (determiners) and *this* and *that* as DD1 (singular determiners). For TreeTagger articles, determiners, predeterminers such as *half* or *all* and postdeterminers such as *former* are not treated separately. Researchers need to be ready to interpret the scope and depth of analysis provided by the tagset and the tagger being used.

Focus 4.4 offers some useful pointers where readers can know more about different tagsets available for the English language.

Focus 4.4 POS recommended POS tagset resources

🔍 **Part of Speech (POS) tagsets for English**

An introduction to CLAWS part-of-speech tagger for English: http://ucrel.lancs.ac.uk/claws/
CLAWS 7 tagset: http://ucrel.lancs.ac.uk/claws7tags.html
CLAWS 8 tagset: http://ucrel.lancs.ac.uk/claws8tags.pdf
CLAWS 7 tagset available on Sketch Engine: https://www.sketchengine.eu/english-claws7-part-of
-speech-tagset/
FreeLing online demo: https://nlp.lsi.upc.edu/freeling/demo/demo.php
POS tagsets available on Sketch Engine: https://www.sketchengine.eu/tagsets/english-part-of-
speech-tagset/

4.2.3   Learner errors and tagging errors

In learner language analysis, Van Rooy and Schäfer (2002) distinguish between tagger errors and learners' errors. They found that incorrect spelling is the main reason behind tagging errors. It is recommended that, while retaining the original spelling, a correct version of the corpus is tagged. There are different ways in which this can be implemented (see Pérez-Paredes (2020) for TEI and XML markup annotation). The following is the POS annotation provided by the Tree-Tagger[10] of the same sentence from ICLE in Table 4.1:

The	DT	the
most	RBS	most
striking	JJ	striking
features	NNS	feature
of	IN	of
our	PP$	our
modern	JJ	modern
world	NN	world
is	VBZ	be
the	DT	the
idea	NN	idea
of	IN	of
progress	NN	progress
which	WDT	which
is	VBZ	be
particularly	RB	particularly
linked	VVN	link
with	IN	with
the	DT	the
industrial	JJ	industrial
revolution	NN	revolution
throughout	IN	throughout
the	DT	the
19th	JJ	19th
century	NN	century

In the next section we explore how corpus linguistics has contributed to the analysis of Learner language by means of word class analysis.

4.3   Researching word classes

We have seen in the previous section how a learner corpus can be tagged using a range of different tagsets and taggers. In this section, we look at research that has used the POS tagging and word classes to explore L2 use.

---

10. URL: https://www.cis.uni-muenchen.de/~schmid/tools/TreeTagger/

4.3.1   Looking at word classes: Applying a contrastive perspective

Learner corpus researchers have widely explored word classes using an application of the contrastive perspective discussed in Chapter 3. Table 4.3 shows a selection of representative research that has looked at nouns, adjectives, adverbs and pronouns. While some of the studies exploring written language use the ICLE and/or LOCNESS (marked with * next to the authors' reference), other researchers rely on the compilation of their own learner corpus data or explore spoken language using corpora such as LINDSEI and LOCNEC. Some of the most relevant findings are provided.

Overall, the research that has examined word classes (Table 4.3) is characterised by the use of a contrastive research methodology which uses corpora as proxies for natural use of the language in authenticated (Widdowson, 1998; Mishan, 2004) language learning contexts where the corpus elicitation tasks are seen as representative of L2 use. In this type of analysis of language use, there is an emphasis on quantifying the occurrences of the items under scrutiny (see Chapter 2), whether these are nouns, adjectives or adverbs, and, in general, comparisons between L1 and L2 data are drawn in terms of overuse and underuse. This analysis is possible thanks to POS tagging (see Section 4.2).

An influential research paper in this area is the above mentioned Granger and Rayson's (1998) study. These authors were interested in ICLE L1 French learners of English. They found that, when compared with L1 English writers, ICLE writers overused determiners (D), pronouns (P) and adverbs (R) significantly, while they underused conjunctions (C), prepositions (I) and nouns (N). Looking at the use of determiners, Granger and Rayson found that French learners overused the indefinite article *a* while they underused *the*. For the authors, this shows that French learner writing fails to conform to the expectations about definiteness in essays and shows areas of L2 use that need the attention of L2 classroom pedagogy. As for the use of pronouns, first and second personal pronouns are overused by ICLE French learners, which may point to the presence of involved discourse that is not expected in essays. Other word classes that were analysed were coordinators and subordinators, prepositions and adverbs. Based on the overuse/underuse patterns across word classes, Granger and Rayson, conclude that L1 French learner writing reveals a marked spoken nature in the essays analysed.

Although overuse and underuse have met some relevant criticism, Granger (2015) claims that these terms are neutral and they do not embody in any way imperialistic or L1 normative assumptions about the ownership of English (Tan, 2005). Granger (2015) argues that the terms overuse and underuse should be used by researchers as a technical term within the domain of learner language research:

> According to Aston (2008, p. 343), these terms should be banned, as they imply that "the learner should at all times attempt to conform to native-speaker norms". This criticism derives from a faulty interpretation of the two terms [...]. Gilquin and Paquot (2008, p. 38), for example, note that "the terms 'overuse' and 'underuse' are descriptive, not prescriptive, terms: they merely refer to the fact that a linguistic form is found significantly more or less in the learner corpus than in the reference corpus" (p. 19)

A common feature that most research in Table 4.3 shares is the use of research results for the purpose of informing teaching practitioners and researchers about usage as revealing aspects of instructed language learning that require further attention. These recommendations use L1 grouping to suggest that specific L2 varieties are characterised by overuse/underuse tendencies, and, often, they focus on learner errors (i.e., Kobayashi, 2008).

Deshors and Gries (2021) have noted that a quantificational contrastive typology of learner varieties (see Chapter 3) has become the trademark of studies similar to those found in Table 4.3. For them, the frequency and distributional patterns of formal elements "in an interlanguage help us describe and distinguish individual types of interlanguage and better understand why learners shape it the way they do" (p. 108). They argue that the assumption behind most of the research in Table 4.3 is probabilistic in nature: Learning a second/foreign language involves increasing knowledge of the frequency of co-occurring linguistic items in the L2 "and distributional differences of formal elements in native and learner language allow researchers to capture traces of non-nativeness [...] which is why over-/underuses of linguistic items in [interlanguage] are central in the field" (p. 108).

Learner language research has followed two distinct pathways when analysing L2 word classes: (a) examining an individual exponent of a word class in comparable corpora; and (b) examining a word class and its impact on language use in comparable corpora. Broadly speaking, contrastive research designs probe into L1/L2 groups so as to discuss emerging sources of variation across the textual evidence in the corpora analysed. In both approaches, there is often a focus on accuracy and comparison with target L1 norms (Housen & Kuiken, 2009) rather than on fluency. More recent research has begun to examine phrasal complexity measures, particularly in the noun phrase (Park, 2017; Díez-Bedmar & Pérez-Paredes, 2020).

In order to understand these standard approaches in learner language research, let us examine in detail two representative studies that have looked at the use of pronouns in L2. We take the following two research articles as robust examples that showcase these two approaches to the analysis of word classes in learner language.

Table 4.3 Some findings about the use of lexical items in LCR

Word class	Research	Findings
Nouns	De Haan (2015)*	A longitudinal analysis of 2 advanced Dutch learners of EFL. LOCNESS used as L1 corpus. Distribution patterns in combination with lexical profiles allow researchers to shed light on how essay writing is acquired and how it relates to the acquisition of competence.
	Flowerdew (2006)	A taxonomy of errors in the use of signalling nouns (*difficulty, process, result*, etc.) in a Cantonese L1 learners of English corpus reveals that the number of uses of such nouns correlates with strong essay writing.
	Kobayashi (2008)*	The authors present a classification of errors in the Japanese ICLE regarding the use of countable and uncountable nouns. Japanese L1 EFL learners' understanding of these uses is mediated by their concept about concreteness and abstractness.
	Park (2017)	The authors used Biber, Gray, and Poonpon's (2011) noun phrase developmental stage index to explore academic writing literacy in a small corpus of Korean EFL learners. While the quantity of nouns used could not be considered an indicator of L2 proficiency, the use of modifiers did.
Adjectives	Bikelienė (2016)*	The authors explored ADJ + *to* and ADJ + *that* sequences in the ICLE and LOCNESS. They found generalised overuse of both patterns in the Lithuanian L1 essays.
	De Cock (2011)	The author extracted all evaluative adjectives in the CH, FR and GER LINDSEI as well as in the LOCNEC. The preferred patterns of use include either attributive or predicative position in the clause. Contrasts between L1 and L2 users are discussed in great detail. This research seeks to inform the teaching of spoken English in ELT.
	Lorenz (1998)*	German L1 advanced EFL learners overuse adjective intensification. They overuse attributive intensification in thematic position, as opposed to LOCNEC writers.
Adverbs	Crawford (2008)*	The author provides evidence about the presence of spoken features in EFL learners' writing. Although no clear different patterns of overuse / underuse were found in the LOCNESS/ICLE essays, some of the textual functions of adverbs such as *here* or *then* are not often found in L2 writing.
	Dong & Lee (2017)	Using a corpus of 3,286 essays contributed by secondary school learners of English, the authors found that learners that used general adverbs more frequently displayed higher competence.

Table 4.3 *(continued)*

Word class	Research	Findings
	Hancock & Sanell (2009)	The authors examined the use of 4 adverbs (*aussi, peut-être, seulement* and *vraiment*) in a corpus of 40 interviews with students of varied competence. The authors suggest that frequency patterns are acquired before sentence position patterns.
	Hasselgård (2015)	The authors examined the use of *-ly* adverbs in the writing of Norwegian L1 learners of English (VESPA) and in a corpus of academic English (BAWE). L2 writers overuse adverbs with a modal meaning and underuse adverbs that have a modifying function in phrases.
	Osborne (2008)*	This study examines adverb placement in the written production of ICLE learners of English from a variety of L1 backgrounds. Non-native-like adverb placement suggests a transfer of syntactic patterns in speakers of Romance languages. However, transfer is not the only explanation, and semantic and phraseological factors may play a role.
	Pérez-Paredes (2010)	This study looks at the occurrence of amplifier adverbs (*absolutely, completely*, etc.), downtoner adverbs (*nearly, only*, etc.), emphatic adverbs (*just, really*, etc.) and adverbs functioning as discourse particles (*well, anyway*, etc.) in spoken L1 & L2 English. Learners rarely made use of amplifiers or downtoners, although the latter were also rare in the L1 data.
	Pérez-Paredes & Sánchez-Tornel (2014)	General adverbs are more frequently used as age increases. Statistically significant differences were found between grade 6 and 10 learners across all three L1 groups in terms of the frequency of use. Secondary school learners of English below grade 9 are more unlikely to use adverbs.
Pronouns	Chang, J.Y. (2015)	Korean learners overused *I* as the opinion provider in English argumentative writing.
	Leedham & Fernandez-Parra (2017)	All student groups make more frequent use of *we* than *I* in Engineering assignments. Greek and Chinese students make higher use of *we* than British students. The authors explore the different purposes for using *we* in Greek and British students' output.
	Stormbom (2018)	Epicene pronouns refer to both sexes. This research examines the use of the epicene pronouns *he, he or she,* and *they* in two L1 and L2 corpora of student writing. Variation found in the L2 data is related to L1 influence.

4.3.2   Study 1. An analysis of the pronoun *I* in two corpora

Chang (2015) examined an individual exponent of a word class in two comparable corpora. In this study, the author chose the pronoun *I* to understand the self-representation of L1 English and L1 Korean writers in corpora of English argumentative writing. Chang sought to explore how the use of this instantiation of a pronoun contributes to the overall quality of L1 Korean learners' argumentative writing. Figure 4.6 shows the steps taken by the researcher when approaching their analysis.

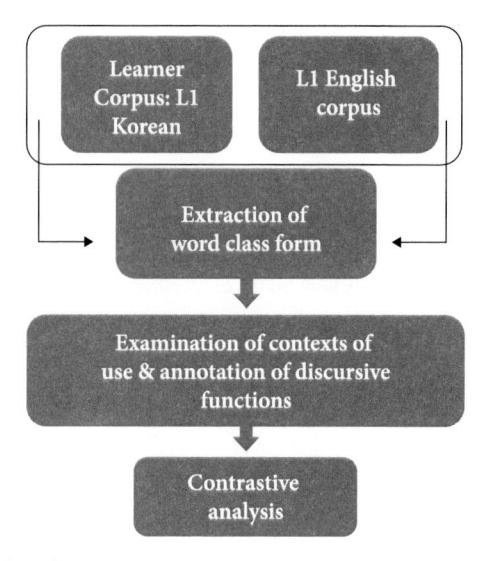

Figure 4.6 Chang's (2015) research steps

For L1 English, the LOCNESS corpus was used. For L2 English, the researcher used the Seoul National University Korean-speaking English Learner Corpus (SKELC). This is a corpus of untimed L2 essays where Korean learners of English were allowed to use dictionaries or other references. The aim of this corpus is to identify the common errors produced by first year University Korean learners of English. Chang used a subset of 340 essays contributed by learners that obtained a score equivalent to iBT TOEFL of 86–99 (i.e. IELTS band 6.5). In both corpora, the instances of the pronoun *I* that do not refer to the writer were excluded from the analysis. Methodologically, this decision generally involves the manual annotation of these uses.

Chang first examined the occurrences of *I* in the data. While the normalised frequency (see Chapter 2) of use of the pronoun *I* in both corpora is diverging, 7.25 /1000 words and 4.32 /1000 words in the L1 Korean and L1 English data, respectively, the average distribution of *I* occurrences across the essays tells a different story: 1.81/ essay and 3.69 / essay in the L1 Korean and L1 English corpora, respectively. A close examination of the spread of these occurrences, however, shows that while *I* is used in 72.7% of the essays in the Korean data, it is only found in 57.1% of LOCNESS essays. However, this frequency-driven approach has met some criticism. Shea (2009), for example, has noted that informing about the frequencies of lexical items in learner data is not enough, as a deeper understanding of these frequencies on learners' use is needed. Annotated corpora can help researchers gain such insights. The use of annotated L1 and L2 English corpora can be used jointly in contexts where a comparison between 2 corpora can help language learners with the same L1(s) increase their understanding about the different linguistic devices that conform the repertoires of different varieties (Granger, 2015) across a variety of genres. As Götz (2021) has noted, annotation allows for fine-grained research questions that can potentially be more relevant for research in the field of SLA or other related areas.

In Chang's (2015) study, some 1200 uses of the pronoun *I* were analysed and coded following a taxonomy of discourse functions: essay commentator, experience provider and opinion provider. Commentator uses (i.e. *As I mentioned above*) tell readers about the organization, purpose and focus of the essay. Experience provider uses describe writers' experiences of facts (i.e., *I am a 21 year old male*). Finally, opinion provider uses communicate the writer's stance or positioning in the essay (i.e., *I think that...*). Chang (2015) found that the experience provider and the opinion provider accounted in the English L1 data for 53.9% ($N=348$) and 36.7% ($N=237$), respectively, "whereas the opinion provider accounted for solely 77.5% ($N=476$) in the [Korean] non-native speaker corpus" (p.96).

The analysis of the two corpora allowed Chang to discover the most frequent 3-word clusters with *I* in the data. In Table 4.4, we can see how these 3-word sequences are different in the L2, left, and L1 English data, on the right.

The analysis of clusters can be of interest to understand patterning and, more broadly, to find and identify usage beyond the 1-word level in corpora. Chang (2015) concludes that contrastive analyses support the notion that, in instructed language learning contexts, it is essential to increase learners' awareness about the discursive use of the pronoun across genres, disciplines and discourse communities.

Table 4.4 Word clusters for the pronoun *I* in the two corpora in Chang (2015)

Top 15 Lists of Clusters for First-Person Pronoun *I*

CEPARG	N	LOCARG	N
I think that	73	I feel that	21
I think it	33	I believe that	12
or why not	31	I do not	11
why or why	30	I think that	9
I don't	29	when I was	8
I think corporal	28	I would like	8
think corporal punishment	28	I have seen	8
why not I	27	would like to	7
so I think	25	that I am	7
think it is	24	if I were	7
but I think	23	I have been	7
corporal punishment should	22	I think it	6
not I think	20	I know that	6
shut down system	20	I know I	6
I think the	20	I had a	6

Note. CEPARG = argumentative writings from the College English Program; LOCARG = argumentative writings from LOCNESS

4.3.3   Study 2. Pronouns in subject positions and transfer effects

Mitkovska and Bužarovska's (2018) study examined the use of pronoun subjects by Macedonian L1 learners of English in the light of the Interpretability Hypothesis (Leal Méndez & Slabakova, 2014). The researchers combined error analysis of learner language in the Macedonian English Learner Corpus (MELC) and a Grammaticality Judgment Correction Task (GJCT) that was completed by language learners between 8 and 15 years of age.

In this research, the authors retrieved all the exponents of the pronoun word class in subject position. They wanted to test whether non-referential subjects are more difficult to acquire by speakers of non-null subject languages. Granger (1996) suggests that "contrastive analysis data helps analysts to formulate predictions about interlanguage that can be checked against CIA data"[11] (p. 46).

---

11. A reappraised CIA conceptualization (Granger, 2015) stresses the role of alternative reference language varieties, fighting the criticism about contrastive analysis that was echoed in

The learners in Mitkovska and Bužarovska's (2018) displayed a variety of English proficiency levels (A1, A2, B1 and B2 CEFR levels). The authors used a corpus of written English of about 500,000 words contributed by some 2000 learners. Each learner wrote an e-mail, a narrative or descriptive piece and four guided conversations. As we saw in previous paragraphs, POS tags allow researchers to retrieve all the items that have been automatically annotated as pronouns. This facilitates the treatment of large amounts of linguistic data. Nevertheless, as we suggested before, it is essential that researchers are familiar with the range of lexical items that have been tagged as pronouns and the tags used. If we, for example, retrieve all pronouns from the 2014 spoken British National Corpus (BNC) (Figure 4.7) on *Sketch Engine*, we will have some 1.7 million concordance lines to examine.

Figure 4.7 Retrieving all pronouns from the 2014 spoken BNC

Sketch Engine uses the Tree Tagger tagset. The "PP.?" query includes personal pronouns ("PP") and possessive pronouns ("PPZ"). Note that uses of *my* as in "My God" are tagged as "PP" while the one for *mine* as in "Did you bring mine?" is tagged as "PPZ". The actual range of items POS tagged as pronouns can be accessed on the "Frequency" option (see Figure 4.5). Other tagsets, however, display a more sophisticated range of tags. The CLAWS 7 tagset has the tag "APPGE" for prenominal uses of the pronoun while the tag "PPGE" has been reserved for nominal possessive personal pronouns. On top of that, CLAWS 7 has further 18 tags that differentiate between person, indefiniteness etc.

Figure 4.8 shows the pronoun word forms in the 2014 spoken BNC. This corpus was tagged with the TreeTagger with Sketch Engine modifications,[12] the same tagset used with the Open Cambridge Learner Corpus.

Bley-Vroman's (1983) comparative fallacy: "The term 'Reference Language Varieties' (RLV) makes it clear that there are a large number of different reference points against which learner data can be set. Alongside the traditional inner circle varieties, which will continue to be used by many researchers, the model also incorporates the possibility of using outer circle varieties as well as corpora of competent L2 user data, as suggested for example by proponents of English as a Lingua Franca" (Granger, 2015, p.17).

12. URL: https://www.sketchengine.eu/english-treetagger-pipeline-2/

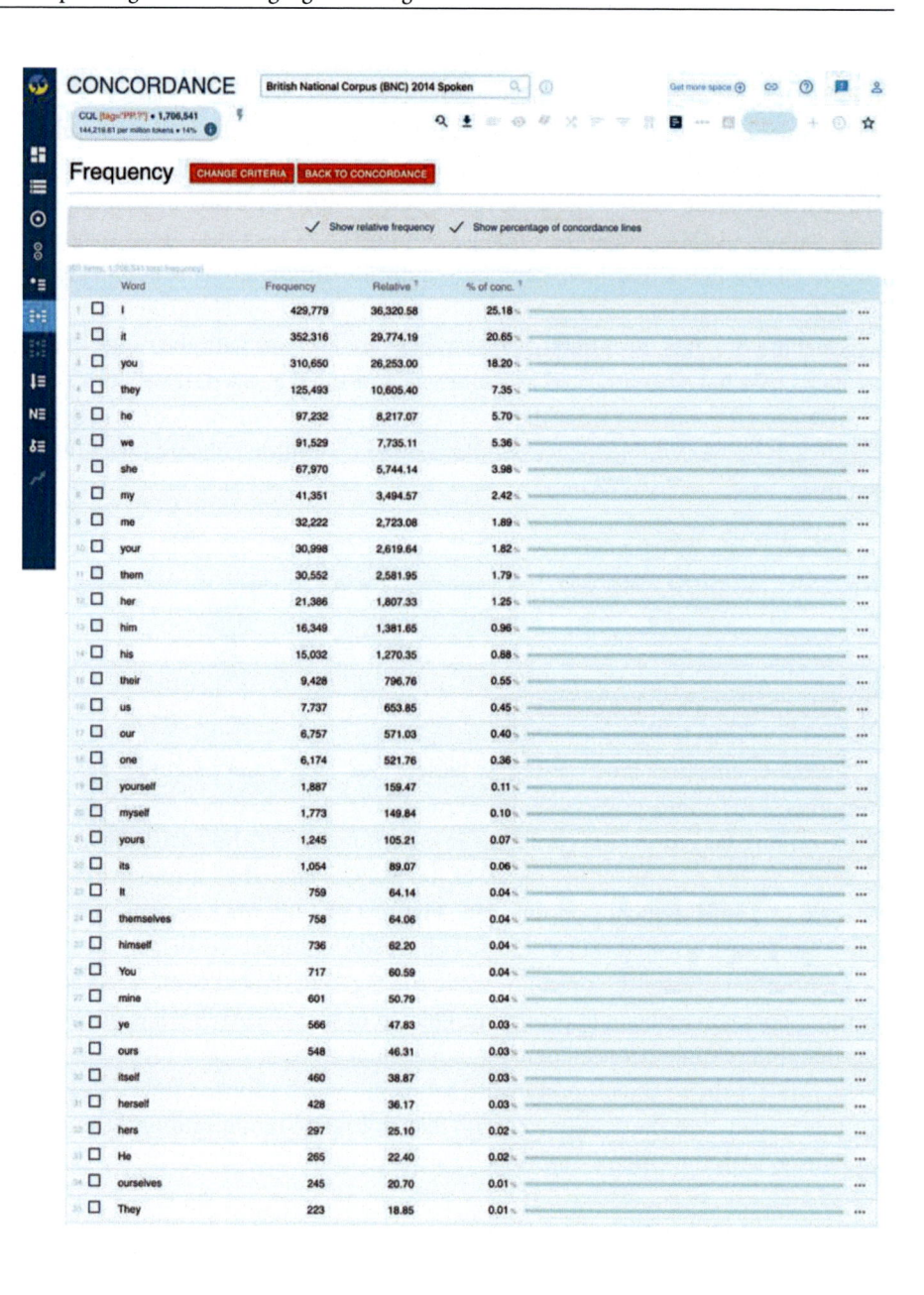

CONCORDANCE British National Corpus (BNC) 2014 Spoken

CQL [>"PP.?"] • 1,706,541
144,219.61 per million tokens • 14%

Frequency CHANGE CRITERIA BACK TO CONCORDANCE

✓ Show relative frequency   ✓ Show percentage of concordance lines

	Word	Frequency	Relative	% of conc.
1	I	429,779	36,320.58	25.18%
2	it	352,316	29,774.19	20.65%
3	you	310,650	26,253.00	18.20%
4	they	125,493	10,605.40	7.35%
5	he	97,232	8,217.07	5.70%
6	we	91,529	7,735.11	5.36%
7	she	67,970	5,744.14	3.98%
8	my	41,351	3,494.57	2.42%
9	me	32,222	2,723.08	1.89%
10	your	30,998	2,619.64	1.82%
11	them	30,552	2,581.95	1.79%
12	her	21,386	1,807.33	1.25%
13	him	16,349	1,381.65	0.96%
14	his	15,032	1,270.35	0.88%
15	their	9,428	796.76	0.55%
16	us	7,737	653.85	0.45%
17	our	6,757	571.03	0.40%
18	one	6,174	521.76	0.36%
19	yourself	1,887	159.47	0.11%
20	myself	1,773	149.84	0.10%
21	yours	1,245	105.21	0.07%
22	its	1,054	89.07	0.06%
23	It	759	64.14	0.04%
24	themselves	758	64.06	0.04%
25	himself	736	62.20	0.04%
26	You	717	60.59	0.04%
27	mine	601	50.79	0.04%
28	ye	566	47.83	0.03%
29	ours	548	46.31	0.03%
30	itself	460	38.87	0.03%
31	herself	428	36.17	0.03%
32	hers	297	25.10	0.02%
33	He	265	22.40	0.02%
34	ourselves	245	20.70	0.01%
35	They	223	18.85	0.01%

36 ☐ We	187	15.80	0.01 %	...
37 ☐ theirs	163	13.78	<0.01 %	...
38 ☐ She	161	13.61	<0.01 %	...
39 ☐ IT	106	8.96	<0.01 %	...
40 ☐ Me	81	6.85	<0.01 %	...
41 ☐ My	72	6.08	<0.01 %	...
42 ☐ Your	58	4.90	<0.01 %	...
43 ☐ yourselves	52	4.39	<0.01 %	...
44 ☐ thou	21	1.77	<0.01 %	...
45 ☐ Her	21	1.77	<0.01 %	...
46 ☐ His	14	1.18	<0.01 %	...
47 ☐ One	14	1.18	<0.01 %	...
48 ☐ Their	8	0.68	<0.01 %	...
49 ☐ Yourself	8	0.68	<0.01 %	...
50 ☐ Us	7	0.59	<0.01 %	...
51 ☐ thy	7	0.59	<0.01 %	...
52 ☐ ME	7	0.59	<0.01 %	...
53 ☐ thee	5	0.42	<0.01 %	...
54 ☐ US	4	0.34	<0.01 %	...
55 ☐ HE	4	0.34	<0.01 %	...
56 ☐ oneself	3	0.25	<0.01 %	...
57 ☐ Ourselves	3	0.25	<0.01 %	...
58 ☐ Yours	3	0.25	<0.01 %	...
59 ☐ Its	2	0.17	<0.01 %	...
60 ☐ thine	2	0.17	<0.01 %	...
61 ☐ Our	2	0.17	<0.01 %	...
62 ☐ Him	2	0.17	<0.01 %	...
63 ☐ 'em	1	0.08	<0.01 %	...
64 ☐ one's	1	0.08	<0.01 %	...
65 ☐ Himself	1	0.08	<0.01 %	...
66 ☐ Mine	1	0.08	<0.01 %	...
67 ☐ Ye	1	0.08	<0.01 %	...
68 ☐ YOU	1	0.08	<0.01 %	...
69 ☐ Ours	1	0.08	<0.01 %	...

Rows per page: 100 ▾   1–69 of 69 |< < 1 /1 > >|

Figure 4.8 Pronoun word forms in the 2014 spoken BNC

The information provided in Figure 4.8 can give researchers a measure of the spread and relative frequencies of the different pronoun word forms used in spoken English as found in the BNC 2014 distribution.

Let us come back to Mitkovska and Bužarovska (2018). The Macedonian language displays both null and overt pronominal subjects but lacks nonreferential subjects. English, however, allows only overt pronominal subjects, both referential and pleonastic non-referential (e.g., it, there). The MELC corpus data revealed that null subjects were more frequent at A1 level, and they decreased gradually at each subsequent level. In the corpus data, null referential subjects were uncommon even in A1 and A2 writing. Referential null subjects correlated with the syntactic complexity of the sentences in which they are found. For the authors null subjects tend to occur in more complex constructions "due to the processing difficulties involving shift of attention learners resort to their L1 patterns" (p. 471). As regards the expletive *it* subject, the corpus data showed that the subject pronoun "tends to be dropped if the subject is non-topical, which leads to the conclusion that the L1 information structure affects the acquisition process" (p. 474). The Grammaticality Judgment Correction Task supported these findings. The researchers argue that "non-referential subjects are more difficult to acquire by speakers of non-null subject languages, as proposed by the Interpretability Hypothesis" (p. 480).

Mitkovska and Bužarovska (2018) is a good example of how complex corpus queries involving POS tags can be used to answer research questions involving the use of formal language features. In the next section, we will explore practical ways to tag a learner corpus.

4.4   How to POS tag a corpus

So far we have explored corpora that are available online through *Sketch Engine* and which have already been POS tagged. In the following sections, we offer two ways in which researchers can tag their own learner corpus.

4.4.1   Tagging a corpus using *TagAnt*

TagAnt is a freeware software (Anthony, 2022b) developed by Laurence Anthony and which works well in desktop environments together with *AntConc*. Users upload their texts and then decide on the language and type of tagging. Two of the options are widely used by most researchers. One is word + POS Tag (selected in Figure 4.9).

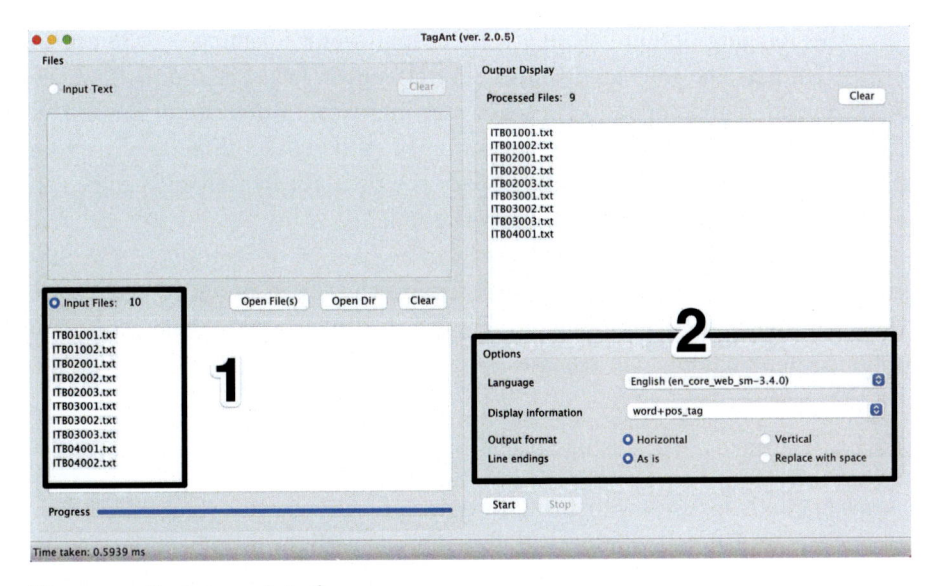

Figure 4.9 *TagAnt* user interface

This will return new files with the following format (Table 4.5):

Table 4.5 POS tagged text using *TagAnt* (word + POS tag)

Original text (ICLE-IT-BER-0002.1)	Tagged text (Word + POS tag)
Nowdays advertisements occupy an important place in our life, I would hardly dare say a fundamental one.	Nowdays_NNP advertisements_NNS occupy_VBP an_DT important_JJ place_NN in_IN our_PRP$ life_NN,_, I_PRP would_MD hardly_RB dare_VB say_VB a_DT fundamental_JJ one_CD._.

The word + POS tag + Lemma (Table 4.6) will return new files with the following format where we can see that the corresponding lemma is appended to the POS tag (i.e., the word advertisements is tagged as NNS and its corresponding lemma is advertisement):

Table 4.6 POS tagged text using *TagAnt* (word + POS tag + Lemma)

Original text (ICLE-IT-BER-0002.1)	Tagged text (Word + POS tag)
Nowdays advertisements occupy an important place in our life, I would hardly dare say a fundamental one.	Nowdays_NNP_Nowdays advertisements_NNS_advertisement occupy_VBP_occupy an_DT_an important_JJ_important place_NN_place in_IN_in our_PRP$_our life_NN_life ,_,_, I_PRP_I would_MD_would hardly_RB_hardly dare_VB_dare say_VB_say a_DT_a fundamental_JJ_fundamental one_CD_one ._._.

Other tagging options include lemma only, word + lemma + POS tag or word + lemma. The software includes several built-in language models that can be downloaded and added to the main user interface. In the case of English, at the time of writing, three models are included, although all three are based on the same popular NLP library Spacy. Spacy is written for Python and can be run independently using relatively easy-to-write code.

Once we have our files tagged, they can be queried on *AntConc*. As we saw in Section 4.2, researchers are advised to explore the tagsets provided in advance. Users can toggle between hiding or showing tags, which gives them a range of options when building their searches.

4.4.2   Tagging a corpus using *Sketch Engine*

Sketch Engine helps users with the POS tagging process when they first upload their corpus files. A dialogue window will present users with the tagging options available. For the English language, TreeTagger with *Sketch Engine* modifications is recommended (Figure 4.10). The second option, Universal generic 1.0, uses so-called universal POS tags from Universal Dependencies (UD) grammar, a cross-linguistic project[13] for many languages mainly based on Stanford dependencies (De Marneffe et al., 2014) and Google universal part-of-speech tags (Lin et al., 2012).

Sketch Engine will let users see both word forms and POS tags (Figure 4.11) and, from the corpus dashboard, download the tagged corpus.

From the *Sketch Engine* corpus dashboard, users can download the POS tagged corpus and use it offline with other desktop tools.

---

13. URL: https://universaldependencies.org/u/pos/index.html

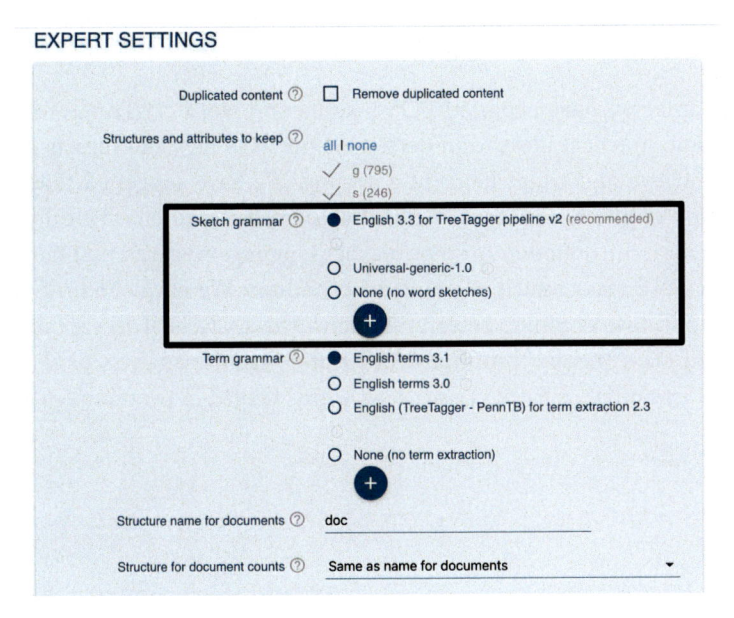

Figure 4.10 *Sketch Engine* tagging options

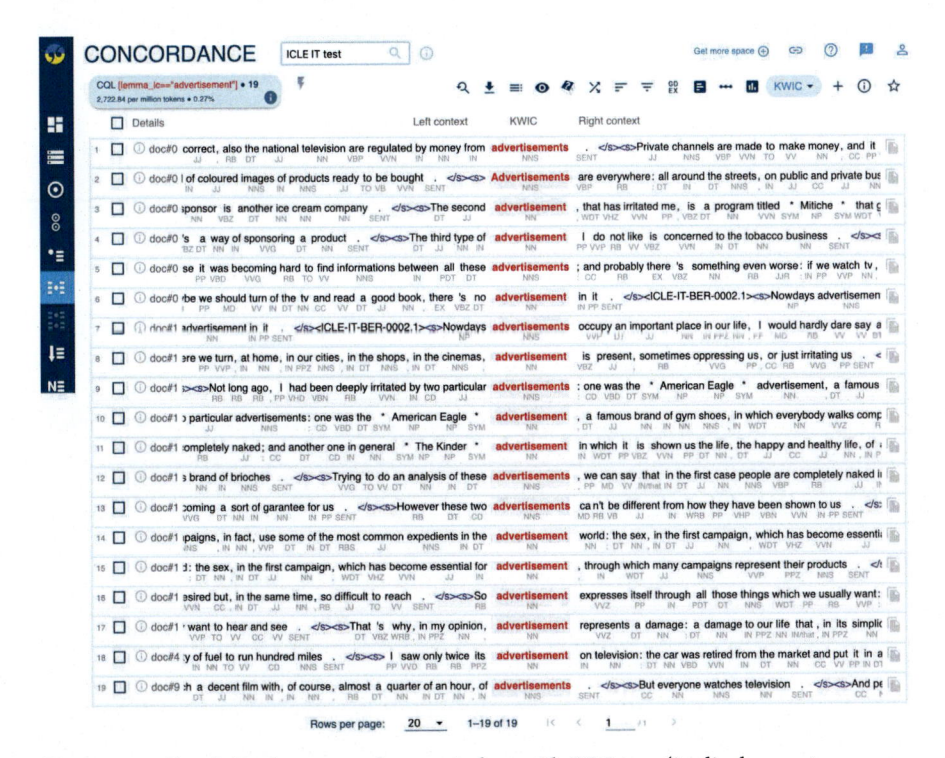

Figure 4.11 *Sketch Engine* concordance window with POS tags (in display, part of the ICLE Italian component)

4.5   Summary

In this chapter we have explored POS tagging and word class analysis. We have offered some practical ideas to understand how POS tags and tagsets may affect how we retrieve and count items in a corpus. We have suggested that a careful examination of the chosen tagset is essential to explore our data critically. We have also offered an introduction to some learner language research that has explored the use of word classes such as nouns or pronouns. We have chosen two studies that exemplify two common research designs: the analysis of an exponent of one given word class (i.e., *I* / pronoun word class) and the analysis of all the word forms that instantiate a word class (i.e. all words tagged as pronouns in a corpus).

CHAPTER 5

Researching phraseology
Collocations

Recommended reading 5.1

Nesselhauf, N. (2005). *Collocations in a learner corpus.* John Benjamins.

This book offers a solid contrastive analysis of the collocations used by both English L2 learners and English L1 writers. Nesselhauf (2005) studied verb + noun collocations in a written corpus of advanced German L1 learners of English of around 150,000 words. In her research, she used the German component of the ICLE (see Chapters 2 and 4). According to the author, of the 2,000 verb-noun collocations, 25% were found to be wrong. She concluded that collocations do not "seem to be taught in a way that leads to their acquisition, and mere exposure only helps to improve collocational performance to a slight degree" (pp. 237–38). Research has corroborated this claim, showing that collocation instruction increases the acquisition of collocational knowledge in language learners. A recent metanalysis (Li & Lei, 2022) has shown that explicit classroom interventions involving L2 collocation learning produce large effect sizes, leading to the claim that the teaching of collocations in the L2 classroom can be beneficial.

L2 corpus research has gradually shifted its attention from the analysis of word classes (nouns, verbs, adverbs, etc.) and individual lexical items (*conclusion, suggest, well,* etc.) to the analysis of phraseology and formulaic language. Moving away from structuralism, which understood language as a self-contained relational structure (Ellis, 2008), corpus linguistics has contributed enormously to the study of recurrent lexical patterns (Granger, 2015, 2024).

This chapter looks specifically at the analysis of collocations in learner language research. We explore the corpus tools and methods that help researchers examine the presence and the use of this type of phraseological unit in corpora. We offer, first, an introduction to the impact of corpus analysis on a phraseological approach to L2 analysis. Section 5.2 shows the ways in which collocations can be researched using corpus methods. Section 5.3 discusses three studies that make use of different collocation extraction techniques and different research designs. They showcase different approaches to the analysis of collocations in learner language research.

5.1   A phraseological approach in learner corpus research

Phraseology is "everywhere in current SLA research" (Ellis, 2008, p.7). Learner research has contributed to this interest in phraseology by using a range of quantitative methods (Granger & Meunier, 2008; Granger, 2015). In this chapter we discuss collocation analysis and how this corpus method can be applied across a range of research designs.

Corpus linguistics methods have facilitated a phraseological approach to language analysis (Sinclair, 1991, 2004) that underlies language (Sinclair, 2004). Sinclair's idiom principle (1991) states that speakers access and make use of their linguistic repertoires as pre-stored preconstructed phrases. Cognitive science and cognitive linguistics have contributed an important body of research to this area, with probabilistic and frequency-based theories of language stressing the relevance of frequency and repetition in driving language comprehension and production (Bod et al., 2003; Bybee & Hopper, 2001; Hoey, 1991, 2005).

The attention paid to word combinations and multi-word units in corpus analysis has enlarged our understanding of formulaic language as opposed to isolated lexical items. Sinclair's (1991) discussion about new units of meaning and the idiom principle, in contrast with the open-choice principle, have largely driven the observation and study of word combinations in a corpus. For McEnery and Hardie (2012), corpus methods such as collocation analysis have shown that there are "aspects of the meaning of a word [or a lemma or other linguistic unit that] are not contained within the word itself [which] subsist in the characteristic associations that the word participates in, alongside other words or structures with which it frequently co- occurs" (pp.122–123). The phrase, not the word, is at the centre of language. Ellis (2008, p.6) put it in the following way:

> Phraseological analyses demonstrate that much of communication makes use of fixed expressions memorized as formulaic chunks, that language is rich in collocational and colligation restrictions and semantic prosodies, that the phrase is the basic level of language representation [...] and that fluent language users have a vast repertoire of memorized language sequences [...] The unit of language is "the phrase, the whole phrase, and nothing but the phrase".

Corpus methods can offer language-driven insights into how L2 learners "construe the world like natives of the L2 [and how] transfer affects L2 phraseology" (Ellis, 2008, p.8), ultimately making meaning in the L2 (Hunston, 2022). However, collocations have been found to be challenging for L2 speakers.

The concept of collocation has allowed a wide range of interpretations (Barfield, 2006). Collocations are often studied as restricted units, sometimes as figurative idioms if the combination displays some figurative meaning. Figure 5.1

shows how this continuum understands restrictions on substitutions of some of the lexical items involved, and whether the meaning(s) of the individual items of the combination is literal or figurative.

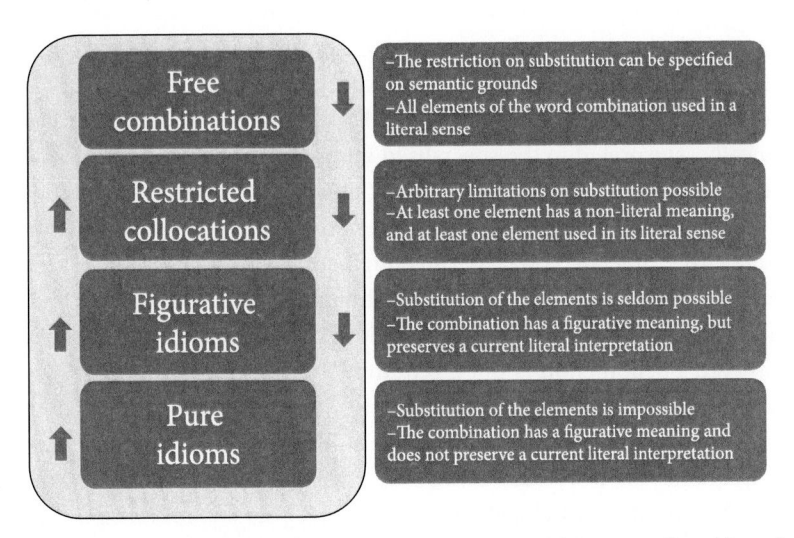

Figure 5.1 Cowie's (1994) phraseological approach. Adapted from Nesselhauf (2005)

For Paquot and Granger (2012), the most frequent units of analysis in LCR have been collocations, phrasal verbs and pragmatic markers in conversation (i.e., *I don't know*). To be concrete, it is Verb + Noun collocations the unit of analysis that has been more widely examined (Choi, 2019; Paquot & Granger, 2012). Unsurprisingly perhaps, most learner language research has found differences in the frequencies of formulaic language in L2 and L1 corpora, where the analyses of co-occurrence have shown a combination of underuse, overuse and misuse (see Chapters 3 and 4). While differences may be attributed to the effect of corpus sizes and, more generally, corpus design issues, learner corpus research often sees these differences as manifestations of both language use and the language learning process. Most of the research in language learners' use of formulaic language has adopted a comparative approach where L2 data is contrasted against L1 comparable corpora or other L2 corpora (Paquot & Granger, 2012).

In Section 5.2 we discuss the necessary steps to carry out a collocation analysis on *Sketch Engine*. We pay special attention to different association measures that can be used and how they may yield different results.

5.2   Introducing collocation analysis

We can define collocations as "co-occurrence patterns [of lexical items] observed in corpus data" (McEnery & Hardie, 2012, p.123). A word w_1 collocates with w_2 when a statistical test establishes that such co-occurrence is evidenced in the corpus (see Chapter 2), potentially revealing aspects of word meaning that go beyond the individual semantics of a given word. For Durrant et al. (2022), collocations are typically interpreted in the specialised literature as pairs of words that are frequently found together and which are, to some extent, bound to each other.

Although there are different approaches to defining collocations (McEnery & Hardie, 2012; Sinclair, 2004), corpus linguists tend to rely either on frequency information or significance testing (Krishnamurthy, 2000). Simple frequency information may be relevant in research designs where statistical significance of the observed phenomenon is not a requirement. In these cases, Log Likelihood (LL) may be instrumental.[14] LL determines whether significant differences of word frequency across different corpora exist. The test shows whether differences in the frequency of words are reflective of the actual variation in language or whether they result from chance occurrences (Szudarski, 2018, 2023). LL > 3.84 indicates a significant difference between two datasets.

The most common approach to identifying collocations is to compare the frequency of a given word within a certain distance of another word to the frequency of that word elsewhere in the corpus. The choice of how far to measure the proximity of two words is critical. This is usually known as the *span* of the node or search term. In Figure 5.2, we can see how researchers can set up the distance between the search term and the context to the left and the right. By default, this ranges between −5 and + 5. The search node in this example is the lemma *feel*.

Most automated methods for identifying collocations involve comparing the frequency of collocates candidates within the window of text surrounding the node against the frequency of that term elsewhere in the corpus. If the frequency difference is sufficiently large, the term being examined is identified as an associated term. Figure 5.2 shows a basic interface with just a few options for the researcher. In *Sketch Engine*, these options can be expanded by selecting ADVANCED Collocations in the interface (see Figure 5.3). In this new dialogue window, we can change the attribute to a POS tag (see Chapter 4) or a word. We can decide on the range of words to the left and to the right that will be examined for the extraction of the collocations. We can also set up a minimum frequency in both the corpus and the selected range.

---

14. Paul Rayson's online log-likelihood calculator (ucrel.lancs.ac.uk/llwizard.html) computes the value of LL using the input provided.

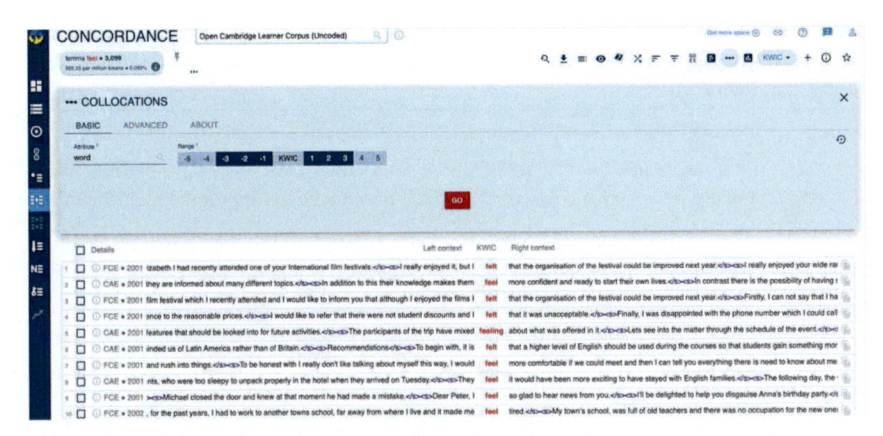

Figure 5.2 Setting the collocation span in *Sketch Engine*

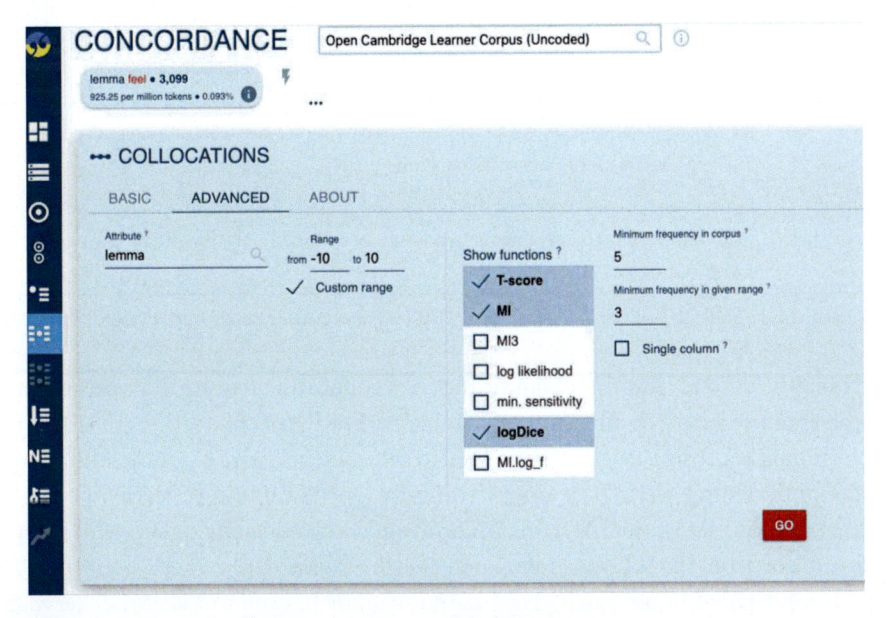

Figure 5.3 Advanced collocation settings in *Sketch Engine*

In this window, users can select different association measures. According to Brezina (2018), these association measures position collocations along two dimensions: frequency and exclusivity. While the former considers the number of instances in which a node (i.e., the search term) and collocate occur together in a corpus, exclusivity "refers to a specific aspect of the collocation relationship where words occur only or predominantly in each other's company" (p. 73). Table 5.1 shows some of the most common measures used in collocation analysis, namely, T-score, Mutual information and logDice.

A critical review of the statistics and the differences among them may be seen in Hunston (2002), Hoffmann et al. (2008) and Baker (2006). The variety of measures

Table 5.1 Some association measures used to measure collocation

Measure	Interpretation
T-score	T-score works well with frequent, non-exclusive collocations (Brezina, 2018). T scores of >2 provide strong evidence of collocability in a corpus (Szudarski, 2018). T-score is very sensitive to corpus size. It may not be the appropriate statistic to compare corpora of different sizes.
Mutual information (MI)	MI measures the strength of association between words W1 and W2.MI works well with relatively infrequent and exclusive collocations (Brezina, 2018). MI scores of >3 provide strong evidence of collocability in a corpus (Szudarski, 2018). Mutual information 3 (MI3) works well with relatively frequent and exclusive collocations (Brezina, 2018).
logDice	This is the test[*] that Sketch Engine uses as a default option to measure collocation strength and identify collocates. It is used when computing collocations from a concordance window. It uses the frequency of the node (i.e., the search term) and the collocate and the frequency of the whole collocation (co-occurrence of the node and collocate). The strength of logDice lies in the fact that it is not affected by the size of the corpus. It can be used to compare scores between different corpora. logDice favours exclusivity of association.
Delta P	Delta P takes directionality of the association (i.e., *sour* and *cream* vs. *cream* and *sour*) into account by producing two values of collocational strength for any pair of words (Gries, 2013).

[*] You can find a guide to logDice in the following URL: www.sketchengine.eu/my_keywords/logdice/

that may be used to determine significance of a collocation require that researchers think about some of the affordances in Table 5.1 The list of collocations returned is determined according to the statistic used to calculate it. Figure 5.4 shows the collocates for the lemma *feel* in B2 learner writing the Open Cambridge Learner Corpus. Three statistics are shown: T-score, MI and logDice. By default, logDice will determine the order of the collocates shown in *Sketch Engine.*

If we decided to use the logDice scores, *confident, comfortable, tired, nervous* and *makes* would be the top five strongest collocates in the B1 data. These are some of the 653 concordance lines found in the data for the collocate *confident*. In brackets we find some of the metadata (see Chapter 2) annotated in this corpus.

> That way they are going to specialise in what they like more and will *feel* more confident.   (FCE Exam. L1 European Spanish. Age 16)

> I certainly improved my knowledge and I *feel* more confident but in my opinion the course, even though, good and adequate, misses on some important skills
> (CAE exam. L1 Italian. Age 26–30)

> First of all, I *felt* confident to say to you that I am one of the ones you are looking for.
> (CAE exam. L1 Portuguese. Age 26–30)

	Word	Cooccurrences ?	Candidates ?	T-score	MI	LogDice ↓
1 ☐	confident	37	244	6.07	9.60	10.40 •••
2 ☐	comfortable	27	543	5.18	7.99	9.53 •••
3 ☐	tired	18	342	4.23	8.08	9.21 •••
4 ☐	nervous	14	259	3.73	8.12	8.97 •••
5 ☐	makes	20	769	4.44	7.06	8.85 •••
6 ☐	happy	30	1,483	5.42	6.70	8.85 •••
7 ☐	disappointed	12	291	3.45	7.72	8.70 •••
8 ☐	relaxed	9	121	2.99	8.58	8.57 •••
9 ☐	ease	7	62	2.64	9.18	8.33 •••
10 ☐	make	42	4,121	6.36	5.71	8.17 •••

Figure 5.4 Collocates for the lemma *feel* in B2 texts in the Open Cambridge Learner Corpus

If we used the MI score, the top five collocates in the B1 data would be *confident, embarrassed, Louise, ease* and *uncomfortable.* As we can see, three of the top five collocates are not even in the top 10 in Figure 5.4: *embarrassed* would be top 21, *Louise* top 11, and *uncomfortable* top 35. Why is this? As seen in Table 5.1, different measures tend to exploit different characteristics of collocational behaviour. While the lemma *feel* and *confident* co-occur 37 times in the data out of a pool of 244 candidates, *Louise* and *confident* co-occur six times out of a pool of 48 candidates. All in all, these two collocates cover 15% and 12.5% of the candidates, a very similar, and high, proportion of the pools. However, T-score works differently. Figure 5.5 shows the same collocation analysis results for the lemma *feel* in the same subset of the Open Cambridge Learner Corpus this time using the T-score as the ranking criterion.

As seen in Figure 5.5, this measure favours very frequent and not exclusive collocates. This is the reason why grammatical words rank very high in the list (e.g., *I, and, you, that,* etc.). This is probably the main distinction between T-score and MI, MI3 and logDice measures: their emphasis on the non-exclusivity of the collocates.

Focus 5.1 offers some practical considerations about collocation analysis.

In the next section, three selected studies showcase how collocation analysis has been used across cross-sectional and longitudinal research designs in the exploration of learners' use of collocations. Along with the corpora used, we will discuss the steps that were followed in each study to extract the collocations from the corpus data.

	Word	Cooccurrences ?	Candidates ?	T-score ↓	MI	LogDice	
1	☐ I	221	77,078	13.86	3.88	6.54	⋯
2	☐ .	205	148,457	12.30	2.82	5.49	⋯
3	☐ ,	164	140,139	10.67	2.59	5.25	⋯
4	☐ and	141	76,660	10.62	3.24	5.90	⋯
5	☐ you	124	42,685	10.39	3.90	6.55	⋯
6	☐ that	78	41,181	7.92	3.28	5.93	⋯
7	☐ to	96	104,922	7.71	2.23	4.90	⋯
8	☐ more	50	10,341	6.79	4.63	7.22	⋯
9	☐ me	50	10,469	6.78	4.61	7.20	⋯
10	☐ very	49	12,440	6.65	4.34	6.94	⋯

Figure 5.5 Collocates for the lemma *feel* in B2 texts in the Open Cambridge Learner Corpus using the T-score

Focus 5.1 Collocation analysis: The basics. Adapted from Pérez-Paredes (2020)

🔎 **Collocation analysis**

Collocation analysis uses significance tests to measure the strength of association between two items. There are different statistical measures that can be used to find out the collocational behaviour of a word, a lemma or n-grams.

AntConc will let us explore collocations by means of, among others, the mutual information (MI) score and the T score.

Sketch Engine uses the logDice score. The logDice score is not affected by the corpus size and it is frequently used to compare scores between different corpora.

Using a combination of MI and T scores can be effective in understanding how language is used by a group of people or in a set of texts.

Collocations that are extracted by using the MI score will be particularly useful to identify what is unique and truly specific in a corpus; collocations found by using a T- score will be helpful when looking at how longer units of text are put together in the corpus.

5.3   Collocation analysis: Representative studies

The three studies in this section represent different approaches to the analysis of collocations in L2. The three studies below (a) show different ways to extract collocations from a corpus, and (b) make use of different research designs. Durrant and Schmitt (2009) (see Section 5.3.1) studied collocations using both association measures and frequency analyses (Chapter 2 in this volume), a not-so-common approach that can be of interest in usage-based accounts of language learning.

Kreyer's (2021) (see Section 5.3.2) focus was on language acquisition and the analysis of longitudinal data of German learners of English. Finally, Wang (2016) examined collocations across a variety of L1 and L2 corpora in order to test L1 interference.

5.3.1 Durrant & Schmitt (2009): Using frequency and collocation strength measures

Durrant and Schmitt (2009) examined the use of collocations in L1 and L2 English corpora using a cross-sectional design (see Chapter 3). They explored the frequency of directly adjacent premodifier-noun word pairs (i.e., adjective noun and noun-noun combinations) in texts written by English native and non-native writers. The authors studied a total of 10,839 word combinations from 96 texts from a course in English for Academic Purposes (EAP). The strength of the collocations was measured by (1) tallying how frequently each of the combinations occurred in the British National Corpus (BNC) and (2) t-scores and mutual information (MI) (see 5.2). The collocations were identified and extracted following these steps:

1. Pairs of adjective noun and noun-noun combinations were manually extracted from the texts. Combinations were not included if they contained proper nouns, acronyms, pronouns, possessives, semi-determiners (i.e., *same, other, former*) or numbers/ordinals. Quotations were excluded from the analysis. These decisions were openly discussed in the research, which favours the interpretation of the results and the replicability of the research.
2. The collocational strength of the extracted word combinations involved totaling how frequently each of the combinations occurred in the BNC and calculating the t-scores and MI scores of the selected pairs.
3. Each collocation candidate was assigned a band. The extracted collocations were divided into 7 bands of t-score, as follows: $t=2-3.99$; $t=4-5.99$; $t=6-7.99$; $t=8-9.99$; $t=10-14.99$; $t=15-19.99$; $MI\geq20$. The MI scores were divided into the following bands: $MI=3-3.99$; $MI=4-4.99$; $MI=5-5.99$; $MI=6-6.99$; $MI=7-7.99$; $MI=8-8.99$; $MI=9-9.99$; $MI\geq10$
4. Each text was given a score and then the four groups of texts were compared using standard inferential statistics, taking each text as an individual case. This differs from other research designs where the whole corpus is taken as an observation case. Accordingly, the percentage of collocations falling into each score band was calculated.

It was found that while L2 EAP writers overuse high-frequency collocations, they underuse strong collocations that are less frequent in the BNC. L2 writers use 20% of their more frequent collocations from the high frequency band in the BNC.

Native speakers, however, take only 14%. An independent sample t-test showed that the difference is significant at the $p < .005$ level. In other words, in the corpora analysed native speakers use more low frequency combinations than non-native speakers. Non-native speakers significantly under utilise collocations with high MI value compared to L1 data. Language learners apparently depend on the most frequent lexical items (as shown in the BNC data) in the language. Their use of collocations with a very high t-score shows that they effectively absorbed many high-frequency formulaic sequences in the target language.

Durrant and Schmitt (2009) suggest that an overuse of very frequent collocations is consistent with usage-based models of acquisition "while accounting for the impression that non-native writing lacks idiomatic phraseology" (p.170). Gablasova et al. (2017) have suggested that corpus-based SLA studies on the collocational use of L2 speakers have revealed that L1 speakers systematically produce collocations with higher MI-score values than L2 users (see Table 4.5). These authors argue that studies so far have focused on the analysis of "formulaic units typical of a particular register or genre and described the frequency of occurrence of these expressions according to these settings" (p.167). They call for further empirical evidence about the degree to which genres and modes of communication affect the strength of association (see association measures in Table 4.5) between words. Durrant and Schmitt (2009) show the impact of using different association scores to measure collocation, as the choice of one score exclusively may bias the findings:

> [...] learners are quick to pick up highly frequent collocations, but less common, strongly associated items (e.g., *densely populated, bated breath, preconceived notions*) take longer to acquire. This trend for overuse of high frequency items and underuse of high MI items tallies with some previous research.　　(p.175)

This study provides empirical evidence of how L2 users access and use collocations as a type of formulaic language. The emphasis on the analysis of frequent collocations resonates with UB models that place great importance on the availability of language in the input as a prerequisite for acquisition.

5.3.2　Kreyer (2021): Studying collocations using a longitudinal research design

Corpora can provide evidence of the learners' ability to acquire formulaicity in a target language. For Lundell (2021) and Paquot and Granger (2012), the acquisition of L2 phraseological competence is slow to develop as phraseological errors change over time "progressively morphing from totally non-native-sounding combinations [...] to units that closely approximate native speaker use" (p.142). While the use of longitudinal corpora has been identified as a promising area of development and application of corpus linguistics analysis (Myles, 2015), the number of existing longitudinal corpora is still low. It is expected that in future years, with the popularisation of corpus research methods and the ubiquity of both written, spoken and hybrid digital communication, the collection and treatment of learner data will become more readily available to language teachers and researchers.

Kreyer (2021) studied verb-noun (V-N) collocations with the verbs *do, give, make* and *take* in a corpus of written data from 83 German learners of English in their four final years of secondary school. He made use of the Marburg corpus of Intermediate Learner English (MILE), a corpus of L2 English from students in grades 9 to 12 of a German secondary school. This corpus presents relevant learner data that can help researchers understand the acquisition on L2 English in pre-tertiary education levels. The corpus tracks the written production of around 90 learners over a 4-year period in 2,852 texts.

Kreyer (2021) adopted a non-statistical approach to the extraction of data from the corpus, that is, association measures such as MI or logDice were not used. Kreyer embraced the notion of collocations in the sense of Nesselhauf (2003) (see Recommended reading 5.1), who sees collocations as combinations of verb and noun where the noun is unrestricted while the verb is restricted, e.g., *take a picture* or *have an experience.* The collocations were identified and extracted following these steps:

1. 6,558 tokens of the highly frequent delexicalised verbs *do, give, make* and *take* were obtained through a python script that identified all tokens of the four lemmata and provided every occurrence together with a full sentence as context.

2. Only 2,120 cases were retained for analysis. Their correctness or incorrectness of use is based on the online version of the *Oxford Collocation Dictionary*[15] (OCD). Kreyer offers in his study a detailed account of the process followed to determine whether the learner collocations were correct or not.

The author found that around 25% of the collocation candidates are atypical and remained unchanged over the four years. Half of all erroneous collocations were interpreted as the result of L1-interference. Although a high degree of variability was found in the learner data, there was a tendency to use a higher number of correct collocations across the years. In Figure 5.6, each line represents an individual student.

---

15. URL: www.freecollocation.com

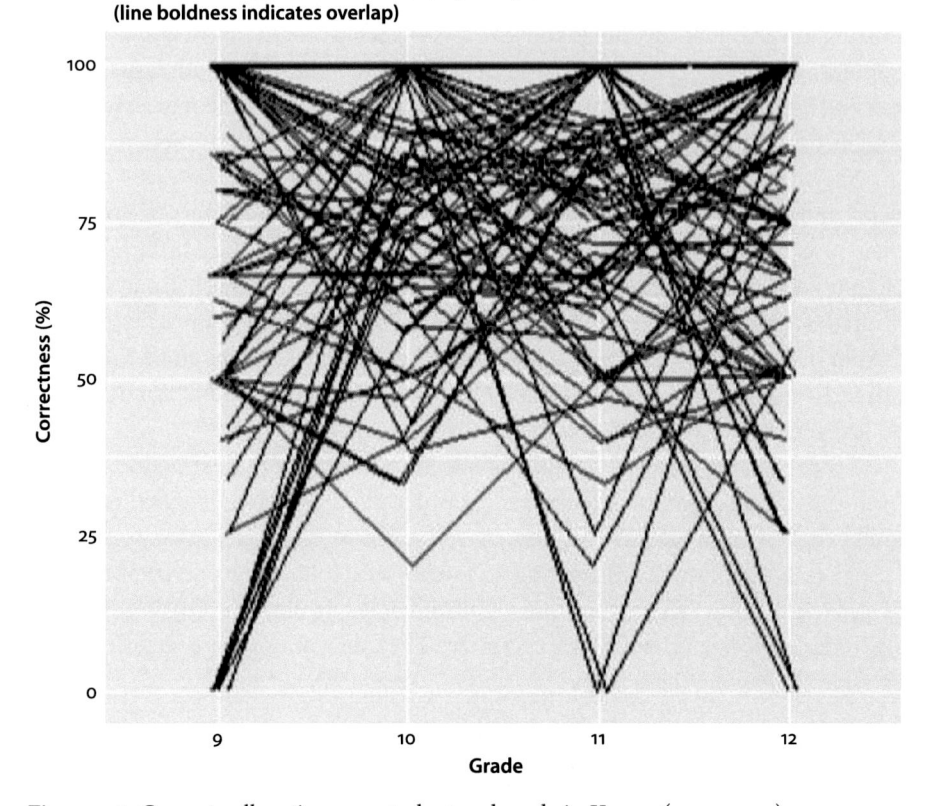

Figure 5.6 Correct collocations per student and grade in Kreyer (2021, p. 114)

Around 75% of all collocations in the data are used correctly. According to Kreyer (2021) "while some students show 100% correct use of collocations over the four years others show different variants of fall-rise or rise-fall patterns" (p. 113). Overall, he found a decrease in the influence of the L1 from grade 9 (58% of atypical collocations explained by interference) to the rest of the grades, ranging from 34% to 41% of all collocations. Although L1-induced erroneous collocations increase over the last three years, the author argues that this may be explained by the learners' drive to engage with complex ideas thus relying on verbatim translations of German verb + noun collocations.

5.3.3 Wang (2016): Delexical verbs + noun collocations in L1 and L2 corpora

Wang (2016) looked at the delexical verbs *have, make, take, give*, get and *do* and noun collocations (DVNCs) in two argumentative essay corpora written by University Chinese and Swedish learners of English: the Corpus of Chinese Learner English (CCLE) and the Uppsala Student English Corpus (USE). These two corpora were put together following the guidelines for the ICLE (see Chapters 2, 3 and 4). Some of the titles used to collect the L1 Swedish argumentative essays were "Sweden should leave the European Union" or "There is no place for a monarchy in a democratic country like Sweden". As for the L1 Mandarin Chinese speakers, essay titles included "It is humane to use animals in experiments" or "We really need the mobile phone".

The researcher also made use of editorial sections from two corpora of L1 English: the Freiburg-LOB Corpus of British English (FLOB) and the Freiburg-BROWN Corpus of American English (FROWN), representative of British and American English varieties, respectively. These corpora were used as the comparative baseline against which Wang tested the use of similar DVNCs in L1 writing. We note that corpus linguistics places great importance in examining naturally occurring data and this is reflected in how the learner data was collected and the type of L1 corpora used. Wang (2016) presents a novelty with respect to those studies mentioned above, since it uses corpora from the L1 of English learners. Two corpora of Mandarin Chinese, the Lancaster Corpus of Mandarin Chinese (LCMC), and Swedish, the Stockholm Umeå Corpus (SUC) were used. Sizewise, most corpora were comparable (around 1 M words each), although the Chinese learner English corpus was made up of 382,256 words.

In order to extract the verb + noun collocations, Wang followed these steps:

1. A wordlist per corpus was created to establish the overall frequency of the verbs analysed in the datasets.
2. Concordance lines for each of the occurrences of the verbs were produced.
3. Concordance lines were manually examined and DVNCs were extracted using Howarth's (1996) criteria, among others, semantic equivalence of the combination with a lexical verb, a copula + adjective, the presence of an abstract noun or the noun being used figuratively.
4. The extracted collocations were quantitatively and qualitative examined across all corpora.

A normalised frequency of 1,077 DVNCs per 100,000 words were found in the L1 Swedish learner data. In the Chinese L1 corpus 954 DVNCs per 100,000 words were extracted. The normalised frequency in the L1 English corpus was 463. The

differences across the three corpora were statistically significant. As in other studies, both groups of learners overused DVNCs when compared with native L1 English writers. However, learners used a narrower range of noun collocations (see
Table 5.2). This finding is in line with Lu's (2016) study of Chinese L2 learners of
English that found that university students tend to overuse a very restricted set
of collocations. This may be the "result of either lack of linguistic knowledge or a
cognitive strategy used to guarantee correct use of collocations" in an educational
context where correctness is particularly relevant (p.145).

For reasons of space, it is impossible to discuss in depth the results of this
research concerning all the collocations studied. If we take *make*, the collocations
that were retrieved from the different corpora are found in Table 5.2. Normalised
frequency per 100,000 words in brackets.

Table 5.2 Noun collocates for *make* across L2 and L1 corpora (Wang, 2016)

Swedish learner corpus	Chinese learner corpus	L1 English corpus data
decision (24)	use (14)	decision, sense (4)
difference, sense (5)	progress (12)	contribution, statement (3)
mistake, change (4)	call, decision (10)	choice, comment, effort,
choice, effort, living, profit (3)	effort (8)	payment (2)
experiment, purchase,	choice (7)	apology, case, change,
statement (2)	contribution (6)	difference, mistake, move,
	point, preparation (5)	name, point, progress, trouble,
	comparison, effect, friend,	use, way (1)
	mistake, sense (3)	

Wang concludes that both groups underused the range of DVNCs available in
English, either because they tended to rely on overuse of collocations that are frequent in their L1s, for example, *make + statement* in Swedish, or *make + contribution* in Mandarin Chinese. Also, the author suggests that some collocations in
the learner data reflect L1 writing conventions. Thus, Wang argues that while Chinese learners tended to "see things in terms of opposites", the Swedish writers were
more willing to "relate an unpleasant event or consequence" (p.124) in their essays,
which resulted in diverging preferences such as *have + advantage* and *take + stand*
in Chinese and Swedish learner data, respectively. The use of L1 corpora allowed the
researcher to fully understand the range of semantic fields associated with the noun
collocates. They included communication (*statement, enquiries*), specific activities
(*journey, splash*), manner (*effort, transition*), transactions (*profit, purchase*), outcomes (*progress, mess*), cognition (*sense, guesses*) and reasoning (*point, connections*). For example, according to the collocations and concordance lines examined,
Mandarin Chinese learners of English do not appreciably use collocations that

denote movement or communication-related meanings. In terms of errors, Wang claims that systematic errors, either grammatical (i.e., determiners, affixation) or lexical (i.e. wrong choice of verb or noun) are a valuable source of information to understand interlanguage development. In the data analysed, 16% of errors were found in the Swedish learner corpus, while the Mandarin Chinese learner corpus displayed 23% of errors. Delexical collocations headed by the verbs *get* and *have* appear to be a major source of problems for language learners. Wang argues that a combined use of L1 and L2 corpora offered interesting insights into the nature of the use of the collocations investigated:

> L1/IL comparisons throughout the study displayed only partial support for L1 influence. To view the learner language along with the source and target languages, the Swedish learners' IL was very close to both, while the Chinese learners' IL was a bit farther away from the TL, but at the same time also bore little resemblance to the L1. [...] As regards those collocations which appeared to be less firmly entrenched in the learners' mental lexicon, the prototypical meaning of a component word might be more susceptible to L1 transfer than the noncentral (e.g. figurative and delexical) meanings.   (Wang, 2016, p. 205)

5.4   Summary

Chapter 5 has examined how collocations can be researched in learner corpora. We have surveyed some of the underlying concepts and corpus methods available (Sections 5.1 and 5.2) and have explored representative research (Section 5.3) that has looked at adjective + noun, noun +noun and delexical verb + noun collocations. The chapter showcases how collocations can be extracted from learner corpora and complements an overview of basic corpus methods already covered in Chapters 2, 3 and 4.

CHAPTER 6

Researching grammatical patterning

Recommended reading 6.1

Hunston, S. (2019) Patterns, constructions, and applied linguistics. *International Journal of Corpus Linguistics, 24*(3), 324–353.

In this paper, Hunston argues that language patterns and the identification of their meaning groups can be used as the basis for the identification of constructions at a consistent level of specificity. For her, the term *construction* can be used to refer to a sub-set of instances of a grammar pattern identified by the occurrence of a limited set of node words. This paper discusses the procedures and the complexities involved in analysing the pattern-construction continuum from a corpus linguistics perspective.

Recommended reading 6.2

Hilpert, M. (2014). Collostructional analysis. In D. Glynn & J. Robinson (Eds.), *Corpus methods for semantics. Quantitative studies in polysemy and synonymy* (pp. 391–405). John Benjamins.

This chapter offers an excellent introduction to the three main types of collostruction analyses: collexeme analysis, distinctive collexeme analysis and covarying-collexeme analysis. Hilpert offers step-step-step guidelines and exemplifies each of these analyses using different case studies.

Recommended reading 6.3

Gries, S. T. (2017). *Quantitative corpus linguistics with R. A practical introduction* (2nd ed.). Routledge.

This book is an excellent introduction to using corpus linguistics methods with R. The book offers step-by-step guidelines to the analysis of frequency, dispersion, collocations and concordances. The reader will find a very useful section devoted to tests and, more generally, to statistical thinking. A selection of case studies is discussed.

A Google group devoted to using R in corpus linguistics can be found here: https://groups.google .com/g/statforling-with-r?pli=1

In this chapter, we explore colligation and related areas in L2 research such as colligation and verb-argument constructions (Römer, 2019). Section 6.1 examines the notion of colligation and practical ways to research colligation in learner data. We showcase two different studies that focus on colligation, illustrating practical ways to explore linguistic data and carry out complex searches that can retrieve grammatical patterns from corpora. Section 6.2 looks at collostructions, showing hands-on techniques to extract collostructions from learner corpora. Section 6.3 looks at research that has examined Verb-Argument Constructions (VACs) in learner corpora.

6.1   Colligation

Colligation analysis is the study of the recurring grammatical behaviour of individual lexical items (Hunston, 2002). Interest in this area of research dates back to the work of Firth (1957a, 1957b), Sinclair (1991) and Hoey (2005) and their studies on phraseological meaning and different forms of *restricted language* analysis (Römer, 2011). As we will see in the studies discussed below, the use of corpora and corpus methods can provide researchers with insights into language learners' pattern variability. Thus, words are *primed* for use in discourse because of the cumulative effects of all the speakers' encounters with the words in a language (Hoey, 2005). A word is primed to occur with a selection of other words known as *collocates* (see Chapter 5 for a discussion on collocations). Similarly, words are primed to occur in certain grammatical positions and grammatical functions known as *colligations* (Firth, 1957a, 1957b). The lexical priming theory (Hoey, 2005, p. 43) suggests that colligation can be defined as follows:

1. the grammatical company a word or word sequence keeps (or avoids keeping) either within its own group (e.g., a noun phrase) or at a higher rank;
2. the grammatical functions preferred, or avoided, by the group in which the word or word sequence participates (e.g., a noun phrase);
3. the place in a sequence that a word or word sequence prefers or avoids.

Some of the examples of colligation patterns discussed in Hoey (2005) include, among many others, the finding that *ponder* is primed to avoid the passive voice, or the fact that the prepositional phrase *in winter* is primed to show relational and material processes[16] in 57% and 26%, respectively, of the clauses analysed in the corpus of The Guardian newspaper texts that Hoey (2005) used in his study. In other words, in a corpus, a word or a word sequence will occur with function words (Biber et al., 1999) such as determiners, prepositions, conjunctions, etc. to reveal preferred or dispreferred functions. McCarthy et al. (2010) illustrate the colligational patterns for *phone*:

---

16. According to Hoey (2005), material processes have an obligatory actor and an optional goal. Relational processes express *being* and have an identifier and an identified, or a carrier, and an attribute.

- noun phrase + participle: *phone-lines jammed*
- verb + prepositional phrase: *yell into the phone*
- verb + to + pro(noun) (+ prepositional phrase): *spoke to her on the phone*
- make + phone call (+ prepositional phrase): *make a phone call to you*
- verb + particle + phone: *turn on the phone*
- verb + phone + particle: *turn the phone on*

Querying a corpus helps researchers discover the grammatical behaviour of a word and its pattern, or patterns, of co-occurrence with other words. This discovery process involves unveiling both the semantic association of the priming, as well as potential grammatical constraints that we can find in the corpus. In the following paragraphs, we showcase two studies that approach a phraseological analysis of learner language by examining the colligations found in the corpora analysed. Their different foci illustrate the broad scope of analysis that characterises different units of analysis in learner corpus research. The first study (6.1.1) looks at the use of colligation around signalling nouns in L2 and L1 corpora. The second study (6.1.2) examines colligations with ditransitive verbs in textbooks and in learner data. The analysis of local grammars (Hunston & Sinclair, 2000) such as signalling nouns and ditransitive constructions facilitate our understanding of how language is used in a particular genre such as argumentative essays. We discuss the corpora that were used in each of the studies and how colligation analysis was approached in each of them.

6.1.1   Colligation in learner language: Signalling nouns

Flowerdew (2006) examined the use of signalling nouns in English L2 essay writing. Signalling nouns are abstract nouns such as *difficulty, fact* or *attitude* whose meaning is made specific by reference to their linguistic context. According to Flowerdew (2010), signalling nouns operate across clauses, both cataphorically and anaphorically, or within the clause. Anaphoric signalling nouns refer back to a word or meaning that has already appeared in the text. Cataphoric signalling nouns refer to a word that will appear later in the text. Flowerdew wanted to understand how L2 English writers used these nouns and whether patterns of misuse (i.e., errors) could be identified in the data.

Flowerdew (2006) made use of a corpus of argumentative essays (450–500 words) of 110,000 words written under examination conditions by Cantonese L1 first year undergraduate students in Hong Kong. A total of 210 essays on nine different topics such as recycling, smoking or transportation were collected. The corpus included a balanced representation of essays that received B+, B, C+, C, D+, and D grades. A larger set of the corpus (ca. 400,000 words) was later incorporated into the International Corpus of Learner English (ICLE).

The focus of the analysis was on characterising the types of errors found in the data. Colligation errors were the most frequent type of errors found in the corpus. Out of a total of 1,451 errors, there were 989 colligation errors, that is, 68% of all errors, 283 incorrect signalling noun uses (19% of all errors) and 153 errors of collocation (10% of all errors). Flowerdew (2006) provides the following examples of colligation errors in the data. The appropriacy of each colligation was checked against the British National Corpus (BNC). The incorrect phraseology is provided in brackets, while the phraseology found in the BNC is provided in square brackets:

- The major argument in supporting the development of country parks (in) [for]
- The chance to suffer lung cancer, heart diseases and respiratory diseases (to) [of suffering]
- Discrimination to smokers (to) [against]
- A great effort on banning smoking in restaurants (on) [to ban]
- The argument on developing country parks (on) [for]

The results showed a correlation between the essay grades and the percentage of errors made ($p < .05$, $r = -.232$), which confirms the hypothesis that in lower grades more errors are made. According to Flowerdew (2006), the acquisition of signalling nouns is a developmental phenomenon which correlates with overall writing ability. The study shows how learners who achieved higher marks used signalling nouns more frequently and with greater accuracy. In a follow-up study, Flowerdew (2010) compared learner language use with that of L1 speakers of English by examining the frequency of signalling nouns across different functions (across clause, cataphoric and anaphoric uses, and in-clause) and the frequency of different in-clause realisation patterns. The L1 English data (110,537 words) was taken from The Louvain Corpus of Native English Essays (LOCNESS) (Granger, 1998) (see Chapter 4). Among many other findings of interest, Flowerdew (2010) discovered that L1 Cantonese learners of English overused certain cataphoric across-clause signalling nouns, which, he suggests, may be partly explained by the emphasis on text types that follow a compare and contrast, advantages and disadvantages pattern. An example of cataphoric across-clause noun is *advantage* or disadvantage as in *In this essay, I discuss the advantages and disadvantages of students using credit cards.*

The steps followed to analyse the signalling nouns in the corpus data can be summarised as follows (Flowerdew, 2010):

1. All signalling nouns in the corpora were identified manually by the researchers;
2. nouns in-clause patterns were identified;
3. nouns in across-clause patterns were identified by locating the signalling noun in the surrounding co-text;
4. each of the uses above was annotated. Annotation was done manually using the codes ANAC (anaphoric across clause) and CNAC (cataphoric across-clause);[17]
5. in-clause patterns were tagged with codes such as ICNP (in-clause signalling noun + np), ICing (in-clause signalling noun + V-ing), ICto (in-clause signalling noun + to) and others;
6. the frequencies of the signalling nouns were categorised into general frequencies per thousand words, or per hundred thousand words, and the means of frequencies of signalling nouns in individual texts in the two L1 and L2 English corpora were also compared; t-tests were used to test the significance of the differences.

In practical terms, identifying a specific type of noun can be approached in different ways. The easiest way to identify this group of nouns would be perhaps to have a POS tag that identifies such nouns (see Figure 4.4). Unfortunately, this is a very specific tag that is not found in most tagsets (see Figure 4.8). Another way to identify signalling nouns is to run a frequency list of nouns in the corpora (see Chapter 4). This frequency list of nouns can provide the researchers with a convenient way to spot the frequency of such nouns in the data. An alternative way to approach this first analysis is to search for a set of signalling nouns identified by the researcher. For example, the 20 most frequent signalling nouns in the LOC-NEC corpus are the following: *argument, problem, case, reason, claim, way, act, example, fact, right, issue, idea, article, time, question, side, effect, evidence, reasoning* and *result*. We could run a complex query on *Sketch Engine* where we search for any lemma of the 20 nouns above that has been tagged as a noun in our data. In the following example, we use the Open Cambridge Learner Corpus to exemplify this search shown in Figure 6.1.

Figure 6.1 shows how a complex search (CQL) can help researchers find target items for further analysis. Table 6.1 shows some useful CQL searches when exploring and retrieving data from the corpus.

---

17. Manual annotation is usually done with relatively unsophisticated text editors such as Notepad (Windows) or TextEdit (Mac). Both save plain text files as .txt, which facilitates the processing of the data in corpus management software such as AntConc or Sketch Engine. Both encode text files as UTF-8 or UTF-16, which is essential when dealing with multilingual texts or texts for language analysis of lesser known languages.

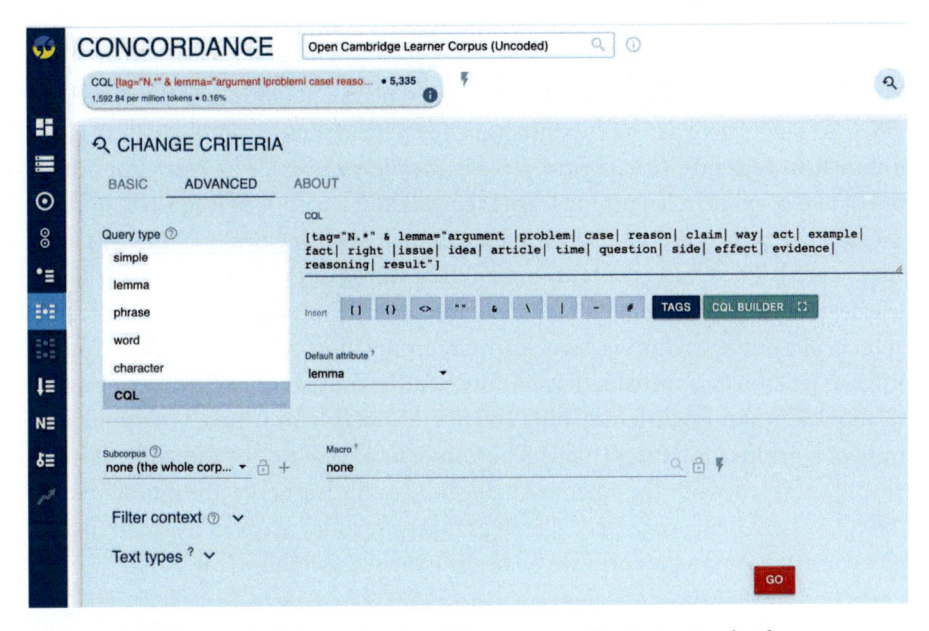

Figure 6.1 CQL search of the top 20 signalling nouns in the Open Cambridge Learner Corpus

Focus 6.1 Using corpus query language (CQL) on *Sketch Engine*

Corpus Query Language (CQL)

CQL searches provide researchers with flexibility in terms of how complex a search can be. CQL searches allow for complex grammatical (i.e. POS tags) or lexical patterns searches that cannot be searched using the simple, lemma, phrase, word or character query type. We can use operators such as AND, OR, NOT combined with POS tags, lemmas, words and positions within structures (as long as they have been annotated in the corpus). The following examples illustrate how to carry out noun-related searches:

- The CQL search [tag="N.*"& lemma="advantage"] [word="of"] returns all instances of the noun lemma *advantage* that are followed by the preposition *of*.
- The CQL search [tag="N.*"& lemma="advantage"] [tag="IN" & word!="of"] returns all instances of the noun lemma *advantage* followed by a preposition except for the preposition *of*.
- The CQL search [tag="N.*"& lemma="advantage"][tag="IN"][]{2,4}[tag="N.*"] returns all instances of the noun lemma *advantage* followed by a preposition with 2 to 4 words in between before a noun. Results include *advantage of going by bicycle* and *advantage of keeping animals on zoos*

For more information on CQL: www.sketchengine.eu/documentation/corpus-querying/ In the following resource, we collect the latest *Sketch Engine* video tutorials: http://www.perezparedes.es /sketch-engine-video-tutorials/

6.1.2   Colligation in EFL textbooks: Exploring priming effects in L2 input

Xu (2015) explored one specific type of text that plays a major role in the input provided to language learners: textbooks. The specific focus of this analysis is the ditransitive verb *give* (e.g., *I gave you my mobile number*). The researcher made use of two corpora: a beginning learner corpus and a corpus of English textbooks. The learner corpus used is The Chinese Learner English Corpus (CLEC) (Gui & Yang, 2002). The CLEC contains one million words of essays written by Chinese learners from five different educational levels. For this study, the author selected a sub-corpus of the beginning-level learners, around 209,000 words. The corpus of English textbooks, approximately 207,000 words, consists of two series of English textbooks: Junior English for China and Senior English for China, both published by People's Education Press (1996). The former had been used by the students in the corpus analysed, while the latter was being used by the learners at the moment when the corpus was being collected. The steps that were followed to analyse ditransitive *give* constructions in the corpora can be summarised as follows (Xu, 2015):

1. All the instances of the lemma *give* were identified in the data. All of them were exported to a spreadsheet for further analysis.
2. Ditransitive constructions were annotated manually and analysed semantically. To-dative (*give* + direct object (DO) + *to* + complement), monotransitive constructions (*give* + DO) and phrasal verbs were also annotated.
3. The uses of *give* were semantically classified in 8 classes including, among others, transfer, communication, permission, enablement, and causation meanings.

The findings support the colligation effect of English textbooks on learners' use of ditransitive *give* constructions. The use of *give* in the English textbooks corpus mainly displays senses of transfer and communication meanings, "with a lack of semantic categories at a more abstract level (enablement and permission meanings)" (Xu, 2015, p. 130). According to the author, a large number of texts included in the textbooks corpus are oral narratives and stories that reflect spoken language features, rather than written language. This may explain the high proportion of pronouns found in learners' written language as well as the limited range of meanings represented in the textbooks corpus. Xu (2015) found that the uses in textbooks show 55% of transfer meanings (e.g., *give someone something*) and 32% communication meanings (e.g. *give someone advice*). No feeling-related or idiom meanings were found. Only 3% of the uses showed causation meanings (*give someone trouble*). In the learner corpus, 40% of the uses show transfer meanings, while 17% show communication meanings.

6.2   Collostructions

Collocation (Chapter 5) and colligation (Section 6.1) analyses originated both methodologically and conceptually as applications of corpus linguistics insights into how grammar and lexis cooperate to generate meaning (McEnery & Hardie, 2012). A substantial part of the analyses carried out by corpus linguists started either with a lexical item (Baker, 2006) or with a part of speech using POS tags (see Chapter 4). However, the concept of 'construction' was not widely researched in the early days of corpus linguistics. Hunston (2021) has argued that while constructions exist in the brain, they have been "often used for regularities observed in corpora, whether or not there is empirical evidence that speakers have them stored" (p. 151).

Stefanowitsch and Gries (2003) coined the term *collostruction analysis* to introduce a new method to identify the meaning of grammatical constructions by determining "the degree to which particular slots [at any level of a given construction] prefer a particular set [...] of lexical items" (p. 211). The authors situate their contribution at the crossroads between construction grammar (Goldberg, 2006) and corpus linguistics. Stefanowitsch and Gries argue that corpus methods such as collocation analysis can only uncover units of meaning that "disregard the grammatical structures in which a search word and its collocates occur" (2003, p. 214). According to Wulff (2021), sentences are not just applications of a rule to a number of words so that they are arranged in a grammatical sequence. For her, sentences are the result of "combining constructions" (p. 176) that are stored in multiple forms in the mental lexicon, with different levels of schematization. Collostructional analysis was therefore designed to research the lexemes attracted to, or repelled by, a construction in particular slots. Such slots exist at different levels of abstraction in linguistic structures. For Hunston (2022), a construction is therefore a unit of any size that matches form and meaning: A construction can be a word (*apple*), a phrase (*the apple of one's eye*), a structure such as the ditransitive (*give someone an apple*) or an abstraction such as subject — verb inversion that has the meaning of "interrogative" (*did you eat the apple*). (Hunston, 2022, p. 152).

Stefanowitsch and Gries (2003) illustrate their approach with the construction [N *waiting to happen*], where the noun headword slot is usually filled, according to the concordance lines extracted from the British National Corpus, with words such as *accident, disaster* or *event*. This type of collostruction analysis is known as collexeme analysis (Stefanowitsch & Gries, 2003). It uses the Fisher exact test to calculate collostruction strength, a statistic that, on the plus side, does not make distributional assumptions and does not need a minimum sample size, that is, it can be potentially used with a relatively small corpus. However, the test is computationally intensive, which may be less apparent given the recent advances in home computer computational power. For Hackstein and Sandell (2023), collostruction analysis allows to investigate quantitatively how strongly a lexeme like *stand* or *tolerate* prefer to occur in the context of a construction such as *cannot* + verb infinitive + OBJ. By means of a contrastive approach, these authors have used collostruction analysis to measure the collostructional strength of English constructions *can't stand sb./sth.* And that of *can't tolerate someone/something* as well as the German *jdn./etw. nicht ausstehen können* compared with that of *jdn./etw. nicht leiden können*.

Collexeme analysis returns the Fisher exact p-values of the collexeme candidates for a given construction in a corpus. For example, Stefanowitsch and Gries (2003) investigated the verb *cause*. Previous corpus analysis had shown that the verb displays a negative prosody, that is, *cause* collocates with words that display a negative connotation. Collostruction analysis allows researchers to examine the collexemes candidates for different constructions. In the case of *cause* used as a verb, three constructions were explored: transitive constructions (A *causes* B), prepositional dative constructions (A *causes* B *to* C) and the ditransitive construction (A *causes* C B). Using the British component of the International Corpus of English (ICE-GB), Stefanowitsch and Gries found important differences across the three constructions in terms of the preferred or dispreferred collexemes.

The steps followed to carry out a collexeme analysis using *AntConc* and a spreadsheet software are summarised below:

1. The researcher finds all the instances of the transitive construction in the corpus. To do this, you can use CQL (see Focus 6.1) or regular expressions[18] and then check out the resulting concordance lines. Save the output and open the file using a spreadsheet software (e.g. Excel, Numbers, etc.). Identify the frequencies of all collocates (all verbs) in the concordance lines.[19]
2. Find all the instances of the dative prepositional construction in the corpus.
3. Find all the instances of the ditransitive construction in the corpus.
4. Find the corpus frequency of all verbs identified in steps 1, 2 and 3. You can do this manually (one by one) or, alternatively, use the advanced search in *AntConc* and paste all the verbs previously identified in the "Use search terms in the list below". Save the results and import it into a spreadsheet software.

---

18. For example, "cause\b*[a-z]" will return instances where "causes" and "caused" are found in the corpus; "\w \w cause\b*[a-z] \w" will return four slots where the search before occurs in the third slot, "\w \w cause_V*[a-z]\b*[a-z] \w" will return four slots where cause is POS tagged as a verb, etc.

19. Prof Martin Hilpert has put together an excellent video tutorial that shows how to use Excel to identify and quantify constructions. URL: https://youtu.be/5Mfv_6kzNXo

5. Build a contingency table for each of the three constructions like this one.[20] A contingency table (Table 6.1) displays the observed frequencies of the variables analysed.

Table 6.1 Contingency table showing construction and token counts in a corpus

	Frequency of *cause*	Frequency of all words (excluding *cause*)	Totals
Frequency of the transitive construction	Frequency here	Frequency here	Total here
cause frequency in the corpus	Frequency here	Frequency here	Total here
Total	Total here	Total here	Total here

6. Now that we have the observed frequencies in the corpus, we can calculate the expected frequency. We can do this by multiplying the total frequency of *cause* in the corpus by the total number of the transitive construction and then divide the result by the total number of frequencies in bold in the table above. The resulting frequency shows the expected number of the frequency of *cause* in the transitive construction, and now the figure can be compared against the frequency in the cell with frequency in italics.

7. Log Likelihood or Fisher's Exact test can be used now to test the strength of the attraction in the corpus data. A qualitative analysis of the results is strongly encouraged to understand how the actual uses relate to the quantitative findings.

Table 6.2 shows the top 5 most relevant collexemes for each of the constructions analysed. Note that the collexemes vary across the three constructions analysed, providing a finer-grained examination of collocational and colligational behaviour in a corpus.

Collostruction analysis offers complementary insights to the widespread analyses of collocations (see Chapter 5) and colligation (see Section 6.1). For Stefanowitsch and Gries (2003), the identification of collexemes in constructions offer more precise results and show "more rewarding perspectives to offer" (p. 236) in language pedagogy. Theoretically, they argue that collostructions support the notion that grammatical structure can be studied as signs that are stored as a "repository of linguistic units of various degrees of specificity" (p. 236).

---

20. We recommend watching Martin Hilpert's video tutorial on collostruction analysis for an extended explanation of how to conduct collexeme analysis: https://youtu.be/5Mfv_6kzNXo

Table 6.2 Collexemes across three *cause* constructions (Stefanowitsch & Gries, 2003)

Transitive construction	Prepositional dative construction	Ditransitive construction
problem	harm	distress
damage	damage	hardship
havoc	modification	discomfort
cancer	inconvenience	inconvenience
injury	famine	problem

While collexeme analysis has had a substantial impact on learner corpus research (Gilquin, 2015; Schweinberger, 2020), other two other types of collostruction analysis (Gries, 2019) are available to researchers: Distinctive collexeme analysis and co-varying collexeme analysis. Distinctive collexeme analysis (Gries & Stefanowitsch, 2004a) quantifies how much words prefer to occur in slots of two functionally similar constructions (i.e., the *will-* vs. the *going-to* future constructions). Co-varying collexeme analysis (Gries & Stefanowitsch, 2004b) quantifies how much words in one slot of a construction are attracted to or repelled by words in a second slot of the same construction. Examples of analysis include the verb slots in the *into*-causative (*trick someone into buying*) or the verb and the preposition of the *way*-construction (*make your way to the top*).

For those familiar with R, Susanne Flach has put together an R script that can be downloaded from https://sfla.ch/collostructions/ and used by researchers to carry out simple, distinctive, and co-varying collexeme analyses.

6.3   Verb-argument constructions in learner language

As seen in Section 6.2, some corpus researchers have looked at constructions as their object of analysis. Among the different types of constructions, verb-argument constructions (VACs) have received a great deal of attention in the corpus linguistics community. This attention may be explained by the fact that VACs are crucial for understanding how arguments, and argument roles, that is, objects, complements, adverbials, etc., are structured and how they contribute to the meaning of clauses and sentences. In construction grammar, an argument is a constituent of a clause or of a phrase that a verb requires to form a complete and meaningful construction. In English, arguments are often noun phrases that are semantically linked to the verb, representing the entities involved in the event or the state that the verb describes. VACs provide a framework for analysing the use of specific constructions, becoming central in studying L2 learners' lexical choices in, for example, transitive and ditransitive constructions. Researchers have suggested that the frequency of certain lexical units have an impact on language learning:

> ... there is a strong tendency for one single verb to occur with particularly high frequency in comparison to other verbs and that the overall distribution of verbs in constructions follows Zipf's (1935) law, which states that the frequency of words decreases as a power function of their ranks in the frequency table. The studies show how the frequencies of verbs influence acquisition, and how Zipfian distributional properties of language usage help make language learnable, for both first and second language learners. (Römer, O'Donnell, & Ellis, 2014, p.953)

For usage-based (UB) theorists, L2 learners acquire constructions through frequency and distribution (Ellis & Ferreira-Junior, 2009), which can be affected by L1 transfer and language typology (Römer, O'Donnell, & Ellis, 2014). So, according to UB theories, L2 acquisition of constructions is mediated by a number of factors, including how learners engage with the presence of constructions in their input. Kim and Rah (2019) has shown that constructional sensitivity plays a role in the integration of argument roles between a verb and a construction. Römer and Berger (2019) used subsets of the Education First-Cambridge Open Language Database (EFCAMDAT) to examine the development of L2 learner phraseological knowledge, confirming expansions of learners' VAC repertoires in terms of types, productivity, and complexity from lowest to highest proficiency levels. Römer and Berger (2019) found that as learners' proficiency increased, their most frequently used phrase-frames became more variable, less predictable, and more functionally complex, and they showed a development from predominantly fixed sequences to more flexible and productive ones, moving in verb-VAC associations toward a native usage norm. These findings about the transition from fixedness to productivity have been confirmed by Lim et al. (2024) in the Cambridge Learner Corpus (CLC) data.

VACs such as the 'V *against* n and 'V *in* n' were investigated in Römer, O'Donnell and Ellis (2014). This study is part of a larger research that has examined 50 constructions from the patterns identified in Francis, Hunston and Manning (1996). The authors conceptualise this study "as a starting point for a systematic analysis of VACs in the [...] British National Corpus (BNC)" (Römer, O'Donnell, & Ellis, 2014, p.953).

Römer, O'Donnell and Ellis (2015) used two different measures of contingency to test the strength of the association between a cue and an outcome. For these authors "the more readily an association between [cue and outcome] can be learned [...], so constructions with more faithful verb members should be more readily acquired" (p.56). These measures were faithfulness, i.e. the proportion of tokens of total verb uses in a particular construction, and directional mutual information, i.e., (MI word → construction and MI construction → word). Figure 6.2 shows the contingency measures for the 20 most frequent verbs in the 'V *across* n' constructions in Römer, O'Donnell, and Ellis (2015). The figure also shows the top 20 verbs ordered by the contingency measure MIc (MI word → construction) and the top 20 ordered according to total corpus frequency. See Chapter 5 for a coverage of the mutual information (MI) measure.

Figure 6.2 Top 20 verbs in the 'V *across* n' construction in the BNC. From Römer, O'Donnell, and Ellis (2015, p. 57)

Verb	Constr. freq.	Corpus freq.	Faith.	MI word → constr	MI constr → word	Top 20 by MIwc	Top 20 by corpus freq
COME	628	143580	0.004	15.607	10.837	SCUD	BE
WALK	243	19994	0.012	17.081	15.155	FLIT	GO
RUN	202	38688	0.005	15.862	12.984	SLANT	GET
CUT	198	17759	0.011	16.957	15.202	SCUTTLE	SEE
LOOK	188	108373	0.002	14.273	9.908	SKID	COME
BE	152	4090106	0.000	8.728	−0.875	SPRAWL	LOOK
GO	139	224168	0.001	12.788	7.375	TRAMP	PUT
MOVE	136	37573	0.004	15.334	12.498	SCURRY	WORK
LEAN	120	4464	0.027	18.227	18.464	FLICKER	CALL
SPREAD	96	5714	0.017	17.548	17.429	STRIDE	START
GET	75	211788	0.000	11.980	6.649	SPRINT	RUN
FALL	66	26023	0.003	14.821	12.514	SKIM	SET
STARE	58	7573	0.008	16.415	15.890	STUMBLE	MOVE
LAY	55	15799	0.003	15.278	13.691	DIFFUSE	PLAY
STRETCH	55	4446	0.012	17.107	17.350	LEAN	LIVE
TRAVEL	51	8290	0.006	16.099	15.443	FLASH	MEET
REACH	50	22300	0.002	14.643	12.559	SPLASH	CARRY
SET	45	38630	0.001	13.698	10.822	HOP	SIT
STRIDE	44	1049	0.042	18.868	21.195	CRAWL	FALL
LIE	44	13190	0.003	15.216	13.890	SPREAD	REACH

Here it is important to appreciate that frequency measures and contingency measures examine different phenomena. The top 3 most frequent verbs in 'V *across* n' are *come, walk* and *run*. However, when, for example, we examine the mutual information word → construction measure, the top 3 verbs are *scud, flit* and *slant* as in the following examples from the BNC:

> And then at last, the summit, with the cloud shadows *scudding across* the huge curved expanse...
> (BNC. Written books and periodicals. From the book *Jane's journey.*)

> A savage look *flitted across* his face and was gone. Guillamon grimaced. 'Fair enough.' They fell silent again.
> (BNC. Written books and periodicals. From the book *The way to Babylon.*)

> The light *slanted across* her skin in such a way the tiny blonde hairs showed like fair fluff. 'I'm trying to persuade Miranda to come back with us to London,' began her father.   (BNC. Written books and periodicals. From the book *Indigo.*)

Römer, O'Donnell, and Ellis (2014) showed that frequency, contingency, and semantic prototypicality drive language processing. The authors maintain that VAC mental representations differ in L1 and L2 English speakers.

While frequency has been covered in previous chapters, the analysis of contingency deserves some attention. Ellis and Ferreira-Junior (2009) analysed L2 learners' use of verbs in three VACs in a learner corpus. They studied the type/token (see Chapter 2) distributions in VACs produced by seven learners of English across 234 sessions in the ESF corpus. Wulff (2021) found that that the verbs that are first learned are those "most distinctively associated with the three different constructions, so rather than frequency alone, it is contingency, or frequency in context that kickstarts the acquisition of these constructions" (Wulff, 2021, pp.176–177). Naturalistic English learning of VACs "is affected by the frequency distribution of specific exemplars in each construction, as well as by their prototypicality and contingency" (Wulff, 2021, p.184).

For Gries (2018), contingency has been crucial in researching collocations (see Chapter 5), colligations and collostructions (see 6.1 and 6.2). Gries argues that the association measures used to calculate contingency can be improved by using the so-called Multiword Expressions from the Recursive Grouping of Elements measure (MERGE). These are the steps followed by Gries (2018) to calculate the MERGE contingency algorithm in a given corpus:

1. Extract all the multi-word units (MWUs) in the corpus. MERGE extracts all 2-gram tokens in a corpus, which may include contiguous 2-grams, as well as bigrams with gaps.
2. The tokens for each 2-gram type are counted, as well as the tokens for each word type and the corpus size.

3. Log-likelihood scores G^2 are calculated. The highest scoring 2-gram is selected as n-gram with the strongest attraction and merged into a unit and all instances of that 2-gram are replaced by instances of the new, merged unit. Accordingly, all frequency information statistics and the corpus size must be updated as new candidate n-grams are created through the co-occurrence of individual 1-grams with tokens of the newly-merged 2-gram.

4. New 2-gram strengths can be calculated and the cycle iteratively repeats from the point at which a winning 2-gram is chosen above; this continues until the lexical association strength of the winning 2-gram reaches some minimum cutoff threshold or a user-defined number of iterations has been processed, after which the output of the algorithm is a corpus, parsed in terms of MWUs, and a list of 1- to n-grams of different sizes, with and without gaps. In a new non-bullet paragraph: "Traditional methods for the analysis of MWEs usually depend on fixed lists, but MERGE takes a data-driven approach. It automatically finds MWEs by grouping words that cluster together based on statistical measures, so there' is less need for manual tagging."

6.4   Summary

Chapter 6 has looked at the analysis of colligation and collostructions in learner corpora. We have also examined the study of VACs in learner language. We have surveyed some of the corpus methods available (Sections 6.1 and 6.2) and have explored representative research (Sections 6.1) that has looked at colligation phenomena in L2 corpora. The chapter showcases how colligations and constructions can be extracted from learner corpora and complements an overview of basic corpus methods already covered in Chapters 3 and 4, as well as the research of collocations in Chapter 5.

PART 3

Researching corpus applications in language learning and teaching

CHAPTER 7

Researching indirect uses of corpora for language teaching and learning

Recommended reading 7.1

Timmis, I. (2015). *Corpus linguistics for ELT: Research and practice.* **Routledge.**

A guide for those involved in English Language Teaching (ELT), including researchers, graduate students, and educators. The book looks at the application of corpus research to key areas such as grammar, lexis, English for Specific Purposes (ESP), spoken grammar, and discourse. The volume provides an overview of key research in these areas, offering an evaluation of how these findings can enhance ELT methodologies.

Recommended reading 7.2

Sinclair, J. (Ed.). (2004). *How to use corpora in language teaching.* **John Benjamins.**

This volume offers a collection of chapters selected and edited by John Sinclair. The volume explores how corpora can enhance language teaching and learning and how researchers can contribute to developing and refining corpora that are tailored to pedagogical needs. By conducting analyses of language patterns, researchers can identify, among others, frequent collocations, grammatical structures, and discourse markers that are often challenging for learners. These insights can inform teaching materials and curriculum development, helping educators focus on high-utility language aspects. The book explores how researchers can address specific learning needs more effectively, building corpora focused on specialized language areas, such as academic writing or professional jargon, to support language for specific purposes.

When surveying corpus research methods and applications in language teaching and learning, it is useful to divide them into *indirect* and *direct applications of corpora*, as summarised in Focus 7.1.

Focus 7.1 Indirect versus direct corpus applications

🔎 **Indirect versus direct corpus applications**

- *Indirect applications of corpora:* Research using corpora that leads to better resources for language teaching (e.g. dictionaries, grammars, word lists, assessments and digital tools).
- *Direct applications of corpora:* Research that focuses on corpus tools or applications and resources that can be directly used in the classroom.

In this chapter, we will look at some of the main indirect applications whereas in Chapter 8 we will look at the direct uses of corpora in the classroom (typically through data-driven learning). In the present chapter, we will survey some of the corpus methods that have facilitated the innovations that corpora have brought about in terms of corpus-informed materials for language learning as well as applications and frameworks that can assist researchers and language teachers in the analysis of text with the help of corpus-derived measures. These indirect applications include dictionary making, grammar learning and corpus-based grammar research, and learner language analysis. The discussion revisits some of the corpus methods covered in Chapters 2–6. A new corpus method, keyword analysis, is presented in this chapter.

7.1 Corpora and dictionaries

Lexicographers have a long tradition of gathering and analysing language so as to facilitate the building of better dictionaries. Famously, the *Oxford English Dictionary* (OED) project had amassed more than three million paper slips of attesting word usage by the 1880s, stored in what nowadays might serve as a garden shed and sorted into pigeon-holes so as to organise them into a meaningful body of text from which the world-famous dictionary could be compiled (McCarthy & O'Keeffe, 2010).

Nowadays it is a given that a modern dictionary is based on corpus data, an approach that can be traced back to the pioneering work of Professor John McHardy Sinclair in the 1980s and the Collins Birmingham University International Language Database (COBUILD) project that he led. Central to this groundbreaking project was the creation of the Bank of English Corpus (McCarthy & O'Keeffe, 2010). It is interesting to note that the project title referred to 'language database' rather than 'corpus'. McEnery et al., (2006) note that the more specific term 'corpus linguistics' was not in common usage until the early 1980s. The coinage of the term is associated with Aarts and Meijs (1984).

Skipping to the present day where corpus use in dictionary creation is a given, the greatest single impact of the use of corpora in dictionary creation is that it moves beyond a reliance on intuition. Pre-corpus dictionaries were often more concerned with the origins or etymology of a word rather than its most up-to-date spread of meaning and usages and they suffered from omissions of some common usages and sometimes contrived examples (Rees, 2022). For example, *The Oxford Advanced Learner's Dictionary of Current English* (3rd ed.), (Hornby, 1974) listed the first meaning of the verb *fire* as: '*set fire to with the intention of destroying*' and the example given is *fire a haystack* (based on Rees, 2022, p. 388). If one goes to a corpus, such as the English Web 2021 Corpus (enTenTen21) of 52.2 billion words, one can find panels of lists of information about *fire* as a verb in milliseconds. Just a tiny segment of the results (Figure 7.1) clearly points to the most frequent sense of *fire* being related to gunfire.

Figure 7.1 An extract of results from enTenTen20 for word sketch of *fire* as a verb

Following Rees (2022), Table 7.1 summarises some of the key corpus tools and methods that can be used for lexicographical research, which gives an insight into the impact of corpus linguistics in the process of contemporary dictionary making.

Table 7.1 Summary of main corpus methods used in dictionary making (based on Rees, 2022)

Purpose in dictionary making	Important consideration(s)
Wordlists (see Chapters 2 and 6)	
Word frequency lists allow for the identification of potential *headwords**	For dictionary making a very large language corpus or corpora is required so as to get the greatest representation of uses (including newly emerging uses).
Multi-word units (MWUs) /N-Grams (see Chapter 2)	
It is important to identify high-frequency multi-word units (MWUs) or N-grams and include them in dictionary entries.	It is important to set a minimum frequency threshold and also to identify what is 'useful' for a dictionary. Not all high frequency MWUs will make it to a dictionary (e.g., *out of the* and *to be a* are very high 3-word MWUs but are unlikely to be in a dictionary).
Keywords (see this Chapter)	
Keywords identify salient words. In designing *The Louvain English for Academic Purposes Dictionary,* Granger and Paquot (2015) drew on the *Academic Keyword List.*	Homonyms pose a challenge (e.g., *table* in the sense of furniture versus the sense of a format for presenting data). The corpus tools cannot disambiguate the meaning, and this will need to be followed up qualitatively (especially through concordances, see below).
Concordances (see Chapters 2)	
Concordances are essential to observe and disambiguate meanings and uses in context, as well as to identify patterns of lexicogrammar.	When choosing an example for a dictionary, tools such as GDEX (*Good Dictionary Examples*) in Sketch Engine can aid lexicographers in finding suitable examples from concordances.
Collocation measures (see Chapter 2 and 5)	
The statistically measure of the strength of the association between words is important for lexicographers. This helps them find the most typical collocations.	Different statistical measures give word association measures (see Chapter 5). T-scores tells us about grammatical behaviour; mutual information (MI) scores highlight restricted lexical collocations. LogDice measure is seen as most useful for lexicographers because the results are not influenced by the corpus size and give an indication of the relative difference in collocation strength.

Table 7.1 *(continued)*

Purpose in dictionary making	Important consideration(s)
Word sketches (see Chapter 6 and this Chapter)	
The word sketch function (*Sketch Engine*) generates summaries of a word's collocation behaviour, using part-of-speech tags and statistical measures of collocates for a given headword. They sort the collocates according to grammatical relation and statistical salience.	It is important to choose a large representative corpus when using word sketches as a lexicographer. Subject-specific dictionaries need to draw on large up-to-date representative corpora.
Word sketch differences (see this Chapter)	
The *word sketch differences* function (*Sketch Engine*) allows for the comparison of the collocational behaviour of two forms and is very useful in researching the senses of words in different domains.	*Word sketch differences* look at collocates of two near synonyms (e.g., *horrible / terrible*) or can look at collocates of a homonym in specific domains. For example, using the sub-corpus settings, the collocates of *table* in a general corpus and be compared with those of *table* in a corpus of academic writing.

* A headword is the word at the beginning of a dictionary entry, the word which the definition or explanation refers to (McCarthy, O'Keeffe & Walsh, 2010)

Clearly, the corpora and corpus tools available to the current day lexicographer greatly enhance the dictionaries that are produced. From the user perspective, a corpus-based dictionary is one that ultimately provides learning advantages, including: (1) up-to-date frequency-based content based on actual usage; (2) evidence-based definitions which derive from quantitative and qualitative corpus research; (3) frequency-based patterns of words including multi-word units, collocates, formulaic language; (4) real examples from spoken and written language. The availability of computational tools such as those described in this book, however, has facilitated the creation of smaller-scale research projects such as the compilation and validation of word lists, which have become popular in the teaching of specialized languages (see 7.4).

7.2   Corpora and grammars

Books about English grammar can be traced back to the 1500s and their existence sprang from the desire to match the grammar books of Latin which were used at the time (O'Keeffe & Mark, 2018). Modern grammars are based on real samples of both spoken and written language from corpora and this development saw three major impacts:

1. a shift from *prescription* about what should be said or written to *description* of what is found in the empirical data (i.e., corpora);
2. a greater understanding of grammar patterns and register; and
3. a gathering momentum to describe spoken grammar as distinct from written grammar.

The start of the era of corpus-informed grammar books is closely linked to two major empirically-based works: Quirk et al. (1972) and Quirk et al. (1985). Quirk's early corpus endeavours resulted in the *Survey of English Usage*. This in turn led to Quirk et al. (1972) and, what Leech (2015) refers to as the mega-grammar, Quirk et al. (1985). Automated Part-of-Speech (POS) tagging (see Chapter 4) has led to major innovation in grammar research because it is now relatively simple to extract instances of even "abstract categories such as progressive aspect or passive voice" (Leech, 2015, p.148).

For a researcher, being able to retrieve all instances of grammatical patterns in a corpus brings its own challenges. It comes with the responsibility, and sometimes burden, of describing what one finds in an unbiased and objective way through what Leech referred to as the "principle of total accountability" (Leech, 2015, p.146). The reality of corpus-based grammar research is that we can reveal patterns that go against received rules and the researcher has to make use of all relevant data and not shy away from patterns that do not appear to fit received paradigms. As Leech puts it, a grammarian using a corpus, "cannot ignore data that do not fit his/her view of grammar, as theoretically oriented grammarians have sometimes done in the past" (2015, p.147). As a result of the principle of total accountability, learners of grammar are getting a more authentic experience of language patterns even though this can bring its own challenges because real usage is not always neat. For materials and grammar book writers and researchers, being totally accountable can pose a dilemma for as we discuss in the case studies below. On the one hand, materials are written for learners following a syllabus, usually one that prepares them for exams. However, rules on the syllabus are not always neatly adhered to in the corpus data. In the following sections, we will show examples of research that make use of some of the corpus methods studied in previous chapters, showcasing their usefulness for researchers interested in developing corpus-informed materials and language analyses in the language classroom.

7.2.1   Study 1: *There is, there's* and *there are: English Grammar Today* (Carter et al., 2011)

When writing the entry of *There is, there's* and *there are* in the corpus-based grammar for learners of English, *English Grammar Today*[21] (Carter et al., 2011), the authors started with corpus evidence based on word and pattern frequency and concordance searches (as illustrated in Chapter 2). This allowed them to *describe* the patterns of use of *there is, there's* and *there are*. To replicate their process, we can conduct a corpus search of the 100 million word British National Corpus (BNC) for patterns of *there is, there's* and *there are* using the CQL search query (based on POS tags) to generate the most frequent patterns of *There BE + plural noun*: [word="There|there"][lemma="be"][tag="NNS"] (see Table 7.2 and Chapter 6 for further insight into complex searches). Any of these patterns can then be examined qualitatively using concordances so as to gain greater understanding of how it is used and to find good examples for the grammar.

Table 7.2 Top 20 patterns from the British National Corpus for the pattern *there + lemma be + plural noun*

	Pattern	Freq.		Pattern	Freq.
1	there are people	179	11	there are things	82
2	there are lots	148	12	There were times	81
3	there are times	138	13	There are people	81
4	there are problems	134	14	there were times	80
5	There are times	115	15	there are differences	76
6	there are others	109	16	there were signs	75
7	There are lots	109	17	there are ways	73
8	there's lots	91	18	there were reports	71
9	there are signs	87	19	there were problems	65
10	there were people	82	20	there are plans	64

However, the results in Table 7.2 show the pattern *There's lots*, i.e., *there + is + plural noun* as the 8th most frequent item but this does not fit with the main paradigm or rule. The pattern can be further explored through concordance lines (Figure 7.3):

---

21. *English Grammar Today* is freely available online through https://dictionary.cambridge.org /grammar

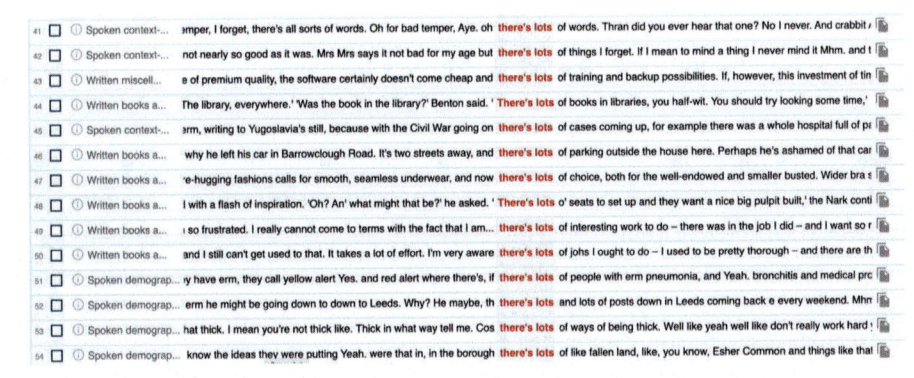

Figure 7.3 Sample screen of concordance lines from the British National Corpus for the pattern *there's lots*

This is a dilemma for authors of a grammar resource for English language teaching. Learners will refer to it to find out how to use grammar correctly for exams, homework etc. Yet, a learner ought to know about this high frequency pattern. For the authors, within the principle of total accountability (see above Leech, 2015 and the afterword of this book), they cannot ignore a pattern like this in their grammar book. To this end, Carter et al. (2011) first described the rules for *There is, there's* and *there are* and then described what they found in the corpus data so that the learner is fully informed:[22]

In speaking and in some informal writing, we use *there's* even when it refers to more than one. This use could be considered incorrect in formal writing or in an examination:

There's three other people who are still to come.
There's lots of cars in the car park.

Figure 7.4 Extract of *there's* from *English Grammar Today* (Carter et al., 2011)

Because corpus software is such a powerful tool in foregrounding patterns of individual words, it has meant that many common patterns that had, in pre-corpus times, gone unnoticed have been brought into focus (as seen in Chapters 5, collocations, and 6, colligation and collostructions). These findings can become part of our teaching materials, as study 2 illustrates.

---

22. The entry for *There is, there's* and *there are* can be seen in full at https://dictionary .cambridge.org/grammar/british-grammar/there-is-there-s-and-there-are?q=there+is

7.2.2   Study 2 linking adverbs and register: *The Longman Grammar of Spoken and Written English* (Biber et al., 1999)

Another major contribution of corpus linguistics to grammar research and resources was the enhanced understanding of the importance of register (i.e., the situational characteristics of a text type, e.g. written academic prose; fictional prose; casual conversation; media interview). In their ground-breaking grammar, *The Longman Grammar of Spoken and Written English* (LGSWE),[23] Biber et al. (1999) used the *Longman Corpus of Spoken and Written English* (LCSWE) and apart from distinguishing grammar patterns across spoken and written registers, they also used the four main register categories of *conversation, fiction, news* and *academic prose* (Conrad, 2019). They justify these four registers on the basis that:

1. they are important, highly productive; and
2. they are different enough from each other to represent a wide variation.

By using a corpus that was designed to represent four registers, the authors of LGSWE were able to offer learners a description of grammar patterns by register. In its coverage of *linking adverbs,* for example, it gives rich register-based information about usage, spoken and written modes and British versus American English varieties (see Biber et al., 1999, p. 886ff) (adapted from Biber et al., 1999, p. 886):

–   four linking adverbs are more common in conversation. *So* and *then* mark result/inference while *anyway* and *though* mark contrast/concession
–   American English differs from British English in terms of its higher frequency of *so* over *then.*
–   Academic prose shows an overall lower frequency of use of linking adverbs compared to conversation, but several occur with notable frequency including *however, thus, therefore* and *for example.*

Other researchers or even a learner, teacher, or materials writer can now readily replicate this type of register-based investigation of a word or a pattern using a corpus such as the Corpus of Contemporary American English (COCA) (https://www.english-corpora.org/coca/) (Davies, 2008). For example, if we take the linking adverbial *however,* we can use the *Chart* function in the COCA interface to generate its profile of use across eight registers (Blog, Web, TV/Movie, Spoken, Fiction, Magazine, News and Academic) (Figure 7.5):

---

23.   Biber, et al. (2021). *Grammar of Spoken and Written English,* published by John Benjamins, revisits the original 1999 edition using the same corpus data.

SECTION	ALL	BLOG	WEB	TV/M	SPOK	FIC	MAG	NEWS	ACAD
FREQ	326096	53474	60578	5109	11339	13641	46003	29228	106724
WORDS (M)	993	128.6	124.3	128.1	126.1	118.3	126.1	121.7	119.8
PER MIL	328.39	415.77	487.53	39.89	89.90	115.29	364.84	240.08	890.92
SEE ALL SUB-SECTIONS AT ONCE									

Figure 7.5 Profile of the frequency of *however* across eight registers in the COCA corpus

As Figure 7.5 clearly illustrates, *however* is used most frequently in academic journals (809.92 times per million words) and, to a lesser degree, in web-pages (487.53 times per million words). The register-specific role of *however* in academic language accounts for the majority of its use.

When researching learner language, being able to zone in on registers can be very useful across different corpora so as to compare learners' patterns of use. Let us take the linking adverbial *moreover*. When we look at its profile of use (see Table 7.3), we can see that, per million words of text, learners appear to overuse it:

Table 7.3 Comparison of frequency per million words of linking adverbial *moreover* across Open CLC, BAWE and BNC (written books and periodicals sub-corpus)

Corpus	Frequency PMW
Open Cambridge Learner Corpus	375.89
British Academic Written English	127.04
British National Corpus, written books and periodicals sub-corpus	36.18

A small corpus that offers interesting comparisons in terms of the use of academic lexis or multi-word units among native versus non-native speaker writers is the Michigan Corpus of Upper-Level Student Papers (MICUSP) (https://elicorpora.info/main), a corpus of over 800 A grade papers (circa 2.6 million words) from a range of disciplines across four academic divisions of the University of Michigan (Humanities and Arts, Social Sciences, Biological and Health Sciences, Physical Sciences). Because the student papers are all A grade papers, it is a useful dataset for the comparison of how words and patterns are used both across disciplines and among native and non-native undergraduate writing. Let us return to one of the linking adverbs discussed above as being high frequency in academic prose (*however*). When we search this by native and non-native writers across disciplines, we see that its profile is rather different, as Figure 7.6 illustrates.

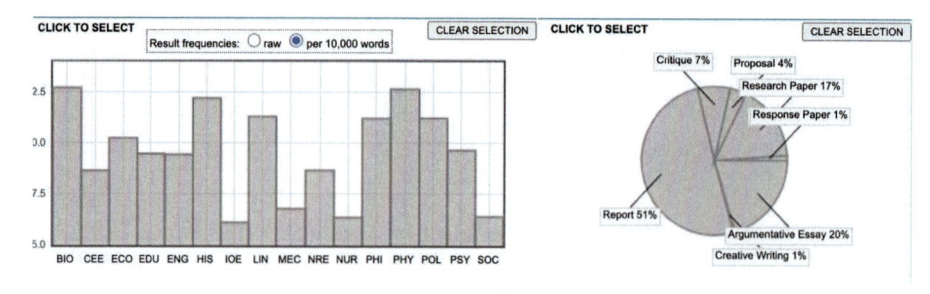

Native speaker writers' use of *however*, per 10,000 words, by discipline[24]

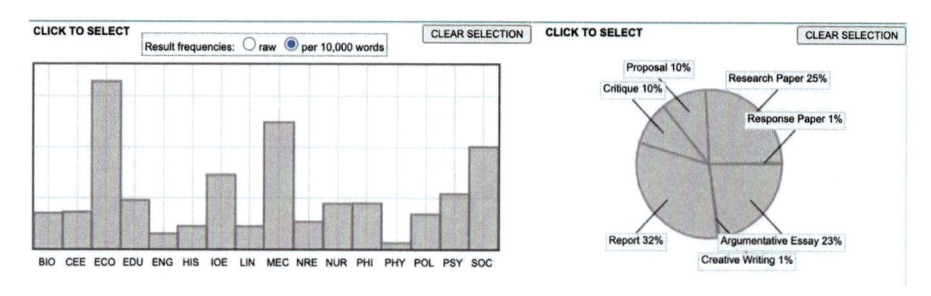

Non-native speaker writers' use of *however*, per 10,000 words, by discipline

Figure 7.6 *However* in native speaker writers versus non-native speaker writers by discipline in the MICUSP

Corpus linguistics highlights the importance of distinguishing between different registers (e.g., conversation, fiction, news, and academic prose) to understand grammar patterns. This approach allows researchers to observe how linguistic features, like linking adverbs, vary significantly across contexts. The frequency and use of linking adverbs, such as *however, so* and *therefore* differ not only between spoken and written language but also between British and American English. For example, *so* is used more frequently in American English, while *however* is prominent in academic prose, emphasising the need for register-specific considerations in language research. Resources like COCA and MICUSP enable researchers to analyse linguistic elements across various registers and compare L1 and L2 language use. Such tools are instrumental in examining the nuances of academic language and identifying potential areas of overuse or underuse among learners.

---

24. Discipline abbreviations in MICUSP: Biology (BIO); Civil & Environmental Engineering (CEE); Economics (ECO); Education (EDU); English (ENG); History & Classical Studies (HIS); Industrial & Operations Engineering (IOE); Linguistics (LIN); Mechanical Engineering (MEC); Natural Resources & Environment (NRE); Nursing (NUR); Philosophy (PHI); Physics (PHY); Political Science (POL); Psychology (PSY); Sociology(SOC)

7.2.3   Study 3. Investigating learner patterns within a register: Academic writing

Register, as we have seen, can be a useful basis for comparison of how words and multi-word units have differing profiles of us. It is a fruitful variable for the investigation of learner language as well as, among others, novice writers' texts. Here we use the N-gram function within *Sketch Engine* to examine patterns of use within the register of academic writing. As a starting point, we use the British Academic Written English Corpus (BAWE) (Nesi et al., 2008).[25] The whole corpus comprises 2,761 samples of proficient assessed student writing with lengths in the range of 500–5000 words.[26] Using the N-gram function of Sketch Engine, set to search for 3-word strings, we generate the following N-gram frequency list (Figure 7.7 illustrates the result for the top 26 items).

These results are useful because they give us what we term as a *baseline* for the most frequent 3-gram patterns in a representative corpus of academic writing in UK university settings. With this baseline, we can then look at learner data and compare different corpora. For example, Table 7.4 illustrates the top 20 most frequent 3-gram patterns in the Learner Corpus of English Essays (ArabCC), a corpus of 957 English essays (224,278 words) written by more than 300 students of The Arab Academic College of Education (all native speakers of the Arabic language).

For the researcher, this offers a springboard for a number of corpus-based investigations. The following showcases the type of potential research questions that learner corpus researchers and corpus linguists may want to explore in terms of the frequency of use of discrete lexical items and patterns:

- Why are the Arabic writers using *a lot of* so frequently?
- Why are the Arabic writers using first person patterns such as *I think that; In my opinion, I want to* and *I believe that* etc. so frequently?
- Quite a few of the top 20 items are on both lists. Are these being used in the same way?

---

25. The British Academic Written English Corpus (BAWE) is a 6.9 million word British Academic corpus of academic works written at universities in the UK, distributed disciplinary areas (Arts and Humanities, Social Sciences, Life Sciences and Physical Sciences) and levels of study (undergraduate and taught masters level).

26. The data here come from the British Academic Written English (BAWE) corpus, which was developed at the Universities of Warwick, Reading and Oxford Brookes under the directorship of Hilary Nesi and Sheena Gardner (formerly of the Centre for Applied Linguistics, Warwick), Paul Thompson (formerly of the Department of Applied Linguistics, Reading) and Paul Wickens (School of Education, Oxford Brookes), with funding from the ESRC (RES-000-23-0800).

N-GRAMS   British Academic Written English Corpus (BAWE)

3-grams, word (items: 100,852 , total frequency: 1,448,032)

	N-gram	Frequency ?		N-gram	Frequency ?
1	in order to	3,179 •••	14	be able to	1,084 •••
2	as well as	2,241 •••	15	a number of	1,069 •••
3	due to the	2,067 •••	16	such as the	1,060 •••
4	the use of	1,602 •••	17	there is no	987 •••
5	one of the	1,601 •••	18	Oxford University Press	971 •••
6	the fact that	1,481 •••	19	the end of	959 •••
7	in terms of	1,456 •••	20	to be a	947 •••
8	there is a	1,362 •••	21	a result of	901 •••
9	part of the	1,260 •••	22	it is not	863 •••
10	can not be	1,260 •••	23	need to be	860 •••
11	can be seen	1,249 •••	24	the other hand	853 •••
12	the number of	1,114 •••	25	the development of	840 •••
13	that it is	1,112 •••	26	it can be	827 •••

Figure 7.7 Top 26 sample of 3-gram patterns by frequency in the British Academic Written English Corpus

– The BAWE shows several fixed patterns such as *in order to, due to the, the fact that, in terms of the.* How are these being used in the BAWE data and how, if at all, are they used in the Arabic learner data?

Focusing on the most frequent item in BAWE and the second most frequent on the ArabCC list (Table 7.4), *in order to,* we can also cross check its use in the MICUSP across native and non-native students (all of whom have received A grade results for their papers). Figure 7.8 shows that this pattern is used much more by native speaker writers compared to non-native speakers. The results show some differences.

When we look at the writing of C2 level learners in the Open Cambridge Learner Corpus (available within *Sketch Engine*), we find that *in order to* is also in the top 3-gram items. We can check if this pattern is also prevalent in the Corpus of Contemporary American English (COCA). As Figure 7.9 clearly shows, it is a pattern that is strongly associated with the academic register (and it tells us that web-based writing, including blogs, also show a prevalence for its use). COCA also shows us that over time, this pattern has been a stable feature.

These studies offer examples of how targeted explorations of language use can inform teaching materials and can guide, among others, the development of language assessment tools. Corpora provide authentic language data collected from real-world contexts, allowing researchers to analyse language as it is genuinely

Table 7.4 Top 20 most frequent 3-gram patterns in Learner Corpus of English Essays (ArabCC) compared with the BAWE

	BAWE			ArabCC		
	Item	Freq.	PMW	Item	Freq.	PMW
1	in order to	3179	381	a lot of	199	887
2	as well as	2241	269	in order to	192	856
3	due to the	2067	248	I think that	186	829
4	the use of	1602	192	I want to	150	669
5	one of the	1601	192	I believe that	140	624
6	the fact that	1481	178	the other hand	129	575
7	in terms of	1456	175	In my opinion	98	437
8	there is a	1362	163	On the other	88	392
9	part of the	1260	151	the fact that	85	379
10	can not be	1260	151	one of the	80	357
11	can be seen	1249	150	do n't have	78	348
12	the number of	1114	134	to be a	74	330
13	that it is	1112	133	because of the	68	303
14	be able to	1084	130	I do n't	66	294
15	a number of	1069	128	a foreign language	65	290
16	such as the	1060	127	the chance to	64	285
17	there is no	987	118	be able to	61	272
18	the end of	971	116	that it is	59	263
19	to be a	959	115	the city center	59	263
20	a result of	947	114	To sum up	58	259

used rather than relying on introspective or hypothetical examples. Corpus evidence enables quantitative assessments, like frequency counts and statistical analyses, helping researchers identify patterns in language use that might not be evident in smaller samples or through anecdotal observation. Taking this evidence to language classrooms needs a thorough understanding of the corpus methods covered in this book. In the following sections, we will explore some tools and applications that can be used to explore learner writing.

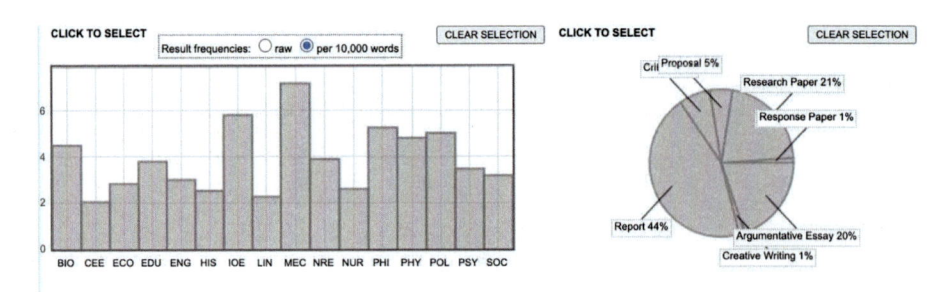

Native speakers' use of *in order to* across disciplines, per 10,000 words

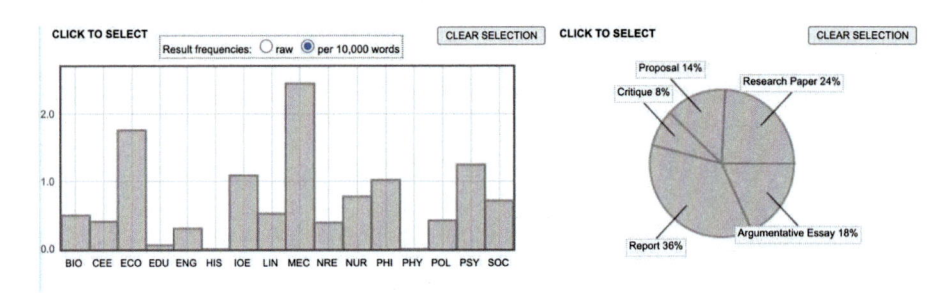

Non-native speakers' use of *in order to* across disciplines, per 10,000 words

Figure 7.8 *In order to* in native versus non-native (A graded) papers in MICUSP, by discipline

SECTION	ALL	BLOG	WEB	TV/M	SPOK	FIC	MAG	NEWS	ACAD	1990–94	1995–99	2000–04	2005–09	2010–14	2015–19
FREQ	91548	17697	18150	3091	9410	4359	9812	5019	24010	10542	9261	8734	8734	8359	10071
WORDS (M)	993	128.6	124.3	128.1	126.1	118.3	126.1	121.7	119.8	121.1	125.2	124.6	123.1	123.3	122.8
PER MIL	92.19	137.60	146.07	24.13	74.60	36.84	77.82	41.23	200.43	87.05	73.96	70.08	70.98	67.77	82.04
SEE ALL SUB-SECTIONS AT ONCE															

Figure 7.9 Chart of use of *in order to* in the Corpus of Contemporary American English (COCA), across registers and time period

7.3   Corpus-based tools to analyse learner writing and texts

In this section we showcase corpus-based tools, resources, and applications that, not having been discussed in the previous chapters, can be used to enhance learning, inform materials design and assessment and provide insights on learning. These resources are facilitated by existing measures and frameworks such as formulas for measuring lexical density or syntactic complexity, word lists, or descriptors about what a learner at a given level of proficiency typically knows in terms of vocabulary or grammar. Some of these tools can automatically calibrate and profile learners' language and proficiency level across a battery of indicators. Others also demonstrate how learner corpora have been used as a resource for their development.

The tools covered in this section provide researchers with robust options for assessing language proficiency in learner texts by using standardised corpora and frameworks, allowing for precise alignment with expected proficiency levels. They offer insights into specific vocabulary and grammar strengths and weaknesses. The automated analysis of various linguistic variables exemplified supports handling larger datasets, which is valuable for language learning research, where large-scale analysis is often required. By leveraging standardised references, researchers can uniformly compare texts, monitor progress, and benchmark across groups. Additionally, the tools in this section help in designing or selecting materials that align with learners' language levels, essential for effective instruction and assessment. The next sub-sections will examine the following selection of tools and applications:

- *Compleat Lexical Tutor* (*Lextutor*): offers a variety of tools for corpus-based analysis, including vocabulary tests, vocabulary profiling, and access to multiple corpora.
- English Profile Frameworks:
  - *English Vocabulary Profile* (EVP): describes vocabulary usage in learner language across the CEFR proficiency levels using the Cambridge Learner Corpus.
  - *English Grammar Profile* (EGP): describes grammar usage in learner language across the CEFR proficiency levels using the Cambridge Learner Corpus.
- *Text Inspector*: a web-based tool for automatic text analysis, including vocabulary, CEFR level profiling, and part-of-speech tagging.
- *Tool for the Automatic Analysis of Lexical Sophistication* (TAALES): analyses lexical sophistication with over 500 indices, including word frequency, n-gram range, and contextual distinctiveness.

7.3.1   Compleat Lexical Tutor

Compleat Lexical Tutor (https://www.lextutor.ca) is a website developed and maintained by Tom Cobb, at the University of Quebec at Montreal, Canada. It is more commonly referred to as *Lextutor.* The website contains many corpus-based applications in one place so its webpage offers a range of further hyperlinks to sub-pages. These, in turn, usually have sub-links to further resources (See Figure 7.10 for an illustration of the home page).

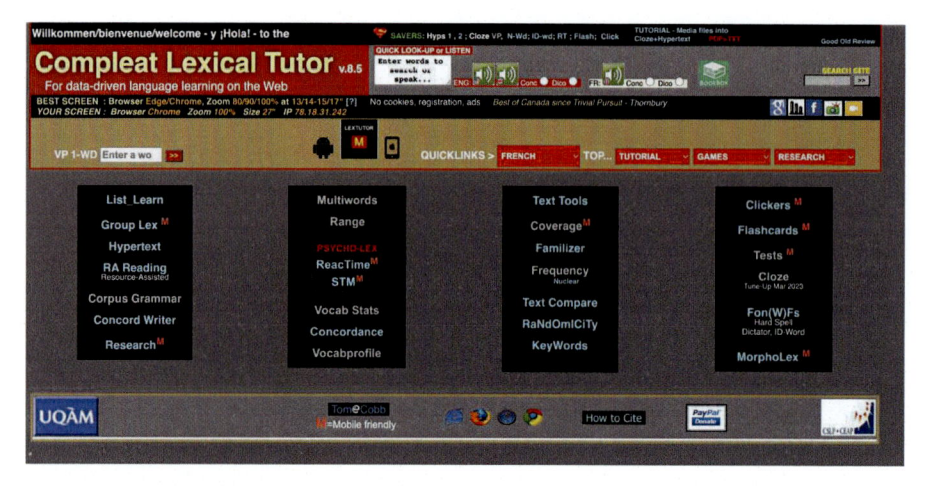

Figure 7.10 *Compleat Lexical Tutor* main webpage

Compleat Lexical Tutor serves both French and English. Given the abundance of tools provided, the website is also a 'one-stop shop', so to speak, for different types of corpus-based text analysis and corpus-based resource applications. It has integrated access to numerous corpora (e.g., the British National Corpus, the Corpus of Contemporary American English) and word lists (e.g. The General Service List, The Academic Word List). Texts that are entered for scrutiny can be analysed with reference to these corpora and word lists. The website has multiple functions and resources. Here, we will show some that, according to our own experience with L2 professionals, can be of interest to language learning researchers.

Compleat Lexical Tutor: Tests sub-page

Within the *Lextutor* sub-page of 'Tests' (see link to *Tests* in the right-hand column in Figure 7.10), there are a number of vocabulary tests available with which users can get their score. In all, there are 14 tests available, mostly in English. Each one has a link to the research paper that explains the test and its validation. In some cases, it offers practice tests in addition to the main test. Examples of tests include vocabulary level tests based on Thorndike-Lorge List (see Laufer & Nation, 1999; Martinez & Schmitt, 2012; Nation, 1990; Read, 1998; Schmitt et al., 2001). One example using the British National Corpus and the Corpus of Contemporary American English is the vocabulary size test (see Nation & Beglar, 2007). This tests vocabulary knowledge across 1000-word bands of the BNC and COCA, from 1st to 14th (i.e., the first band tests knowledge of a sample of words from the 1000 most frequent content words in the corpora, the highest band tests knowledge of words that occur infrequently). Figure 7.11 illustrates the test items for the 14th band, which tests vocabulary knowledge of items that have a very low frequency in the BNC, such as *marsupial, augured, bawdy,* which occur 87 (0.77 PMW), 17 (0.15 PMW) and 73 (0.65 PMW) times respectively in the BNC.

Fourteenth 1000

1. CANONICAL: These are **canonical** examples.
   a. ○ examples which break the usual rules
   b. ○ examples taken from a religious book
   c. ○ examples that are regular and widely accepted
   d. ○ examples discovered very recently

2. ATOP: He was **atop** the hill.
   a. ○ at the bottom of
   b. ○ at the top of
   c. ○ on this side of
   d. ○ on the far side of

3. MARSUPIAL: It is a **marsupial.**
   a. ○ an animal with hard feet
   b. ○ a plant that grows for several years
   c. ○ a plant with flowers that turn to face the sun
   d. ○ Jan animal with a pocket for babies

4. AUGUR: It **augured** well.
   a. ○ promised good things for the future
   b. ○ agreed well with what was expected
   c. ○ had a colour that looked good with something else
   d. ○ rang with a clear, beautiful sound

5. BAWDY: It was very **bawdy.**
   a. ○ unpredictable
   b. ○ enjoyable
   c. ○ rushed
   d. ○ rude

6. GAUCHE: He was **gauche.**
   a. ○ talkative
   b. ○ flexible
   c. ○ awkward
   d. ○ determined

7. THESAURUS: She used a **thesaurus.**
   a. ○ a kind of dictionary
   b. ○ a chemical compound
   c. ○ a special way of speaking
   d. ○ an injection just under the skin

8. ERYTHROCYTE: It is an **erythrocyte.**
   a. ○ a medicine to reduce pain
   b. ○ a red part of the blood
   c. ○ reddish white metal
   d. ○ a member of the whale family

9. CORDILLERA: They were stopped by the **cordillera.**
   a. ○ a special law
   b. ○ an armed ship
   c. ○ a line of mountains
   d. ○ the eldest son of the king

10. LIMPID: He looked into her **limpid** eyes.
    a. ○ clear
    b. ○ tearful
    c. ○ deep brown
    d. ○ beautiful

--** END OF TEST **--

Figure 7.11 Example from vocabulary level tests in *Lextutor,* illustrating sample of questions to test vocabulary knowledge in the 14th band (i.e. the 14th least frequent 1000 word band based on the BNC)

Another test that is hosted within this sub-page of *Lextutor* is the Phrasal Vocabulary Size Test (PVST) developed by Martínez and Schmitt (2012) to address what the creators saw as a deficiency in vocabulary knowledge testing, namely that they are based on single word items and did not include formulaic sequences (e.g., *at all, so far, take over, take for granted*). The PVST is based on

Martínez and Schmitt's (2012) PHRASal Expressions List (PHRASE List), which comprises the 505 most frequent non-transparent multiword expressions in English (i.e., phrasal items that are not easily comprehended from context). The test is especially intended for receptive use and, as with our previous example, the test items are banded according to frequency with reference to the British National Corpus. The test of the 505 items is across 5 bands of 1000 (see Figure 7.12 for an extract from the test based on some of the first 1000 band of items.

First 1000 __[Go 2]

1. GO ON: It will **go on.**
    a. ◯ sleep
    b. ◯ repeat
    c. ◯ be fast
    d. ◯ continue

2. LEAD TO: No one knows what it will **lead to.**
    a. ◯ want
    b. ◯ have inside
    c. ◯ cause in the future
    d. ◯ find

3. SO THAT: He sat **so that** they could do it.
    a. ◯ to make it possible that
    b. ◯ because
    c. ◯ very slowly and then
    d. ◯ before

4. AT ALL: I don't like it **at all.**
    a. ◯ all the time
    b. ◯ in any way
    c. ◯ at first
    d. ◯ sometimes

Figure 7.12 Sample of test items from Phrasal Vocabulary Size Test (PVST) by Martinez and Schmitt (2012), within *Lextutor,* focusing on the first 1,000 BNC vocabulary band

Compleat Lextutor: Vocabprofile — Phrase Profiler

For a researcher interested in examining phrasal items, *Lextutor* website also offers a subpage which allows for texts to be profiled or analysed in terms of how many phrasal items they have across the following phrasal lists (Table 7.5). This page is called *Phrase Profiler* and is accessed via the *Vocabprofile* link on the main webpage (https://www.lextutor.ca/vp/collocs/)(see Figure 7.10).

Table 7.5 Phrase Profiler tools in *Lextutor*

List / number of items	Detail	Further reading
Academic Collocations List / 2,469 collocations	Based on the 25 million-word Academic Corpus of Academic English (PICAE). Particularly interesting is the connection between the ACL and the single word AWL (Academic Word List).	Ackermann & Chen (2013)
Oxford Academic Phrasal Lexicon (written) / 370 phrases	Based on the 71-million-word Oxford Corpus of Academic English (OCAE) containing academic texts published by Oxford University Press across four disciplines such as: arts and humanities and social sciences; Phrases are grouped by function, for example "specifying topics and relations between ideas" (*in terms of, in relation to*, etc.)	Therova (2020)
Oxford Academic Phrasal Lexicon (spoken) / 250 phrases	Based on an aggregation of the following corpora: the Oxford Corpus of Academic English (OCAE), the fiction subcorpus of the Oxford English Corpus (OEC), the spoken element of the British National Corpus (BNC) and a subset of the British Academic Spoken English (BASE) corpus. Phrases are grouped across 15 categories, grouped by function, for example "signposting and focusing in lectures/lessons" (*I was going to, I want to talk about*, etc.)	Therova (2020)
PHRASal Expressions List (PHRASE List) / 505 phrases	Based on a mixed methods approach described in Martinez and Schmitt (2012) which used the BNC to identify N-grams for analysis that were then filtered according to *core* and *auxiliary criteria*. The 505 items are divided across 5 frequency bands of 1000 words based on the BNC.	Martinez & Schmitt (2012)
Sentence Transitions List / 296 phrases	No methodological information is available on how this list was compiled. The 7esl.com website defines a transition word (or phrase) as something that demonstrates the relationship between two portions of the text or spoken language. The list is divided functionally across numerous categories such as *reason* (e.g., given that), *cause and effect* (e.g. as a consequence), *emphasis* (e.g. obviously, to clarify); addition (e.g. *not to mention, additionally*); contrast (*nevertheless*); condition (e.g. granted that)	While no academic paper is available on this list, there is extensive detail on the webpage of 7esl.com https://7esl.com/transition-words/

Let us take a learner text such as the following 275-word essay on *Preventative versus proactive medicine*, written by an ESL student (from McNamara, 2020):

Some people may say that we wouldn't need drugs or any other complex treatment if prevention becomes a priority for our communities. In contrast, the staunch defenders of curative medicine maintain that focusing healthcare on prevention frameworks is not the answer. In fact, could both things be part of the same solution?

Although we cannot ignore the fact that both concepts have a deep significance in medicine, claiming that prevention is more important than care treatments could evince a reductionist understanding of medical science. As an example of this, we could mention hereditary or rare diseases. These kinds of pathologies can affect even the healthiest person. Therefore, axing resources in investigation and care treatments would result in a defeat of the Hippocratic oath. On the other hand, prevention and promotion ought not to be neglected, and governments should implement more supportive policies to back up these services. Unfortunately, the budget allocated for this area all over the world hardly exceeds 5% of the total invested in health care, and paradoxically, this is the main reason why communities spend a considerable amount of money on all kinds of preventable diseases. One example of this vicious circle could be smoking, which is one of the first causes of death in the world and, at the same time, one of the most avoidable noxious habits.

In conclusion, I believe that interventionist medicine should not be placed in a secondary position, since it represents the engine behind the most impressive and significant discoveries in medical science. However, prevention and promotion programs are key factors in the success of medicine saving lives, and government funding should reflect this.

Figure 7.13 275-word essay on *Preventative versus proactive medicine*, written by an ESL student (from McNamara, 2020)

We can use the tools listed in Table 7.5 to profile the vocabulary use in the text in Figure 7.13. Table 7.6 illustrates what the tools can tell us the following about this one text and the corpus methods involved:

Table 7.6 Summary of results from *Lextutor Phrase Profiler tests* based on the text from the ESL learner in Figure 7.13

Tool used from *Lextutor* and related corpus method	What the analysis tells us (Numbers in brackets show the occurrences in the learner text in Figure 7.13)
Academic Collocations List / testing for 2,469 collocations Collocation and frequency analyses	The text has 2 collocational phrases from the EAP ACL: *considerable amount* (1); *key factors* (1). This equates to 0.73 phrases per 100 words.
Oxford Academic Phrasal Lexicon (written) /370 phrases Frequency analyses	The text has uses of 7 phrases from the OAPL (written): *kinds of* (2); *an example of* (1); *at the same time* (1); *of the total* (1); *result in* (1); *the fact that* (1) This equates to 2.55 phrases per 100 words

Table 7.6 *(continued)*

Tool used from *Lextutor* and related corpus method	What the analysis tells us (Numbers in brackets show the occurrences in the learner text in Figure 7.13)
Oxford Academic Phrasal Lexicon (spoken) / 250 phrases Frequency analyses	The text has 5 phrases from OAPL (spoken) list: *all kinds of* (1); *an example of* (1); *at the same time* (1); *one of the most* (1); *the fact that* (1) This equates to 1.82 phrases per 100 words
PHRASal Expressions List (PHRASE List) / 505 phrases Frequency analyses	The text has 4 phrases from the PHRASE list: *all over* (1); *at the same time* (1); *back up* (1); *result in* (1) This equates to 1.45 phrases per 100 words
Sentence Transitions List / 296 phrases Frequency analyses	The text has 8 words and phrases from the Sentence Transitions List: *Although* (1); *As an example of* (1); *However* (1); *In conclusion* (1); *In fact* (1); *On the other hand* (1); *Therefore* (1) This equates to 2.91 phrases per 100 words

7.3.2 English Profile frameworks: *English Vocabulary Profile* and *English Grammar Profile*

Other tools and frameworks can be used to analyse a text such as the one above. Two profile databases that were developed using corpora and aligned to the Common European Framework of Reference for Languages (CEFR) (Council of Europe, 2001) are the *English Vocabulary Profile* and the *English Grammar Profile*. The CEFR was established as a benchmark for language competence (Jones & Saville, 2009) and comprises six levels of competence, from A1 (lowest) to C2 (highest), that have become a common currency in language education. It resulted from a Council of Europe project in the early 1990s which established a set of 'can-do' statements defining what is minimally required for each stage in the framework across grammar, vocabulary and skills development as well as functional and notional objectives. These performance-based 'can-do' statements, or 'Reference Level Descriptors', evolved from the collective judgements of a body of experts and are not language specific.

Various researchers and organisations have sought to localise or refine these descriptors for specific languages and learner corpora are central to this process (see Chapter 3). For example, in English, Cambridge University Press initiated the *English Profile* project with various academic and other stakeholders (see Harrison & Barker, 2015). Within this research endeavour, a substantial amount of empirical corpus-based work went into developing resources such as the *English Functions Profile* (Green, 2012), the *English Vocabulary Profile* (Capel, 2015) and the *English Grammar Profile* (O'Keeffe & Mark, 2017). The *English Vocabulary Profile* (EVP) and the *English Grammar Profile* (EGP) now form online resources that can be used as a reference point for competencies in vocabulary and grammar across the CEFR levels.

English Vocabulary Profile (EVP)

If we take a look back at the learner text above on *Preventative versus proactive medicine* (Figure 7.13), we can search for individual words in the EVP and see where they are on the CEFR. For example, we can see within the EVP tool that the words *prevention* and *priority* are at B2. This means that a learner is not expected to know them until this level. Other words like *promotion*, are a little less straightforward because they are polysemous. The word *promotion* in the text in Figure 7.13 is used to mean health promotion. As illustrated in Figure 7.14, the EVP shows us that *promotion* in the sense of (1) being given a more important role within an organisation, and (2) advertising are words that are placed at B2 within the CEFR while, the use that we find in the learner text, in the sense of *encourage* (encourage something to happen or develop) is a C1-level use of the word.

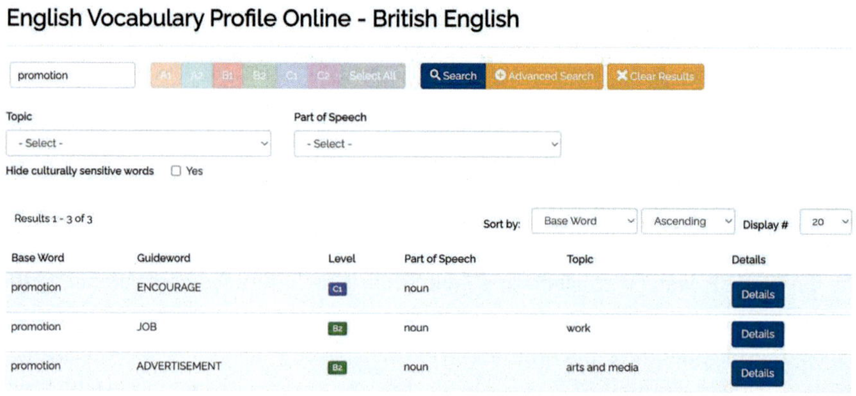

Figure 7.14 English Vocabulary Profile for *promotion*

Some of the words in the learner text are not in the EVP because they are too low frequency (e.g., *pathologies, paradoxically, reductionist*). However, these can be plotted against the British National Corpus or the Corpus of Contemporary American English to see which frequency band they align with, as we shall discuss below (see *Text Inspector*).

In summary, the EVP offers research-driven information about when a learner is expected to know a word and its related meanings. It also includes information on multi-word units, idioms and collocations. As we shall illustrate below, this kind of mapping of a learner's use of lexis within the EVP can be done automatically using an application called *Text Inspector*. First, let us explore the *English Grammar Profile*.

English Grammar Profile

The *English Grammar Profile* (EGP), like the EVP, is an online searchable database. It comprises of over 1,200 empirically derived competency statements about the grammar that a learner is expected to know at a given level. The research-driven results are based on a detailed analysis of the Cambridge Learner Corpus (CLC) using some of the methods discussed in this book. The methodology behind the building of the EGP is described in detail in O'Keeffe and Mark (2017). Essentially, the EGP lists what learners at each of the six CEFR levels 'can do' with grammar in English. By way of illustration, we can look at some of the grammatical structures in the learner text on preventative versus proactive medicine (above) and see what level they are aligned to in the CEFR within the EGP.

Figure 7.15 (a screenshot from the EGP) shows us, for example, that the modal verb *ought* in its negative form is not normally used until C2 level. When we look at the ESL learner text, we find that this form is used and so it offers one marker of grammatical sophistication.

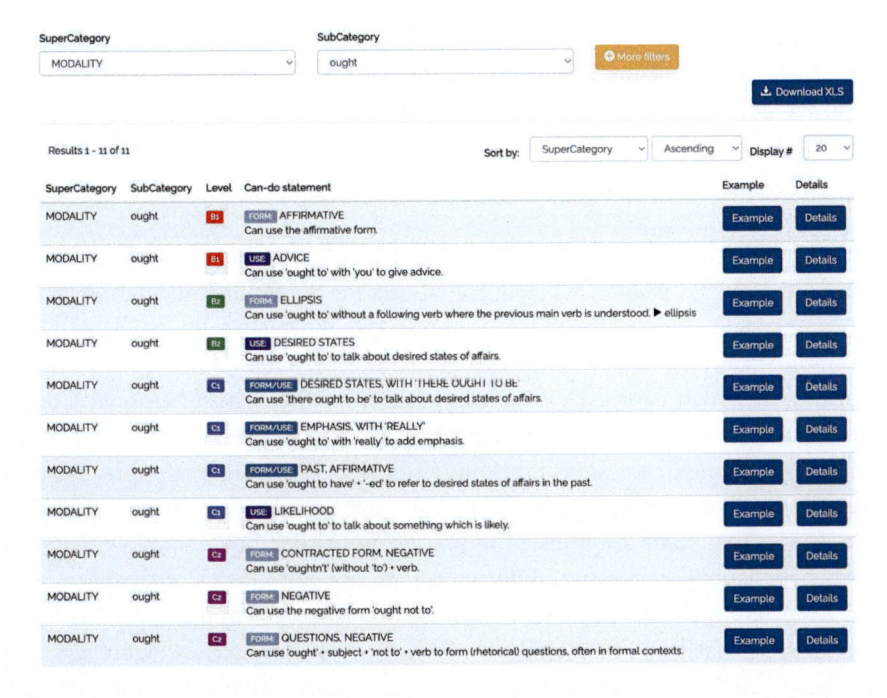

Figure 7.15 Screenshot from *English Grammar Profile* relating to modal verb *ought* competencies

By way of another grammar example from the learner essay on preventative versus proactive medicine above (Figure 7.13), let us take nominalisation. This involves the forming of nouns or noun phrases from other parts of speech, usually a verb or adjective (See Figure 7.13, *the staunch defenders of curative medicine* rather than *those who stanchly defend curative medicine*). When we look at nominalisation in the EGP, we see that it is a competency that is aligned with C1 noun phrase grammatical competency (Figure 7.16).

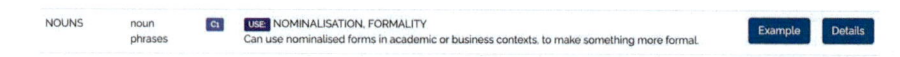

Figure 7.16 Screenshot from *English Grammar Profile* illustrating nominalisation in noun phrases

Building on the EGP, Ishii and Tono (2018) have curated an inventory of grammar items in their analysis of Japanese learners of English. One of their findings showed a substantial underuse of certain grammatical items across levels of proficiency. Interestingly, these items were outside those typically characterised as underused by Japanese learners (e.g., relating to articles and prepositions). In other words, one of the outcomes of the research that drew on the Cambridge Learner Corpus EGP results was new insights into the patterns of use (or underuse) of this cohort of learners.

7.3.3 *Text Inspector*

Text Inspector,[27] a web-based resource, allows for the automatic analysis of texts (Text Inspector, 2018). It can be useful in the analysis of learner language as it automatically generates results across a range of measurements. It draws on benchmarks such as the EVP and statistics from the British National Corpus, among others. For example, if we enter the earlier learner text on preventative versus proactive medicine, we get a listing of how its vocabulary use spreads across the CEFR (Figure 7.17).

Notice that some are unlisted words. As discussed above, some words in the text, such as *evince, curative, reductionist*, are not ones that learners even at C2 are expected to know. However, we can explore these low frequency items within *Text Inspector* as part of the analysis of this text. For instance, as Figure 7.18 illustrates, we can see the learner is using words that align with the 10k–20k; 20k–30k;

---

27. https://textinspector.com/ (Accessed 10th November, 2024). It is important to note that only some of its analyses capabilities are available in the free version.

Summary				
Word List	**Types**	**Tokens**	**cumul% Types**	**cumul% Tokens**
A1	59 (36.20%)	146 (53.87%)	36.2%	53.9%
A2	24 (14.72%)	36 (13.28%)	50.9%	67.2%
B1	24 (12.27%)	21 (7.75%)	63.2%	74.9%
B2	34 (20.86%)	42 (15.50%)	84.0%	90.4%
C1	7 (4.29%)	7 (2.58%)	88.3%	93.0%
C2	2 (1.23%)	2 (0.74%)	89.6%	93.7%
Unlisted	17 (10.43%)	17 (6.27%)	−100%	−100%

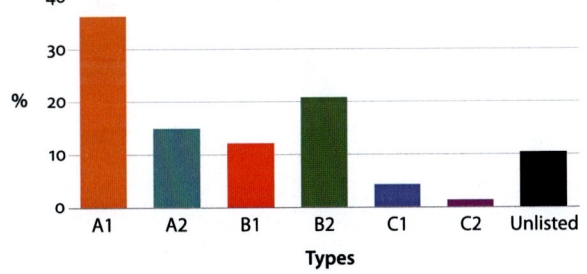

Figure 7.17 Profile of ESL learner vocabulary use across the levels of the CEFR using Text Inspector

30k–40k and 50k–60k frequency bands in the BNC. These words are considered low to extremely low frequency (i.e., rare words). You will also notice from Figure 7.18 that the application tags the text for part-of-speech.

10K-20K (Total: 7 = 4.19%) (cumul%: 93.4%) (Hide words)	**20K-30K** (Total: 4 = 2.40%) (cumul%: 95.8%) (Hide words)	**30K-40K** (Total: 3 = 1.80%) (cumul%: 97.6%) (Hide words)	**50K-60K** (Total: 3 = 1.80%) (cumul%: 99.4%) (Hide words)
oath NN (1)	interventionist JJ (1)	reductionist NN (1)	evince VV (1)
hereditary JJ (1)	avoidable JJ (1)	healthiest JJS (1)	Hippocratic JJ (1)
paradoxically RB (1)	curative JJ (1)	axing VVG (1)	pathologies NNS (1)
healthcare NN (1)	preventable JJ (1)		
staunch JJ (1)			
frameworks NNS (1)			
noxious JJ (1)			

Figure 7.18 Words used in ESL learner text within the 10k–20k; 20k–30k; 30k–40k and 50k–60k frequency bands in the BNC

The aforementioned ESL learner text is part of a batch of five essays, written across one term (see Chapter 2). We can enter the full batch of five ESL texts from the ESL mini-corpus and examine them in various ways using *Text Inspector*. Figure 7.19 shows comparisons between the data from the ESL learner in comparison with the EVP and the BNC in relation to 'lexical sophistication'. By looking at vocabulary indices alone, *Text Inspector* profiles this learner's work at C2. As we illustrate below, further indices can also be applied to a larger batch of work from this student.

Lexical Sophistication: English Vocabulary Profile

EVP: % OF WORDS (TYPES) AT A1 LEVEL	37.11	C2 ▼
EVP: % OF WORDS (TYPES) AT B1 LEVEL	16.15	C2+ ▼
EVP: % OF WORDS (TYPES) AT B2 LEVEL	14.15	C2+ ▼
EVP: % OF WORDS (TYPES) AT C1 LEVEL	4.26	C2+ ▼
EVP: % OF WORDS (TOKENS) AT B2 LEVEL	8.90	C2+ ▼

Lexical Sophistication: British National Corpus

BNC: % OF WORDS (TYPES) AT 0-1K LEVEL	50.99	C2 ▼
BNC: % OF WORDS (TYPES) AT 10-20K LEVEL	5.21	C2 ▼
BNC 50TH PERCENTILE (TYPES)	835.00	C2+ ▼
BNC 60TH PERCENTILE (TYPES)	1575.00	C2+ ▼
BNC 70TH PERCENTILE (TYPES)	2722.50	C2+ ▼
BNC 80TH PERCENTILE (TYPES)	4452.50	C2 ▼

Figure 7.19 Lexical Sophistication Results from *Text Inspector* on five ESL text from one student based on the *English Vocabulary Profile* and the British National Corpus

The *Text Inspector* interface can also conduct an automatic breakdown of the metadiscourse markers that are used in a text. For example, Figure 7.20 shows the results when the five learner ESL texts were analysed in terms of the learners' use of metadiscourse markers.

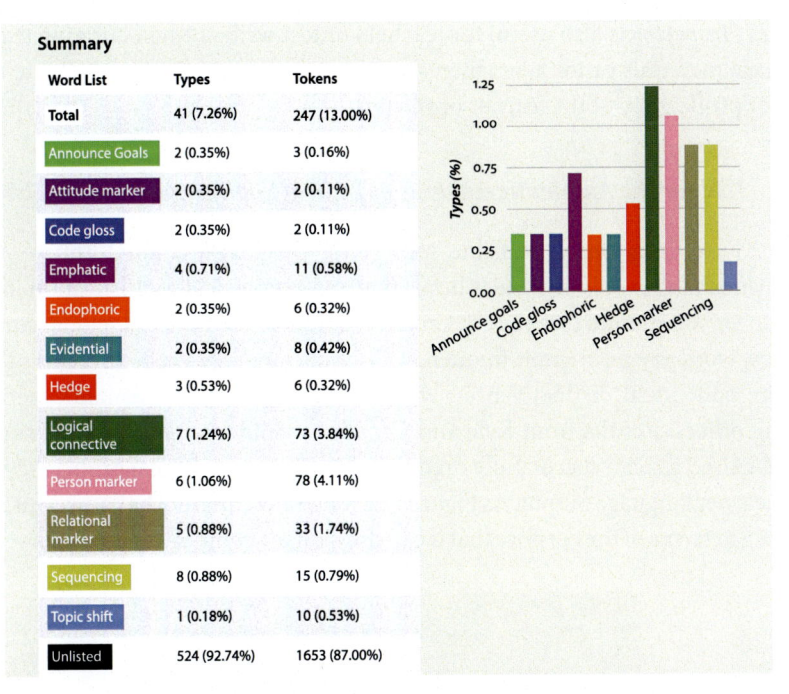

Figure 7.20 Metadiscourse Results from *Text Inspector* based on analysis of five ESL learner texts

Additionally, the application can generate an overall statement about a learners' level of proficiency based on their use on 29 different indices. Figure 7.21 shows us that across the five texts from the ESL student (see Chapter 2), their level is pitched at C2 level based on the various indices.

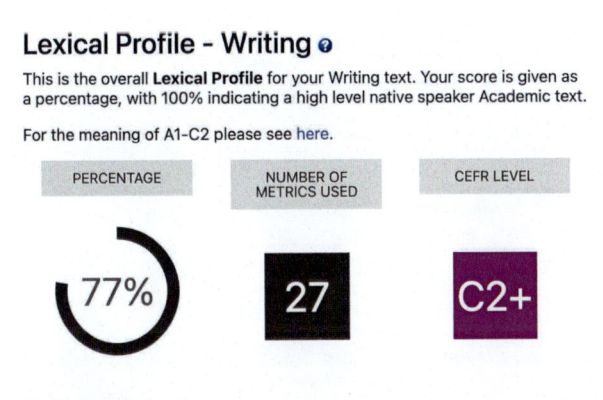

Figure 7.21 Summary Lexical Profile of one learners' ESL texts using *Text Inspector*

Text Inspector is also useful for teachers or test writers when curating texts for language materials or for assessments so as to ensure that they are suitable to the level of proficiency of the learner or the test.

7.3.4 *Tool for the Automatic Analysis of Lexical Sophistication* (TAALES)

TAALES 2.0 is a freely available tool (Kyle & Crossley, 2015) (https://www .linguisticanalysistools.org/taales.html) that analyses lexical sophistication in texts using over 500 indices (see Kyle & Crossley, 2018). These indices include word frequency, word range, n-gram frequency, N-gram range, N-gram strength of association, contextual distinctiveness, word recognition norms, semantic network, among others. Results from Kyle and Crossley's validation study (2018) suggests that *TAALES 2.0* can successfully predict holistic scores of lexical proficiency in L1 and Learner language output. As Figure 7.22 illustrates, this tool has powerful under pinning in terms of the corpora that it can draw on for comparison.

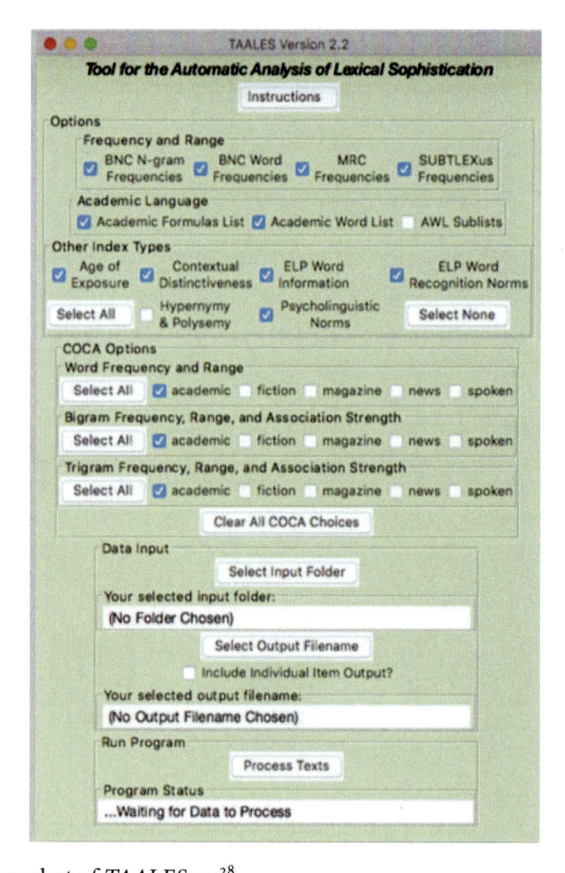

Figure 7.22 Screenshot of *TAALES* 2.2[28]

This tool can have many applications in the analysis of spoken and written texts. As the developers detail, *TAALES* indices "inform models of second language (L2) speaking proficiency, first language (L1) and L2 writing proficiency, spoken and written lexical proficiency [and] genre differences".[29]

7.4   Exploring the aboutness of texts and corpora: Keyword analysis

Some of the corpus methods discussed so far facilitate the identification of frequent items in corpora. Keyword analysis (see also Chapter 2) is similar in this respect. Key analysis is a corpus research method that automatically identifies terms with an unusually high frequency in a target corpus compared to a reference corpus (Gillings et al., 2023; Pérez-Paredes, 2020, 2024). Its main purpose is to uncover distinctive words that capture the central themes, styles, or viewpoints within the analysed texts. The "aboutness" of a corpus (Scott & Tribble, 2006) refers therefore to the primary topics, themes, or subjects that characterise its content. The keywords reflect the main ideas or focus of the texts, giving a snapshot of what the corpus is "about."

This method is especially helpful because it allows researchers to identify notable linguistic elements, removing potential researcher biases. Keyword analysis is often used in fields like critical discourse analysis to examine how specific groups or ideas are represented, for example, in media portrayals of minorities (Gillings et al., 2023) but it has become useful in languages for specific purposes and L2 material development (Flowerdew, 2002).

Keyword analysis operates by comparing the frequency of words in a target corpus (the corpus being analysed) with a reference corpus (often a larger, general corpus). Here we offer a simplified breakdown of the process. The reference corpus is ideally large and representative of the language or genre being analysed. AntConc or Sketch Engine can be used to calculate the word frequencies in the target and the reference corpora. For each word, the software determines how often it appears relative to the total number of words in each corpus, producing normalised frequencies for accurate comparison. The software applies statistical tests, such as the *Log-Likelihood* or *Chi-Square* test, to evaluate which words are significantly more (or less) frequent in the target corpus than expected. Words with significantly high frequency in the target corpus become "keywords." The

---

28. Image from https://www.linguisticanalysistools.org/taales.html (Accessed 30th September, 2021).

29. Quotation taken from TAALES website https://www.linguisticanalysistools.org/taales.html (Accessed 30th September, 2021).

software generates a ranked list of keywords, highlighting terms that stand out in the target corpus compared to the reference corpus. This list may indicate themes, topics, or biases unique to the target texts. Then, researchers often examine the *concordance lines* (see Chapter 2) to understand how these words are used in context, revealing specific nuances or representations within the target text.

Through the aforementioned process, keyword analysis can reveal unique linguistic features and thematic focuses, supporting studies in language learning research. One of the main of areas of application is building wordlists that provide instructors and material developers with an objective way to decide which words to focus on (Dang, 2019). An excellent example of the use of keyword analysis is Gilmore and Millar (2018). The authors identified the terms that frequently occur in civil engineering research articles, distinguishing them from general and academic English. Their analysis compared words from the Specialized Corpus of Civil Engineering Research Articles (SCCERA) with established wordlists like the New General Service List (NGSL) and New Academic Word List (NAWL). This process categorised keywords into general, academic, and discipline-specific words — those unique to civil engineering not present in NGSL or NAWL. Their approach enabled the construction of a wordlist that highlights core vocabulary in civil engineering, addressing both commonly used and discipline-specific terms. It also identified key lexical bundles and phrases typical of the field, which contribute to a specialised understanding of civil engineering discourse and support pedagogic applications for English for Specific Purposes (ESP) instruction.

Other methodological approaches of keyword analysis include its use in the analysis of interviews and focus groups with lecturers of English as Medium of Instruction (EMI) context (Curry & Pérez-Paredes, 2023; Pérez-Paredes & Curry, 2023).

7.5   Summary

In this chapter we have reviewed some of the many indirect applications of corpus linguistics in language teaching and learning. Corpora and learner corpus research, we have shown, contribute to better dictionaries and grammars. Additionally, corpus-based frameworks, such as the EVP and EGP, also based on learner corpus data, facilitate research-led exams, materials and syllabi. We have also shown some of the tools that a language teacher who is interested in using corpus-based applications and interfaces can use to examine the language that their students are using with reference to corpora. These tools can also help us explore learner corpora from a comparative perspective, especially across registers, genres, and disciplines.

We have also showcased interfaces and applications that help test and/or profile learner writing, namely *Lextutor* and *Text Inspector*. Tools such as these can offer a myriad of opportunities to language teachers interested in researching the language used by a cohort of learners. For researchers interested in greater detail in terms of the level of automatic analysis of texts, they can avail of even more advanced tools such as *TAALES*. Finally, we have explored the use of keyword analysis in language learning research.

CHAPTER 8

Researching direct uses of corpora
for language teaching and learning

Recommended reading 8.1

Pérez-Paredes, P. (2022). A systematic review of the uses and spread of corpora and data-driven learning in CALL research during 2011–2015. *Computer Assisted Language Learning,* *35*(1–2), 36–61.

Like Boulton and Cobb (2017), several others have looked systematically at research in the field. This paper focuses on DDL and the use of corpora in language learning using different approaches and sampling parameters. The author traces the spread of DDL and corpora in language learning and teaching across five major CALL-related journals between the period: 2011–2015. He found that DDL studies represented 4.2% of all published papers on CALL during this time frame. The main focus of research was found to be the use of concordancing and collocations when developing university students' writing skills. Contrary to previous research, access to technology was not identified as an impeding factor. Syllabus integration and a lack of contribution from language teachers other than researchers emerged as threats to the mainstreaming or normalisation of corpora use.

Recommended reading 8.2

Zare, J., & Aqajani Delavar, K. (2023). A data-driven learning focus on form approach to academic English lecture comprehension. *Applied Linguistics,* *44*(3), 485–504.

This study proposed a new task-based language teaching (TBLT) type using DDL in a combination with form-focused teaching so as to test how more attention could be brought to target forms through structured DDL Focus-on-Form (FonF) tasks that aimed to enhance academic listening. The participants were drawn from 124 Iranian undergraduates, randomly divided into an experimental and a control group. The methodology is described as quasi-experimental validating quantitative data triangulation model. This involved an intervention of 12 45-minute sessions for both the DDL-treatment cohort and the control cohort. Results from the pre- post- and delayed post-tests generated quantitative findings which were then triangulated using interviews with the experimental cohort. These interviews bring a strong learner voice to the research and greatly enrich the insights on learning. The findings suggest that the DDL FonF tasks result in both short and longer terms improvements in learners' comprehension of English academic lectures and the authors conclude that integrating DDL and FonF TBLT approaches bring about enhanced academic listening comprehension through increased noticing, metalinguistics awareness, discovery learning and agency.

Recommended reading 8.3

Forti, L. (2023). *Corpus use in Italian language pedagogy: Exploring the effects of data-driven learning.* Routledge.

As well as offering a comprehensive summary of the evolution of and work in DDL, Forti provides an extensive overview of DDL in the context of teaching Italian and makes important links between theory and practice. Apart from bringing focus to an under-represented language in DDL studies (i.e. Italian), the book gives in-depth coverage to research in the field and the gaps therein, especially in relation to research design and methodologies. Particularly useful for researchers is the focus on empirical study design for DDL, highlighting the importance of addressing research questions that focus on issues of language acquisition as well as pedagogical operationalisation. The book showcases and evaluates a variety of approaches and discusses variables that can be looked at. Forti stresses that classroom-based empirical studies need to be aware that the nature of DDL tasks and activities will determine the activation of specific SLA learning processes. With this in mind, she advises, the data collection needs to tap into those processes so as to make the evaluation of their effects possible. The book includes a chapter that explores the development of Italian L2 competence from both the etic dimension (relating to language gains) and the emic dimension (relating to learner attitudes) focusing on the development of phraseological competence. For researchers, this material is useful in terms of illustrating how data collection instruments can be constructed to match the specific learning aims of a pedagogical intervention. It shows how it is possible to take into account a range of variables that specifically pertain to the chosen learning aims, and how these can be analysed through mixed-effects modelling.

Research on corpora in language learning is typically divided into the analysis of both *indirect* and *direct applications* (Figure 8.1). Indirect applications refer to the use of corpora as a means to enhance resources for language teaching while direct applications refer to research that focuses on pedagogical interventions, applications, or resources in the language learning classroom where language learners interact with corpora (see Chapter 7). Leech (1997) used the *indirect-direct* distinction on the following basis:

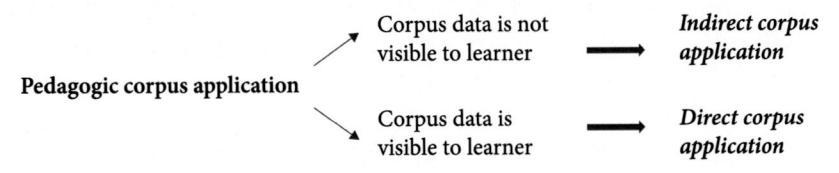

Figure 8.1 Indirect versus direct corpus applications, based on Leech (1997)

This chapter focuses on researching the direct uses of corpus data in the language classroom.

The notion of bringing corpus data to language learners can be traced back to McKay (1980) who first published activities for paper-based materials to encourage noticing from corpus-derived examples (Boulton, 2017). The term Data-Driven Learning (DDL) is widely associated with the work of Tim Johns at the University of Birmingham, who coined the term a decade later (Johns, 1990). Johns and King's (1991) early definition of DDL is still often cited: "the use in the classroom of computer-generated concordances to get students to explore the regularities of patterning in the target language, and the development of activities and exercises based on concordance output" (p. iii). Clearly, this definition points to the notion of students working directly with concordance lines (so as to identify patterns of language) as being at the heart of a DDL pedagogy. As we shall discuss, the degree to which the selection of these concordance lines is curated or mediated by the teacher can vary. A more recent and broader definition of DDL by Boulton and Pérez-Paredes (2024) states that DDL is the use of corpus tools and techniques for learning or using a second language.

Since the 1990s, DDL has gained much popularity and it has been shown to have a positive effect on language learning (Boulton, 2017; Boulton & Cobb, 2017, see Section 8.2). However, it is not, as yet, a mainstream approach to language teaching. In this chapter, we shall look at studies that investigate and evaluate DDL and we shall also examine how more research might be carried out so as to help to investigate how DDL might work in a more mainstream manner. We will also focus on the areas of second language acquisition that relate to DDL and which merit further work.

8.1   What does DDL look like in practice?

Here we examine some typical DDL activities that a learner might encounter in the classroom. For DDL to happen, the corpus methods studied in previous chapters are essential. At the core of DDL is the concordance line from a corpus (see Chapter 2). A teacher will either choose a concordance line for students to work on or will guide the students (to varying degrees) in a search of a corpus to generate a concordance line as their starting point. As stated in the opening paragraph of this chapter, the former approach is referred to as *indirect* or *hands off DDL* while the latter is referred to as *direct* or *hands on DDL*. We shall return to these concepts in greater detail in Section 8.2.

Figure 8.2 shows an example of an indirect hands off DDL task, along with a concordance line from the freely available Corpus of American Soap Operas (available on the English-Corpora.org).

Examine the 20 concordance lines in Figure 8.2 for the word *eye*. Work with your partner and prepare a short presentation on three uses and patterns of the word that are new to you. Use your dictionary to help prepare your presentation.

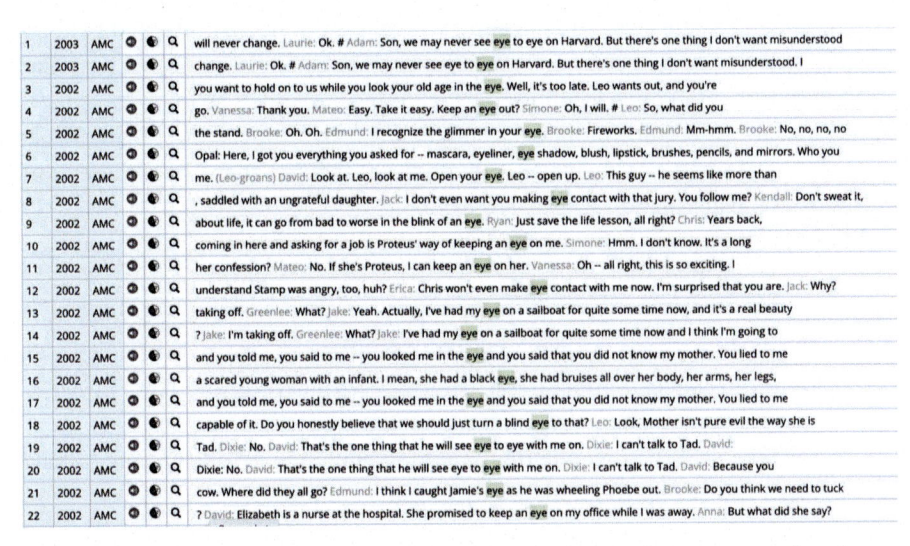

Figure 8.2 Example of an indirect hands off DDL task (concordance extract of *eye* from Corpus of American Soap Operas (available on the English-Corpora.org)

Such an activity, as exemplified in Figure 8.2, might generate noticing of patterns and uses (see Table 8.1):

Table 8.1 Possible patterns and uses of *eye* based on analysis of concordance lines in Figure 8.2

Idioms	see eye to eye [with someone] on [something]; in the blink of an eye; have your eye on [something]; to turn a blind eye to something; catch someone's eye; keep an eye on [something/someone]; keep an eye out for [something/someone]; look [something/someone] in the eye.
Formulaic patterns	make eye contact with [someone]; to have a black eye
Collocates of *eye*	black, glimmer; mascara; eyeliner; eye shadow.

Let us reflect on this activity from a learner's perspective:

- It requires the reading of 20 truncated lines from American soap opera scripts, leading to quite an intense and decontextualised reading experience;

- It requires the learner to read from the node word (*eye*), at the centre, outwards to the left and to the right. This is very different to the normal left to right reading orientation in English;
- It also requires the ability to read along the vertical axis of the node word to the left and to the right so as to audit whether there are any repeated patterns of words that come before or / and after *eye*. For example, such a vertical scan will spot that the node is followed by *on* four times out of 20;
- It appears to require inductive thought processes, where the learner looks at language patterns, formulates hypotheses, checks these hypotheses and induces a pattern and / or use. For example:
  - hypothesis: *eye* is frequently followed by preposition *on,* this might have a specific meaning or use;
  - check hypothesis: 2 of the four *eye* + *on* patterns are preceded by the verb *keep* while 2 are preceded by the very *have.*
  - Induced concepts about these patterns: *keep an eye on* and *have my eye on* have different meanings and both are idiomatic. The first means to watch or take care of someone or something while the second means to have seen something you wish to buy or get.

Let us now consider another activity, adapted from Poole (2018). Poole (2018) uses the Corpus of Contemporary American English (COCA) for this task. In Figure 8.3, we generate patterns from *Sketch Engine for Language Learning* (SKELL).[30] This is an example of a direct hands on DDL approach. Figure 8.3 illustrates some of the panels of collocate information that a learner using SKELL will generate and then explore:

Conduct a corpus search using SKELL for the collocates *beautiful* and *attractive* and compare these so as to answer the question: Can *beautiful* and *attractive* be used in exactly the same way?

Again, let us consider some of what might to be noticed and intuited from the learner's perspective. In response to the question in the task 'Can *beautiful and attractive be used in exactly the same way?*', it is possible, though not in any way guaranteed, they will conclude that this is not the case, based on observations such as the following from their corpus searches:

- The nouns modified by *beautiful* are usually concrete and often animate. When they are animate, they refer to females (*beautiful* + *woman, girl, lady, daughter*);

---

30. URL: https://skell.sketchengine.eu

BEAUTIFUL

nouns modified by beautiful		verbs with beautiful	
1. woman	beautiful woman	1. look	look beautiful
2. beach	beautiful beaches	2. create	create beautiful ,
3. scenery	beautiful scenery	3. sound	sounds beautiful
4. girl	beautiful girl	4. consider	considered beautiful
5. garden	beautiful gardens	5. be	is beautiful
6. countryside	beautiful countryside	6. produce	produces beautiful
7. landscape	beautiful landscape	7. appear	appear beautiful
8. view	beautiful views	8. feel	feel beautiful
9. flower	beautiful flowers	9. call	called beautiful
10. surroundings	the beautiful surroundings	10. mean	, meaning beautiful ,
11. place	a beautiful place	11. find	find beautiful
12. island	beautiful island	12. smell	
13. setting	a beautiful setting	13. stay	stay beautiful
14. lady	beautiful lady	14. seem	seem beautiful
15. daughter	beautiful daughter	15. see	see beautiful

ATTRACTIVE

nouns modified by attractive		verbs with attractive	
1. proposition	an attractive proposition	1. find	find attractive
2. portion	certainly return . Attractive portion of content .	2. look	look attractive
3. alternative	an attractive alternative to	3. prove	prove attractive
4. destination	attractive destination for	4. appear	appear more attractive
5. element	outstanding website ! Attractive element of content .	5. consider	considered attractive
6. target	an attractive target for	6. seem	seem attractive
7. option	an attractive option	7. sound	sounds attractive
8. woman	attractive woman	8. become	become more attractive
9. prospect	an attractive prospect	9. rate	rated attractive
10. feature	attractive feature	10. perceive	
11. female	attractive female	11. play	playing attractive ,
12. football	attractive football	12. feature	
13. offer	attractive offer	13. remain	remain attractive
14. foliage	attractive foliage	14. offer	
15. package	attractive package	15. be	is attractive

Figure 8.3 Example of a direct hands on DDL approach (with screenshots of panels of verb and noun collocates for *beautiful* and *attractive* from SKELL)

– Most of the verbs used with *beautiful* are mental process and sense items: *look, sound, appear, feel, smell, see, create, consider, mean*.
– Several of the verbs that collocate with *attractive* appear to be more tentative: *look, appear, consider(ed), seem, sound, perceive*.

As with the previous example, for a learner to arrive at such observations (at all), it requires a process of hypothesis formation based on patterns, hypothesis checking and formulation. Şahin Kızıl (2023) summarises the benefits across the following three sequential points in this process for learners based on previous work:

1. By quickly looking through and assessing many authentic language samples in concordance lines, learners can observe and analyse the target language so as to form and test hypotheses (see also Cotos, 2014; Lenko-Szymanska & Boulton, 2015; Samoudi & Modirkhamene, 2020);

2. Unlike traditional deductive approaches (where the grammar rule is presented and then practised), DDL allows for a discovery approach to learning where learners can extrapolate rules and then explore regularity of patterns within the concordance lines (and in so doing can learn through an inductive approach) (Flowerdew, 2015);

3. By not treating grammar and lexis as separate entities, DDL takes a lexico-grammatical approach to language pedagogy where learners can notice patterns easily and efficiently through identification of recurrence in concordance lines and can ultimately reuse these in their own output (Meunier, 2011).

As we move forward in this chapter, we will return to this process. First let us consider how DDL is typically researched and evaluated. For a researcher, typical questions arise around the effectiveness and efficiency of DDL overall compared with traditional methods or in relation to a specific area (e.g. forms of vocabulary, grammar; skills such as writing). Others are interested in investigating whether learners at different levels benefit from this approach while some studies also inquire about student and teacher attitudes towards it.

8.2   How has DDL been researched?

In this section we examine how DDL has been researched through three studies. We will also point to areas of DDL that need greater exploration. Our three examples span different areas of interest within DDL research though they have some overlap. The first study compares the use of indirect hands-off DDL and direct hands-on DDL within lower-level learners; the second examines the effect of concordancing on writing in relation to complexity, accuracy and fluency (CAF) measures, while the final study also uses CAF measures to examine DDL used in the context of revision writing. Note that studies 1 and 2 are both set in Iran but, while the participants share the same L1, other variables differ and they have quite a differing focus and methodology. Study 3 is set in Turkey but has a lot in common with study 2 from a methodological perspective.

Study 1

Saeedakhtar, A., Bagerin, M., & Abdi, R. (2020). The effect of hands-on and hands-off data-driven learning on low-intermediate learners' verb-preposition collocations. *System*, 91 102268.

This research paper contains some typical elements of a DDL study. First, it has a specific research question in relation to the effectiveness of an aspect of DDL. Its focus is on the teaching of verb-preposition collocations by Iranian learners of English who are at pre-intermediate level. It sets up a quasi-experimental study over a period of time with an experimental group and a control group. It uses pre-tests, immediate post-tests and delayed post-tests. The study also includes an attitudinal survey based on Likert scale questions. The background, methodology and the main findings of the study are described below.

Background to the study

Existing work in DDL has focused more on upper-level proficiency learners. Most previous work has compared the direct use of DDL with other traditional approaches rather than with its opposite, the indirect use of DDL through off-line concordances (often on paper). Many studies have shown that hands on DDL has a positive effect on vocabulary, L2 collocations and grammar learning. Several works on hands off DDL show promising results for L2 collocations and grammar. However, only a limited number of studies have directly compared direct DDL (hands on, DDDL) and indirect DDL (hands off, IDDL) approaches. These studies have concluded that both types of DDL are effective for teaching collocations.

Aim of the study

The study compared the use of DDDL and IDDL in lower-intermediate learners' knowledge of English verb-preposition collocations. Specifically, it addressed two research questions: (1) whether DDDL and IDDL improve Iranian secondary school learners' L2 collocations differently; (2) what the learners' attitudes towards DDDL and IDDL are in terms of learning L2 collocations and whether these attitudes change over time.

Methodology

A total of 60 female Iranian lower-intermediate secondary school students (aged between 16–18 years) participated. A proficiency test was used to ensure that all participants were at the same level. The cohort were divided into an experimental group of 40 and a control group of 20. The experimental group was further divided into a group that would have a direct hands on (DDDL) treatment and one which will have an indirect hands off (IDDL) treatment. To address RQ 2, an attitudinal survey was devised. All instruments were first piloted.

In the quasi-experimental phase, participants took part in 10 extra-curricular classes. The focus of these classes was to learn a list of 66 verb-preposition collocations (selected based on frequency and other principles).

Hands on DDDL group

Students were given some training on how to use the corpus and each class started with a list of verbs that students had to search for using *AntConc* and identify preposition collocations. A teacher was available to assist and engage in dialogue with the students in the laboratory. Students completed gap fill activities to reinforce the target patterns and made notes on at the end of each session.

Hands off IDDL group

Students were given guidance on how to use hands off DDL materials and the teacher presented the collocations for each class via paper-based concordances. Students completed gap fill activities to reinforce the target patterns and made notes on at the end of each session.

Control group

The language teacher taught collocation lists in a traditional explicit manner in each class. Students completed gap fill activities to reinforce the target patterns and made notes on at the end of each session.

A pre-test was administered in the second session to all cohorts to measure the learners' initial knowledge of verb-preposition collocations. An immediate post-test was conducted on all participants which focused on 30 of the 66 target collocations. The experimental group (DDDL and IDDL cohorts) also completed a questionnaire as part of the post-test session. Two weeks after the immediate post-test, a delayed post-test was administered to all participants.

Main findings

–   There was a significant difference between the experimental (DDDL and IDDL) group as a whole and the control group in terms of success in learning collocations in the immediate post-test.
–   There was no significant difference between the two experimental sub-groups in the immediate post-test (i.e. DDDL and IDDL).
–   The delayed post-test showed that not only had the experimental groups outperformed the control group, but also the IDDL group did better than the DDDL group in terms of accurate verb-preposition collocation recognition.
–   In summary, regarding RQ 2, the questionnaire showed positive findings in relation to attitudes to DDL. The role of dialogue with the teacher during the

sessions was noted, as were levels of difficulty and anxiety in relation to DDL in the initial session. Nine in ten participants reported that DDL was more effective than traditional resources, such as dictionaries, for learning collocations and 80% reported that the study motivated them to continue using corpora. Most participants, 95%, thought that they needed dialogue with the teacher so as to benefit from DDL. In relation to their attitudes to DDL over time, almost all said that they had problems in the first session (98%). All participants noted that they felt anxiety in that session but said that they subsequently became used to it thanks to dialogue with the teacher (93%). The majority of participants (95%) said that by the end of the sequence of classes, they had become more relaxed with DDL. Overall, 90% found DDL helpful for learning collocations.

This study confirms that (1) direct and indirect DDL both improve accuracy in collocation recall, and (2) both approaches to DDL are effective for teaching collocations even at lower levels. However, Saeedakhtar et al.'s (2020) findings differ from some studies (Boulton 2009, 2012; Daskalovsk, 2015; Huang 2014) which conclude that direct DDL was not appropriate for lower levels learners (because they may potentially mistake nearness of words with collocation — that is, taking items that happen to occur before or after the node as a collocation when it may not be).

What is typical about this study is that it has identified a specific question in relation to the use of DDL and set up a quasi-experimental study and an attitudinal questionnaire. It has implemented an intervention to the experimental group and has had a control group who covered the same content in the same period to compare with. It has measured the outcome of the treatment phase through an immediate and a delayed post-test and has also collated the findings of the questionnaire.

Some relevant methodological considerations emerge from this study:

1. The study gives us deep insights into forms of DDL in relation to one very specific language pattern (verb-preposition collocations) among secondary school learners of English at lower-intermediate level where English is a foreign language. Two important questions are related to how generalisable these findings are, how we can compare the results from this study with those from another study on another aspect of collocations, in a different DDL treatment, within a different setting (age, level, L1 background)

2. The study included a pre-test, post-test and delayed post-test. Delayed post-tests are important and insightful. This is because immediate post-tests will capture declarative knowledge that is explicit to the learner from the recent treatment within the study. In other words, it is knowledge that they have just

consciously acquired. This knowledge may or may not go on to be stored subconsciously in the longer term.[31]

3.   The study includes an attitudinal questionnaire and so brings in the students' voice. This instrument is useful to know more about their initial challenges and anxieties with DDL as a pedagogy. Often this is not captured in classroom-based studies. It also gains insight into the role of the teacher in the DDL treatment. What we do not know is the role of the teacher played in the control group treatment. Another missing element in many studies is that we do not gain any perspective from the teacher. An important 'under the radar' point to keep in mind about this study is that it gives some clues as to the role of the teacher in mediated the learning process (e.g. in DDDL, the teacher will have guided queries in the right direction and will have offered timely explanations, in IDDL the teacher, by curating the language examples for the concordances will have guiding the learning path and will have also added explanations). A point to take from this in designing a study is to consider capturing both the teacher's voice and process as part of the methodology.

We will return to some of the above points in studies 2 and 3, both of which look at DDL in the context of writing using complexity, accuracy and fluency (CAF) measures. CAF indices are seen as objective and reliable measures for appraising writing quality and development in both first and second language contexts (see Lu, 2010; Luo, 2016; Wigglesworth & Storch, 2009). Some of the measures (especially those of fluency and some complexity indices) are based on the close analysis and annotation of T-units which are defined as "one main clause with all subordinate clauses attached to it" (Hunt, 1965, p. 20). More recently, phrase complexity measures such as noun phrase elaboration and nominal modifiers (Díez-Bedmar & Pérez-Paredes, 2020; Kyle, 2016) have increased the range of CAF measures beyond clauses. Coming back to traditional CAF measures, a learner's writing can be broking up into its constituent T-units and these can then be divided into Error Free T-Units (EFTs). Measures are calculated in relation to Mean Length of Error Free T-Units (MLEFTs) and total number of clauses (C) and Error-Free Clauses (EFC) as illustrated in Figure 8.4 and contextualised in Case studies 2 and 3.

In study 2, we stay with an Iranian context so as to show a comparative within the same L1 background but where the learners who are participating in the study are university undergraduates at an intermediate level.

---

31. Many would argue that what is stored subconsciously is not directly connected with consciously acquired knowledge. For more on conscious and subconscious learning and the importance of delayed post-testing in SLA, see Han & Finneran (2014).

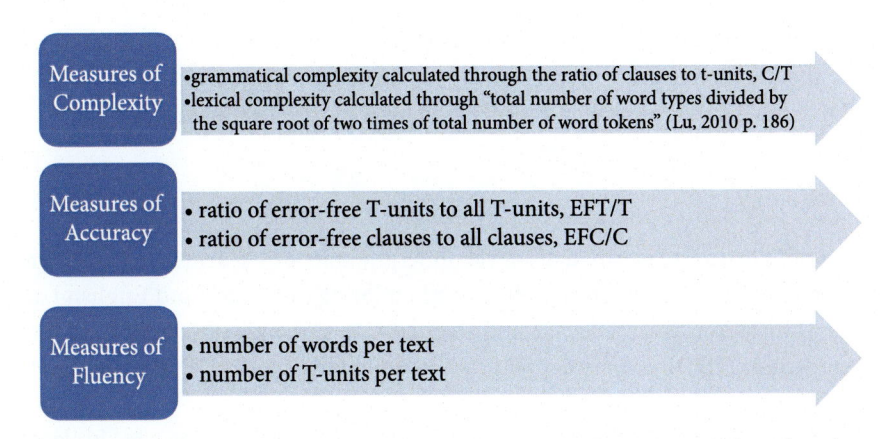

Figure 8.4 Summary of CAF measures used in Şahin Kızıl (2023, p. 1386) based on (Lu, 2010; Luo, 2016; Wigglesworth & Storch, 2009)

Study 2

Samoudi, N., & Modirkhamene, S. (2020). Concordancing in writing pedagogy and CAF measures of writing. *International Review of Applied Linguistics in Language Teaching, 60*, 699–722.

The participants were intermediate-level undergraduates on an English Language Translation programme. This study had a broader focus. It examined whether DDL had an effect on complexity, accuracy and fluency (CAF) measures in learners' writing. Similar to study 1, it was concerned with exploring whether DDDL (hands-on) or IDDL (hands-off) worked best within this context.

Background to the study

The authors took the perspective that, despite the amount of research output on the pedagogical applications of DDL since the turn of the century, results have been ambiguous. This study, thus, explored the application of both native-speaker and local learner corpora, attesting the effect of direct vs. indirect DDL activities on 39 EFL learners' development in CAF measures of writing.

Aims of the study

The study addressed three research questions: (1) Is there a significant difference in the writing complexity scores for the non-DDL (NDDL), direct DDL (DDDL), and indirect (IDDL) groups while controlling for their pre-test complexity scores? (2) Is there a significant difference in the writing accuracy scores for the NDDL,

DDDL and IDDL groups while controlling for their pre-test accuracy scores?, and (3) Is there a significant difference in the writing fluency scores for the NDDL, DDDL, and IDDL groups while controlling for their pre-test fluency scores?

Methodology

A total of 39 learners intermediate-level undergraduate EFL learners, 19 males and 22 females, ranging in age from 19 to 26 and majoring in English and English Language Translation, were selected and divided into three groups: NDDL control (14 students); DDDL experimental group (13 students); and IDDL experimental group (12 students).

In the quasi-experimental phase, all three groups attended nine weekly classes including two sessions for the pre-test and post-test. The experimental groups also attended two one-hour sessions: one teaching general paragraph writing information and one introducing concordancers. The pedagogic focus of each teaching unit related to an aspect of writing (e.g. *cause, linking word, effect*). The topics for the treatment phase were arrived at through the error analysis of Iranian ELF learners' writing and were also informed by the problematic areas identified in the textbook Arnaudet and Barret (1990) which is widely used in this context. Corpus data used in the experimental groups involved: (1) a mini local learner corpus of 120,000 words based on paragraphs written by a parallel group of EFL learners from the previous academic year (errors that were seen as affecting comprehensibility were corrected); (2) the academic sub-section of the Corpus of Contemporary American English (COCA) which contains 100 journal papers and The Michigan Corpus of Upper-level Student Papers (MICUSP), a collection of 2.6 million words containing 830 papers that received an A grade (from both native and non-native users of English). A questionnaire based on Sripicharn (2002) was also administered to all participants for the purposes of gathering participant background information (e.g. English learning background, learning strategies, familiarity with concordances etc.). All groups took a pre- and a post-writing test in the first and last treatment sessions. The concordancing tool Antconc was used by the DDDL group. Printouts of concordance lines were used by the IDDL group and the control group used the traditional course materials including Arnaudet and Barret (1990). The treatment comprised a semester-long module on paragraph development.

DDDL group

A total of 7 units (or lessons) were administered on themes and topics relating to writing and supported by hands on DDL activities. Two one-hour training sessions on how to use corpora were provided in advance. At each session, participants wrote a paragraph relating to the session.

IDDL group

A total of 7 units (or lessons) were administered on themes and topics relating to writing and supported by paper-based DDL activities using concordance print-outs developed for the treatment (including concordances where the node was blank and learners had to figure out the missing word, structured questions based on the concordances that focused learners inductively on patterns). Two one-hour training sessions on how to use corpora was provided in advance. At each session, participants wrote a paragraph relating to the session.

Control group

A total of 7 units (or lessons) were administered on themes and topics relating to writing using a traditional approach using teacher-led explanations, a textbook and follow-up exercises. At each session, participants wrote a paragraph relating to the session.

Pre- and post testing

A pre- and post-writing test was given to all groups at the first and last treatment. These data were handwritten and were subsequently converted into electronic format. This allowed for detailed annotation of T-units in line with Hunt (1965, p. 20) (see above). Error Free T-units (EFT) which are core to measuring accuracy were analysed and used in the measure of fluency in terms of their mean length (MLEFT) (see Figure 8.4). Writing complexity, which in this study was limited to grammar, was calculated using the total number of clauses divided by the total number of T-units (and therefore only refers to syntactic, rather than lexical, complexity).

Main findings

RQ 1. Is there a significant difference in the writing complexity scores for NDDL, DDDL and IDDL groups while controlling for their pre-test complexity scores? No significance difference was found across the three groups.

RQ 2. Is there a significant difference in the writing complexity scores for NDDL, DDDL and IDDL groups while controlling for their pre-test accuracy scores? IDDL was found to be more effective in terms of improvement in writing accuracy than NDDL and DDDL.

RQ 3. Is there a significant difference in the writing complexity scores for NDDL, DDDL and IDDL groups while controlling for their pre-test fluency scores? The IDDL approach was found to be significantly more effective in terms of improving fluency than the DDDL and the NDDL approaches.

In summary, Samoudi and Modirkhamene's (2020) study found that:

- IDDL activities had significantly positive effects on learners' writing development in terms of fluency and accuracy;
- the cohort who received the DDDL treatment did not perform better than those the IDDL or NDDL approaches;
- no obvious advantages were found for either DDDL or IDDL instruction as compared with the traditional (NDDL) method in terms of writing complexity.

These findings are in contrast with many studies that found direct DDL had positive effects on foreign language writing (e.g. Liu & Jiang, 2009; Yilmaz, 2017). However, Samoudi and Modirkhamene note that the results confirm Boulton's (2010) findings in his review of studies on the application of the direct DDL method. Contrasting findings in this area point to the methodological challenge in this type of research. For instance, while Samoudi and Modirkhamene examine learners' development within the context of CAF measures of writing, other studies may use quite different methods and arrive at different conclusions. Liu and Jiang (2009) focused on the use of DDDL in error correction through an observation study and compared pre- and post-test results using descriptive statistics. Given the generalisability of results within a CAF framework across the field of SLA, it is important for researchers of DDL to amass more evidence on the impact of both indirect and direct approaches on learner development.

Reflecting on study 2, we can see that it has some elements in common with study 1, but it is difficult to compare them or their findings as their focus differ. While both tested IDDL and DDDL, their overall focus and methodology differed substantially. Study 1 looked at an element of form while study 2 looked at a skill. Case study 1 used a narrow pre, post- and delayed post-test design that tested a specific list of items that had been the focus of the treatment (verb-preposition collocations) while study 2 used an existing First and Second Language Acquisition measure, CAF, to derive measures based on much more open pre- and post-test. There was no delayed post-test in study 2. Study 1 captured the students' reflections in its design whereas study 2 did not.

So far, from studies 1 and 2, we can see certain gains emerging in relation to the effectiveness and efficiency of DDL is some respects. What we are not gaining from either of these studies is an insight into why DDL is sometimes effective. We have data from the start of the study and from the end but perhaps more developmental information would be more informative as to what happens during the study period. For example, evidence of the trajectory of the type of learning that took place within the experimental and the control groups. This would require more sampling across stages within the treatment.

Let us look now at another study which also draws on CAF to look at writing.

Study 3

Şahin Kızıl, A. (2023). Data-driven learning: English as a foreign language writing and complexity, accuracy and fluency measures. *Journal of Computer Assisted Language Learning*, 39(4), 1382–1395.

In this study, Şahin Kızıl pointed to the lack of research on the effectiveness of DDL in the context of students revising their writing. Additionally, the researcher pointed to the lack of connection by most previous work on writing development with CAF measures as an objective and reliable measure of writing quality. Their goal, therefore, was to investigate the effect, if any, of DDL on revising writing using a quasi-experimental approach. To this end, having recruited 31 university-level B1 level Turkish learners of English, they set up an experimental and a control group. The experimental group received instruction on how to consult a corpus when revising their writing while the control group continued using the traditional resources (such as dictionaries, textbooks and teacher explanations).

Background to the study

Despite extensive research on the use of DDL in developing various aspects of the writing skill, few studies have looked at DDL in the context of revising writing. Among studies that do exist, very few use CAF measures in their investigation despite the objectivity and reliability of its indices of writing development.

Aims of the study

The study aimed to examine the effectiveness of using DDL in revision writing by using CAF measures to compare development in writing performance across a treatment and a control group. Specifically, it addressed the following research questions: (1) Is there a significant difference between the writing performance of DDL and non-DDL groups in terms of complexity of their writing? (2) Is there a significant difference between the writing performance of DDL and non-DDL groups in terms of accuracy of their writing? (3) Is there a significant difference between the writing performance of DDL and non-DDL groups in terms of fluency of their writing?

Methodology

The study recruited 31 undergraduates who were all around 19 years old and non-English majors based at a Turkish university, with an English language proficiency level of B1. Participants were recruited and formed two parallel writing classes: the experimental DDL group of 13 (10 female and 3 male) participants and the control group of 18 (14 female and 4 male) students. All had around 9 years' experience of learning English and none had used DDL before. Both groups were taught by the same instructor and received the same amount of instruction time and followed the same writing syllabus over a 12-week period. Two instruments were used for data collection: (1) a questionnaire to collect personal information on participants (age, language learning background, dictionary and computer use, familiarity with DDL etc.) and (2) pre- and post-tests that involved eliciting students' writing (within timed sessions of 50 minutes).

DDL group

The treatment involved a 12-week programme. Each week entailed 3 sessions on a specific aspect of writing. Students were then required to write and submit the first draft of the writing task out of the classroom time. This was then marked by underlining the parts that needed correction or improvement. The revision tasks took place in the computer lab. In revision sessions, students were assisted in both understanding the feedback and in deciding the appropriate corpus query and guidance. Upon revising their work, students were provided with feedback indicating appropriate and inappropriate revisions. Initial sessions involved training on the use of corpus tools as a resource of revision writing.

Control group

The same course was followed as the DDL experimental group and the same steps were followed but instead of discussing how to use a corpus query to help in revision, the teacher aided their use of dictionaries and reference sources. Initial sessions involved training on the use of dictionaries, collocation dictionaries, thesauri, grammars and other resources of revision writing.

Pre- and post testing

Pre- and post-treatment writing samples were analysed using CAF measures (summarised in Figure 8.4). Clauses, T-units, clauses per T-units and errors were identified and coded and this allowed for the calculation of error free T-units, etc. as detailed in study 2. However, unlike study 2, this research measured both lexical and grammatical complexity (see Figure 8.4).

Main findings

RQ 1. Is there a significant difference between the writing performance of DDL and non-DDL groups in terms of complexity of their writings? There was a significant difference in lexical complexity in the writing produced by the DDL group. However, there was no significant difference between the two groups in terms of grammatical complexity.

RQ 2. Is there a significant difference between the writing performance of DDL and non-DDL groups in terms of accuracy of their writings? No significant difference was observed between the DDL and the control group.

RQ 3. Is there a significant difference between the writing performance of DDL and non-DDL groups in terms of fluency of their writings? The DDL group outperformed non-DDL group.

In short, it was found that the DDL group outperformed the non-DDL group in producing fluent and more lexically diverse writings. The use of online concordancing in the students' revision process seemed to have a positive impact leading them to write lexically diverse and fluent papers. Like studies 1 and 2, IDDL was observed to have a greater impact, albeit from different perspectives and within differing designs and treatments.

The three studies, by way of a sample of DDL research around the time of writing, illustrate some of the richness of the work that is ongoing and which typically looks at DDL among difference cohorts of learners in comparison with control groups. As Boulton and Cobb (2017, p. 381) conclude, based on their meta-analysis of all empirical studies on DDL up until mid-2014, "DDL is a flourishing field". However, it can be challenging to navigate all of these studies, especially when methodologies may vary and their findings may at times be contradictory. This is where meta-analyses are useful and, as Vyatkina (2016) has noted for a relatively young field, DDL has accumulated enough empirical studies to lead to several research syntheses (see Pérez-Paredes, 2022) and meta-analyses.

By way of parting reflection on the three studies, let us consider their differing pedagogical contexts. We know that they differ in terms of types of learners and their proficiency level; they also differ in terms of the type of study:

– Study 1 – 60 lower intermediate' high school students in Iran (16 to 18 years old).

– Study 2 – 39 intermediate level undergraduates majoring in English/English Language Translation in Iran (19 – 26 years old).

– Study 3 – 31 B1 level undergraduates who were not English majors in Turkey (c. 19 years old).

Apart from these three different contexts and participants' educational level (high school, undergraduate English majors, and non-English majors), we know nothing about what their normal baseline experience of learning English has been. Boulton and Cobb (2017) note in their meta-analysis (see Section 8.3) that one fifth of all DDL studies had been carried out in Asia, with half of these taking place in Middle Eastern contexts. These studies were found to have the largest effect sizes, that is, the strength of the treatment was higher (Plonsky & Oswald, 2014) in these contexts than in other parts of the world. Boulton and Cobb (2017) note that the previous finding is counterintuitive given that the prevailing educational preference in Asia has traditionally been teacher-fronted which is the antithesis of DDL. They posit that DDL may offer such a contrast to the traditional norm that it may have a novelty value that is greater in these contexts compared to, for example, Europe where inductive student-centred educational approaches are valued and promoted with a problem-solving focus (and in these contexts, they found DDL to have comparatively lower effect sizes). This leads us on now to look at meta-studies of DDL. In the next section, we look more closely at what meta-analyses tell us in relation to DDL. When results across many studies are scrutinised and aggregated in a systematic way, we can get a bigger picture on whether DDL is effective or not and in which circumstances. These analyses can also point out some weaknesses which we discuss also in the sections that follow.

8.3   Research into DDL through meta-analysis and meta-studies

Meta-analysis is the statistical process used to bring studies together and arrive at summative statements about what all of the empirical research up to a given point in time tells us. It involves selecting all possible studies within a time period, usually within broad criteria in a given research area, averaging their effect sizes and drawing conclusions on the effects of treatments or interventions. According to Loewen and Plonsky (2016, p. 112), meta-analyses "yield a view of the domain in question that is more objective, transparent, and systematic than traditional literature reviews". There is usually a phase of narrowing down of the studies that will be analysed until a body of work is identified which can is considered 'meta-analysable'. These studies are then analysed and systematically (statistically) compared to arrive at combined results across them. As previously mentioned, DDL has involved numerous empirical studies from the outset of this emerging field. Boulton and Cobb (2017), in their meta-analysis first identified 205 works that met the initial criteria for inclusion in their study. This batch was then reduced to 64 once master's theses, posters, conference presentations, qualitative studies, and those that lacked key elements such as pre- or post-tests, were eliminated. As we saw from the three studies in Section 8.2, aggregating results across common variables can be challenging without a meta-analysis. A meta-analysis allows for results to be viewed across many variables by calculating effect size (i.e. the difference between the average, or mean, quantitative outcomes between two different intervention groups). Cohen's d is commonly used as an effect size index, where an effect size is considered small ($d = 0.2$), medium ($d = 0.5$), or large ($d \geq 0.8$).

In Boulton and Cobb's (2017) meta-analysis, various variables were aggregated. In doing so, effect size results from the pre- and post-tests (P/P) treatments are measured separately to the control and the experimental group treatments (C/E). That is, P/P measures the effect sizes within the experimental group while C/E gives a measure across groups. Here is a summary of just some of Boulton and Cobb's (2017) findings across different study variables:

Publication type

(1) journal articles showed higher effect sizes over PhD studies in P/P whereas PhD studies were found to have overall higher effect sizes over journal papers in relation to C/E designs; (2) there was a higher effect size in ranked journals compared with unranked for both P/P and C/E measures; (3) shorter papers had higher effect sizes generally for P/P and C/E.

Design type

- Population: more participants in a study correlated with larger effect size in the P/P design while fewer participants in a study meant larger effect size in the C/E design.
- Data collection instruments: (1) when multiple choice was used as an instrument, there was quite a large effect size; (2) constrained constructed responses (focusing on specific items with limited response options) showed the highest size effect in P/P but lowest in C/E; (3) free-writing tests showed large effect size in C/E and medium in P/P designs.

Populations

Here we can learn much for future studies because part of the information was not consistently available across the body of research in DDL. This limited the authors in their ability to draw more conclusions from this important variable in language learning research:

- Age: the age of the participants was only provided in a small number of studies.
- Year of study: this was generally available.

- Gender: this information was only available in some studies and those that did include it did not separate the results by gender.
- Cultural background: one fifth of studies took place in Asian contexts, with half of these in the Middle East.
- First language background: studies that involved Asian and Middle Eastern first languages showed the largest effect sizes on P/P (except for Japan) and mixed results for C/E designs.

Proficiency

Boulton and Cobb note that it was particularly difficult to appraise this variable because of different proficiency tests used and differing terminology (e.g. compare the terms describing proficiency in studies 1, 2 and 3 — low-intermediate, intermediate level and B1 level, respectively). Here again is a learning point for future empirical studies. As discussed in Chapters 3 and 4, for the purposes of comparability, it is best to define the participant's level using a common reference point such as The Common European Framework of Reference for Languages (CEFR). Despite this, Boulton and Cobb note (1) moderate to large effect size in most cases, with the exception of lower intermediate in P/P while C/E results show the largest effect in social sciences and lowest in hard sciences.

Treatment

Studies differed, some integrated DDL into courses while some provided DDL sessions in laboratory-like conditions. (1) Both contexts showed large effect sizes except for C/E designs in laboratory conditions; (2) the length of intervention was not always explicit and when it was, it varied from short (2 hours or less), medium (3 – 8 classes) and long (more than 10 classes). P/P designs yielded the largest effect size in medium to short treatment periods; C/E comparisons showed medium to large effect sizes in long-term interventions.

How DDL was used in implementation (direct DDL v indirect DDL)

(1) DDDL tended to show large effect sizes while overall learners using printouts in IDDL mode did less well. (2) Where small bespoke corpora were created for use in the intervention, there was a strong effect size; large corpora (100–200 million words) also produced large effect sizes while intermediate sized corpora (1–29 million words) yielded mixed results; (3) Brown, BNC and COCA were the most commonly used corpora. Overall, in relation to corpus type, C/E designs showed more substantial effect sizes than P/P designs; (4) Of the 51 DDDL studies, 15 used more than one software programme and the reminder only used the English-corpora.org interface (COCA). Only COCA and *Lextutor* were found to produce effect sizes.

Objective variables

(1) most studies look at DDL in the context of General English, resulting in large effect sizes; (2) English for Specific Purposes showed quite a good effect size while EAP yielded a very small effect six for C/E; (3) in terms of what type of language was being examined, some focused on skills (but with a major paucity of work on speaking and listening). Writing had a medium effect size for P/P designs and negligible for C/E. The majority of studies looked at DDL for lexicogrammar and vocabulary learning, with fewer looking at grammar or discourse in isolation. While it was challenging to categorise these studies (e.g. vocabulary studies of collocation could overlap with lexicogrammar), Boulton and Cobb did conclude that, it seems that DDL is a strong methodology for lexicogrammar, especially in P/P comparisons.

Boulton and Cobb's (2017) meta-analysis paints a positive picture of the value of DDL based on the research that they systematically scrutinised. Across 84 variables in 25 categories (aligned to those commonly used in meta-analyses), they found 60% large, 24.5% medium and 15% small or negligible effect sizes based on the findings summarised in Table 8.2.

Table 8.2 Summary of Boulton and Cobb's (2017) meta-analysis effect sizes across variables

	Within group designs (P/P)	Between group designs (C/E)
Total large effect sizes	49	47
Total medium effect sizes	20	19
Total small effect sizes	8	5
Total lower than small effect sizes	1	11

Consistent large effects lead Boulton and Cobb (2017) to conclude from their meta-analysis of 64 studies, that DDL is suitable for both undergraduate and graduate students, for intermediate to advanced levels, for general as well as specialised academic purposes, for local and large corpora, for hands-on concordancing and paper-based exploration, for learning and reference purposes, and especially for vocabulary and lexicogrammar. In summary, Boulton and Cobb (2017) found that DDL seemed to work well in almost any context where it has been extensively tried.

To close this section on how DDL has been studied, let us look at some summary points that were made by Boulton and Vyatkina (2021). Their study, which we discuss in Section 8.4, looked at research trends in relation to DDL empirical studies from 1989–2019 (identifying 489 publications). While they were not systematically examining quality in terms of instruments and methods in these studies, they make an important checklist for researchers in terms of the rigour that is needed for the field. Reflecting on three decades of empirical work on DDL, they note the following in relation to some studies (Boulton & Vyatkina, 2021, p. 82):

- statistical analyses have frequently been insufficiently robust;
- reporting practices (of results) have been non-standard;
- despite persistent calls for greater sample sizes and longer study duration, there has been no growth trend in relation to these in actual studies.
- despite the growing and more diverse geographical spread in terms of where DDL is used as a pedagogy, across regions and first languages spoken by DDL participants, English is still heavily dominant as the target language.
- research has overwhelmingly been conducted with university students in language-for-general-purposes classes (usually relating to English). While they acknowledge the obvious convenience of using university students as participants in terms of convenience sampling, there is much to be done with longer, ecological settings to investigate how DDL may be used outside class, after the end of a course, or in non-university (professional, primary and secondary schools) contexts. They call for greater collaboration, both within and between institutions, more outreach to language teachers in form of open access corpora, accessibly written DDL guides as well as training opportunities

Overall, Boulton and Vyatkina (2021) found that much the DDL research over the last three decades covers similar ground, "with many studies confirming that DDL 'works'" (p. 83) and they, like others, call for innovation in how DDL is researched. In the next section, we will explore some important dimensions of DDL that have not received enough research attention. Our focus will be on how methodology can contribute to cross-fertilisation within different fields in language learning research.

8.4   Towards an enhanced research agenda for DDL: Linking with SLA

As Boulton and Vyatkina's 2021 review shows, conclusions to articles on DDL research frequently allege the benefits of DDL to higher-order skills such as critical thinking, independent thinking, and autonomy, but lack any direct focus on testing these. For the authors, future innovative research will advance this challenging yet highly promising direction, aligning with the essential theoretical development of DDL and fostering its cross-fertilisation with broader SLA research and related fields, such as educational psychology. In the next section, we shall explore this theme in greater detail.

8.4.1   DDL and its associative links to constructivism

Reflecting back to the examples of the typical direct and indirect DDL activities that we showcased in Section 8.1, we can see how they seem to require the learner to engage in a process of inductive learning. Over the years, many proponents of DDL have applauded this student-centredness and aligned it with the constructivist theory of learning.

Constructivism is a term linked to educational psychology where processes and concepts such as induction, inference, hypothesising, learner-centredness and discovery learning have played a role. As O'Keeffe (2021a) notes, such constructivist ideals have been lauded in DDL. For example, going back to the early days of DDL, Johns (1994) sought to cut out the middleman as far as possible so as to give direct access to the corpus data and so as to allow learners to build up their own profiles of meaning and use. Corpus data was seen as offering "a unique resource for the stimulation of inductive learning strategies — in particular the strategies of perceiving similarities and differences and of hypothesis formation and testing" (Johns, 1994, p. 297). In its purest form then, O'Keeffe (2021a, p. 261) points out, DDL was seen as open discovery rather than a teacher-curated or mediated focus on language input, where learners will discover as salient [...] any new language input, based on their own [..] explorations". The cognitive rationale is that increased exposure to input through DDL will result in an increase of the likelihood of a given item becoming noticed by a learner.

A consistent view across DDL literature is that its core pedagogical benefit lies in its potential to encourage learners to construct their L2 knowledge independently by exploring the linguistic data from corpus input (Boulton & Vyatkina, 2021; Cobb, 1997, 1999; Collentine, 2000; Flowerdew, 2015). The associative link to constructivism is seen as a pedagogical hallmark for DDL. However, it is problematic is that this long-held and widespread consensus has not been experimentally explored or proven (O'Keeffe, 2021a). For researchers interested in examining how, or whether, DDL enhances L2 acquisition, there is a need to explore how learning takes place if at all for some or all learners. In order to do this, greater links to theory are needed. On one level, a broader theoretical range is required to examine the pedagogy of DDL. On another level, greater depth of insight is needed through the lens of SLA concepts to examine the microprocesses of L2 acquisition that foraging through concordances might bring.

There has been some emerging research that looks at DDL through differing theoretical lenses. For example, Chang (2012) explores the types of cognitive skills with which DDL engages. This study was small in scale. Involving seven doctoral students, it evaluated a web-based corpus interface developed to enhance authorial stance. One of the research aims was to investigate whether DDL fostered a constructivist environment which would prompt learners' inference of linguistic patterns so as to attain deeper understanding. Chang found that the application of higher-order skills, such as inference, was infrequent. The study reported that users deployed more lower-level cognitive skills such as making sense and exploring as their main learning processes. Other studies that deployed quasi-experimental methods to explore learners' ability to induce rules and self-correct include Todd (2001) and Gabel (2001). As Papp (2007) notes, while both of these studies report positive results, neither of their research designs captured students' ability to induce patterns and self-correct (see also Pérez-Paredes et al., 2012; Forti, 2023).

Methodologically, it is imperative that the various variables involved be controlled. The research should control for variables, including the degree of mediation, the cognitive processes, as well as learner characteristics beyond age, L1 or gender and explore their level of competence accurately and within a framework such as the CEFR which allows for comparability. This would allow for more fine-grained and comparable results and a better understanding of how different factors influence language learning through DDL. Similarly, research that examines the cognitive processes involved in language learning, particularly in relation to noticing and attention, should present a more robust operationalization of these constructs across a diverse DDL-input scenarios (Zhang, 2022; Zalbidea, 2021). This could enhance the understanding of how learners interact with language data and the implications for their learning outcomes.

8.4.2   DDL and links to sociocultural theory

Constructivism, in the context of discovery learning, has been criticised because it can lead to learners *wandering off* on independent pathways where they can go astray in terms of learning outcomes (O'Keeffe, 2021a). In the context of DDL, there is a possibility that learners can get lost amid the data and induce or infer incorrectly (or neither induce nor infer anything). To counter this, there is need for teacher mediation of some kind (e.g. where the teacher carefully structures the task or curates the examples). For example, in study 1 (Saeedakhtar et al., 2020), the role of dialogue with the teacher during DDL sessions was identified by the learners as crucial to their learning and to the reduction of the initial anxiety that they felt. This type of 'scaffolding' is important and more research into its role in DDL is needed. The term was originally coined by psychologist Jerome Bruner to refer to the use of some kind of supporting mediation in the learning process within a sociocultural theory (SCT) paradigm.

Though some concepts and practices of SCT-based pedagogies are a good fit for DDL, the theory and related principles receive far less attention in the literature where constructivism is usually a given in terms of underlying theory (see O'Keeffe, 2021b for a detailed discussion).

Some key SCT-related concepts that are important for DDL include the development of learner agency and self-regulation and the role of mediation (by the teacher and learning peers) (O'Keeffe, McCarthy, & Carter, 2007; Cobb & Boulton, 2015; Flowerdew, 2015). Learner agency refers to empowerment, whereby the student takes control of learning rather than assuming a passive role in a transmissive relationship with the teacher. The enhancement of learner agency is cited, though not empirically explored, as one of the main advantages of DDL by O'Keeffe et al. (2007). It is argued that learners can be trained to operate independently to develop skills and strategies and, in the process, they can "surpass instructional intervention and become a better, self-regulated learner" (O'Keeffe et al., 2007, p.55). Flowerdew (2015) identified this SCT connection as important to the evolution of research into how learners best learn in DDL and pointed to some early studies that involved exploring learner agency: Cobb (1999) and Chau (2003). While these studies were not designed to measure learner agency experimentally (e.g. findings were observed from delayed post-tests), their results suggest positive outcomes, as does Zare and Aqajani Delavar (2023) study which we discuss below, see also Recommended reading 8.2.

Also, central to the Vygotskyan notion of SCT is the idea that cognitive processes are mediated and that language is one of the most important tools in this activity (see Swain, 2006). Through dialogue, higher-order cognitive processes are shaped and re-shaped. Within the classroom, mediation may happen through a teacher or a peer or it may involve the self, through private talk or inner speech. Essentially, it is via mediation, manifested through dialogue, that we learn because, in this collaborative process, we engage in the co-construction of knowledge. Clearly, while there is some overlap between SCT and constructivist tenets, fundamentally, an SCT view of DDL moves away from the notion of a learner independently grappling (Cobb, 2005) with the data in a discovery process to a focus on the nature of such grappling and how it can be supported in order to lead to enhanced learning opportunities through self-regulation or mediation by peers or a teacher. It would be most interesting and insightful to build up a knowledge base around teacher, peer and private talk (and inner speech) when individual learners are grappling with concordance lines. Crosthwaite et al., (2019) tracked individual corpus user engagements and look-ups in their study and this offers much insight but if teacher, peer and inner speech could also be added to this type of study design, it would be really useful in the exploration of self-regulation.

An interesting study from the perspective of mediation is Huang (2011). This study explores the role of mediation through intra- and interpersonal dialogues in the acquisition of grammar through DDL. Though small in scale, this 14-week study of undergraduates examined 10 groups of three learners. Peer-to-peer (i.e. learner) dialogues were recorded and students also kept logs. The findings reflected a link between higher performance and engagement with peers in negotiating form-focused episodes, leading to correct conclusions. Huang (2011) is tentative about the findings from her study because of the sample size and the many variables that were not controlled within the study. As O'Keeffe (2021a) notes, what is important about this study is that its research gaze expanded to include a core concept within a learning theory (in this case SCT) in relation to DDL. "Despite the many possibilities for seams of DDL research in relation to SCT", O'Keeffe (2021a, p. 263) notes, "large-scale studies that robustly investigate the role and nature of mediation and scaffolding in terms of the use of DDL do not yet exist".

Designing DDL activities that openly incorporate SCT principles, such as collaborative learning, scaffolding, and the use of cultural artifacts can be useful to evaluate their impact on promoting language learning. Longitudinal studies that track learners' language development over time while using DDL in collaborative settings can help researchers understand how social interactions and cultural contexts influence the acquisition of language and patterns. As a complement to pre and post-tests, data collection methods could include interviews, focus groups, and observations of group work. Similarly, investigating how social interactions influence learners' noticing and attention to language forms during DDL activities, possibly involving eye-tracking or screen-capturing technologies, can only increase our understanding of the role of mediation and collaboration in classroom contexts.

8.4.3   DDL and SLA

So far, we have talked about DDL and the need for greater research focus on the theoretical underpinnings of its pedagogy. There has also been a growing call for more links to be made between SLA and DDL (Flowerdew, 2015; O'Keeffe, 2021a, 2021b; Papp, 2007; Pérez-Paredes, 2022; Vyatkina 2016). This is not a one-way call for DDL researcher to look at their practice through the lens of SLA. As O'Keeffe (2021a) argues, within the field of SLA, there are so many exciting research questions being asked in relation to noticing, attention, salience, usage-based models of acquisition of constructions, to name but a few, where DDL could add insight from the perspective of individual learners by enhancing our understanding of the cognitive processes that second language learning entails within DDL (p. 269). Zare and Aqajani Delavar's (2023) study of DDL in the context of task-based learning and form-focused instruction, which we discuss below, is an interesting example of how DDL research can engage more with SLA research questions and designs.

Boulton and Vyatkina (2021) conducted a systematic study of empirical research in DDL over three decades (1989–2019), uncovering 489 separate publications. They converted these publications into a corpus of over 2.5 million words (the corpus is sub-divided into five time periods). Their main focus is on the concluding sections of the papers so as to explore what recommendations for future research are proposed in each time period (within these conclusions). They used manual coding and semi-automated corpus keyword analysis to explore whether those points are in fact addressed in later publications as an indication of the evolution of the field. Overall, they noted that the body of empirical work in DDL research has been growing exponentially (e.g. there were almost 200 empirical studies published between 2016–2019). Of relevance to the need for greater research theoretical links and underpinnings in DDL studies, they concluded that "it would seem necessary to push further and expect theories to drive continued development" rather than pinning constructivism, noticing theory or sociocultural theory in an "attempt to justify the approach after the event (Boulton and Vyatkina (2021, p.82). This is precisely what DDL research methodology urgently needs, i.e., to pose research questions and designs that do not focus exclusively on what Stockwell has termed as techno-centrism (Stockwell, 2022) and to explore the feasibility and impact of these theories of importance in the broad field of language learning.

Focus 8.1 summarises some SLA concepts that have been mentioned in relation to DDL over the years (Johansson, 2009; Papp, 2009; Flowerdew, 2015; Vyatkina 2016; Lee et al., 2019; Pérez-Paredes, 2022; O'Keeffe, 2021a, 2021b; Boulton & Vyatkina, 2021) and which merit in-depth empirical scrutiny in the future. Notice the relevance of these SLA concept in evolving DDL research.

Essentially, as argued by Boulton and Vyatkina (2021), O'Keeffe (2021a) and Pérez Paredes (2022), there is a need to move the focus of research on the use of DDL away from solely quasi-experimental studies that are often small in scale and often focused on assessing language gains in between and within group designs. Advocates for change see the potential that DDL-based research can make to theories of learning and theories of acquisition. Broadening our research gaze can inform these areas of pedagogy and applied linguistics. An interesting example of this is Zare and Aqajani Delavar's (2023) study (see recommended reading 8.2), in which they examine DDL in the context of task-based language teaching (TBLT) by looking at a focus-on-form (FonF) DDL approach using a triangulated research design that leads to insights for DDL in the broader context of applied linguistics and SLA research. As Gabrielatos (2005) noted, DDL offers the learner a type of condensed exposure that can aid pattern-based learning and this aligns well with a UB model of acquisition which holds that cognitive mechanisms are triggered through experiencing language patterns.

Focus 8.1   SLA concepts that are key to evolving DDL research (based on O'Keeffe 2021a and 2021b)

🔍   **SLA concepts and DDL research**

---

1. Involvement load hypothesis (Laufer & Hulstijn, 2001; Lee et al., 2019)

What is it?

This concept comes from vocabulary studies and proposes that the more a learner is involved in learning a word, the higher the chance that the word will be retained. The notion of load is linked to the *need* (how much the word is needed to complete an exercise or task); the *search* (the cognitive effort that is involved in figuring out or looking up the meaning of the new word) and the *evaluation* (the judgement process involved in working out whether the new item is suitable for the context of a given task).

What kind of research questions need to be addressed?

Lee et al, (2019) make the connection between involvement load hypothesis and DDL. Given the effort needed by the learner in the inductive process of working with concordances, it would be fruitful to examine the three processes of *need, search* and *evaluation* in comparison to a control group (who use traditional resources).

---

2. Input flooding (Hernández, 2018)

What is it?

Input flooding refers to repeated exposure of a target form through many embodiments (examples) so as to improve the chances of noticing (and ultimately acquiring) of that form.

What kind of research questions need to be addressed?

DDL aligns well with this notion because it offers intensive exposure to a target form. Research is needed to appraise whether this leads to noticing and acquisition? Does it depend on variables such as level of proficiency, type of form (vocabulary, grammar, etc.), first language, and so on? Hernández's (2018) research (on discourse markers) tells us that input flooding does not work for all forms and that it works best when there is explicit attention or focus and explanation. More research on input flooding, across variables, and with and without explicit mediation by the teacher, is needed in the context of DDL.

---

3. Input enhancement (Sharwood Smith, 1981; Wong, 2005)

What is it?

This refers to the making noticeable (or salient) of selected language items so as to bring learners' conscious attention to them (e.g. using a different colour font for the target structure).

What kind of research questions need to be addressed?

DDL's use of key word in context (KWIC) concordance formats (see Section 8.1) offers an obvious testbed for degrees of input enhancement (from purely concordance level to teacher mediation). With new applications which allow for the alignment of video clips to KWIC formats, text versus video enhancement could also be compared with a control format such as paper-based text enhancement (e.g. coloured font).

Focus 8.1 *(continued)*

4. Noticing Hypothesis (Lai & Zhao, 2006; Schmidt, 1990, 2001)

What is it?

The Noticing Hypothesis essentially holds that input cannot become intake for a learner if it is not first consciously registered as salient, i.e. noticed.

What kind of research questions need to be addressed?

In DDL literature, it is taken as a given that this approach promotes noticing but little or no micro-detail is available on the nature of noticing across variables such as: L1 transfer, type of form (vocabulary, grammar, skill, discourse), age of learner, level of proficiency, direct versus indirect DDL, etc. Any work on calibrating what leads to (better) noticing through DDL would be valuable.

5. Attention, salience and input processing theory (Van Patten, 1993; Van Patten & Benati, 2010)

What is it?

Attention and salience are key to the concepts of noticing (see above) and in turn are a precursor to the process of encoding language input (input processing). If a form is noticed (made salient) and given attention, it is active in the learners working memory and may be processed in the short-term consciousness and ultimately stored in the sub-conscious long-term (and available for automatic retrieval). Input processing research focuses on how learners first perceive and process new linguistic forms within the learning/acquisition process.

What kind of research questions need to be addressed?

Much is yet to be known about the processes that are involved when a learner encounters language data in a concordance. Research is needed across variables such as: L1 transfer, type of form (vocabulary, grammar, skill, discourse), age of learner, level of proficiency, direct versus indirect DDL, etc. This type of research would benefit from recall protocol instruments as well as eye and screen tracking devices.

6. Usage-based model (Ellis, 2006; Tomasello, 2003).

What is it?

The usage-based (UB) perspective on first and second language acquisition holds that frequent exposure to patterns of language (constructions) contributes to models of associative cognitive learning (Tomasello, 2003; Ellis, 2006; see Chapters 5 and 6). Within this process, learners map forms and meanings in their minds. This is seen as a process whereby learners intuitively identify and organise constructions or form-function mappings based on encounters with relevant exemplars in the communicative environment (Ellis, Römer, & O'Donnell 2016). Ultimately, while the process of learning involves conscious attention and noticing of constructions and form-function mapping, the internal reorganising of one's system of knowledge of the language is done at a subconscious or implicit level (see Han & Finneran, 2013, p. 373).

Focus 8.1 *(continued)*

What kind of research questions need to be addressed?

Learning is largely determined by frequency of exposure to new language within the usage-based model of acquisition. The more often constructions are experienced and understood together, the more entrenched they become (O'Keeffe, 2021a). It is believed that learners subconsciously acquire first the constructions that they encounter most frequently in the input that they receive. This theory has obvious relevance for DDL and, as Römer (2019) and O'Keeffe (2021b, 2023) have shown, it may hold the key to better understanding why learners at lower levels may need concordance input to be carefully calibrated to their stage of form-meaning mapping. Also, as Chapter 3 details (by examined through part-of-speech sequences), the nature of form-meaning mapping is developmental in terms of the types of patterns acquired across levels of proficiency and this is very salient to calibrating DDL input. More research into the link between the nature of DDL input, level of proficiency and degree of form-meaning mapping is required.

A final and important point made by many is that the overwhelming majority of DDL research has been conducted on the use of DDL in English language teaching contexts, with research on Languages Other Than English (LOTEs) lagging behind (Boulton & Vyatkina, 2021; Vyatkina 2023). Boulton and Vyatkina (2021) found that, 430 out of 489 DDL studies published up to 2019, targeted English. German was the second most frequent target language but was represented by only 17 studies, which accounts for 3% of all DDL research and 31% of the 53 studies that addressed LOTEs (Vyatkina, 2023). Important work is emerging on LOTEs, as noted by Asención-Delaney et al. (2015), Chambers (2019) and Vyatkina (2023), among others. Vyatkina (2023) offers an excellent example of this in respect of German. Work on DDL and the teaching of Italian is the focus of Forti (2023) and what is important about this work is the scope and depth of its research focus and methodology.

8.5   Summary

In this chapter, we have looked closely at research that has been undertaken in terms of evaluating whether DDL works as an approach. As we have seen, studies usually involve a quasi-experimental approach and are sometimes aided by triangulation of instruments such as questionnaires or interviews. We observed that there have been many such studies over the years and that the area has merited a number of meta-analyses and systematic reviews. Such summative analyses offer us great insight into the aggregated findings of from studies over three decades. They also point to methodological weaknesses that need to be addressed, triggering reflection and a call for changes in how DDL is being researched with an emphasis on the need for more rigour (e.g. inclusion of pre-, post- and delayed post-tests). They have also pointed to the need for more depth and scope in terms of research questions. Essentially, we have reached the point where existing research shows that DDL works but we need more research into why it works, how it works, and with whom it works best. These three questions need a theoretical lens so that they can be viewed through existing second language acquisition paradigms. This kind of research requires a broadening of scope and methodology. Rife for exploration are the connections between usage-based perspectives and DDL. Opening up the study of DDL applications in the classroom to a broader research gaze brings so many opportunities for an enhanced understanding of how L2 acquisition happens.

Coda

Corpus methods have made significant contributions to language learning research by offering tools and data that can be used to track and analyse, among others, learner variability and language development (Lu, 2022). In sum, they have allowed researchers to:

1. Examine how various learner- and task-related factors influence L2 variation;
2. Analyse the impact of different input factors on second language processing and production;
3. Track longitudinal language development in learners, which helps our understanding of both group trends over time and individual differences in progress and,
4. Profile both inter-learner and intra-learner variability in second language acquisition.

This book has shown how automated and semi-automated corpus analysis programs are essential for both scaling these analyses and providing accurate and detailed language feature extraction. In this Coda, we offer some reflections on the challenges and opportunities for CL methods in language learning research.

Corpus linguistics, SLA studies and learner corpus research: Some challenges

A key challenge for corpus linguistics in SLA studies is specifically how to bridge the gap between a descriptive, pattern-oriented focus, and the theoretically-driven, experimental nature of some areas of SLA research. Other challenges include limitations in corpus size, scope, representativeness, diversity, issues with annotation quality, and the inability to comprehensively address the dynamic and multifaceted nature of second language learning processes beyond the corpus. These barriers hinder the integration of corpus linguistics findings into broader SLA theoretical frameworks (McEnery et al. 2019).

The methods discussed in this book cover the corpus design and compilation, the tagging and annotation of the data, as well as quantitative and qualitative analysis procedures. Despite the potential benefits that LCR can offer to SLA research, there has been not enough interaction between these two fields (McEnery et al.,

2019). This is partly because corpus studies tend to focus on the analysis of patterns of language use rather than engaging with theoretical frameworks that are central in SLA research. CL is particularly effective at identifying norms and frequent patterns through statistical analysis of large datasets. However, SLA research is often theory-driven and relies on experimental methods to explore complex, atypical cases that can test theories of language learning. Mitchell (2021) has claimed that corpus researchers have a somewhat different theoretical orientation on L2 learning. Thus, it is relatively accurate to say that corpus-based studies in the 1990s and 2000s have tended to focus on overuse and underuse phenomena rather than explaining underlying mechanisms of language acquisition, which has limited their implications for SLA theoretical frameworks. However, if there is one SLA theory that has attracted the attention of corpus linguists this is usage-based theories, demonstrating that it is possible to bridge these two approaches when there is alignment in research focus. Central to usage-based theories is the idea that exposure to language input, particularly the frequency of specific forms and structures, drives learning. Corpus tools enable the examination of input data, revealing the frequency distributions and co-occurrence patterns that learners encounter, thus informing theories about emergent linguistic structures. Corpora are instrumental in studying the role of formulaic expressions and multi-word units in second language acquisition. Through corpus analysis, language learning researchers can observe how learners process and utilize these chunks, which are pivotal in developing fluency and language competence. Corpus data also complement dynamic systems approaches often associated with usage-based theories. By analysing corpora, researchers can track variability and change in learner language over time, which helps model the non-linear and adaptive nature of language learning. The development of tools for corpus analysis, such as concordancers and frequency analysis software, has expanded the methodological toolkit for usage based research. These tools allow for detailed examinations of phenomena like distributional learning and the role of constructions in language acquisition.

Although learner corpora have grown in size, they are sometimes not large enough for detailed analyses, especially when multiple factors are combined, such as learner proficiency, task type, and language variety. This results in data sparsity, which can prevent researchers from conducting in-depth analyses involving multifactorial variables. The available data are sometimes unbalanced, which, depending on the point of comparison, might hinder robust comparability across different categories. The design and construction of learner corpora can sometimes limit their usability in SLA research. Learner corpora are designed to capture learner language at a point in time or over a period of time. Whether they may be used to address research questions that were not conceived at the time of their construction, it is only for researchers to say.

Nevertheless, revisiting corpus compilation criteria should be a common practice that informs the community of researchers in this area. We believe that critical perspectives on building learner corpora can only generate fruitful conversations around how to conceptualize the language already present in corpora, as well as new design features to be implemented in future efforts. For example, Pérez-Paredes and Mark (2024) have suggested that an issue in spoken learner corpus interviews is variability in how participants, both learners and interviewers, perceive and execute the task. Learners often struggle to align with the genre of interviews, while interviewers oscillate between passive observers and active facilitators. Many existing learner corpora can be narrow in scope, focusing mainly on written argumentative essays and missing other genres and registers of language use that are crucial for SLA studies. We call for diversification in data collection methods that reflect authentic spoken interaction. Beyond interviews, incorporating tasks that mimic real-life contexts could enrich the understanding of learner language.

Spoken learner corpora are limited in quantity and tend to be challenging to create due to the need for high-quality audio recordings, which often require controlled environments that may reduce the naturalness of the data. Paquot et al. (2024) have stressed that advances in automatic assessment tools that use learner corpus data are still limited. Although some progress has been made, aspects such as pragmatic competence are difficult to evaluate automatically, underscoring the need for further development in this area.

Advances in computational technology have facilitated the use of annotated corpora. However, annotations are not always precise, particularly for learner data, which tends to have more variability and errors compared to native speaker data. Although automated annotation systems like part-of-speech tagging are available, their accuracy often degrades on learner data, leading to inaccuracies that can affect the interpretation of corpus-based studies. The adoption of metadata standards for learner corpora (Paquot et al., 2024) will increase data consistency, comparability, and quality. The LC-meta Version 2 (Paquot et al., 2024) supports the FAIR principles, that is, making data findable, accessible, interoperable, and reusable. Technological advances will continue to have a positive impact on annotation precision and issues of comparability.

Pragmatic aspects of language and natural interaction are difficult to study using current learner corpora due to the limited availability of well-balanced spoken corpora. Existing spoken corpora often lack the variability and natural interaction contexts necessary to explore pragmatic competence comprehensively, which is a major component of SLA research.

The gap between descriptive foci and the theoretical orientation of SLA poses challenges, yet usage-based theories illustrate that bridging this divide is achievable.

Corpus methods enhance our understanding of input exposure and emergent linguistic structures. However, corpus limitations, such as issues of representativeness and annotation quality, constrain their utility. Spoken learner corpora and diversified data reflecting authentic interaction could address these gaps, advancing, among other areas, pragmatic competence research. Technological and methodological improvements promise to enhance corpus precision and applicability in SLA theory and practice.

Corpora in language learning and teaching

Götz and Granger (2024) have noted that the four most important tools and approaches for developing learning and teaching materials and experiences are the use of learner corpora for reference tools, data-driven learning (DDL), CALL applications that offer targeted feedback and integrate learner language data, and textbooks that include frequently encountered language items. In this book, and in O'Keeffe (2023), we note that the future of corpus linguistics methods is closely linked to DDL and the usage-based (UB) model of language acquisition. The UB model emphasizes the importance of exposure to frequently used form-meaning pairings, which leads to the entrenchment of these patterns as grammatical knowledge in the mind of the learner. This approach highlights the role of language patterns in both first and second language acquisition. Götz and Granger (2024) have emphasised the need for enhanced partnerships between researchers and educators to ensure that findings from LC research are effectively integrated into teaching practices and materials. It is urgent to incorporate corpus linguistic methods and DDL into teacher education programmes to equip educators with the necessary skills and knowledge and to emphasise the use of local, teacher-generated learner corpora for creating contextually relevant teaching materials, thus increasing learner motivation and engagement.

CL methods will need to be more carefully curated to suit different learner proficiency levels. This means moving away from purely exploratory DDL towards more structured approaches that can facilitate the learning of beginners by making use of multimodal tools and context-rich inputs (O'Keeffe, 2023). Corpus-driven approaches such as DDL can accelerate language experience through structured exposure to patterns that are sensitive to learners' developmental stages, thereby aiding faster acquisition of grammatical knowledge. However, traditional corpus linguistics methods largely rely on text-based data, which lacks the rich, multimodal context present in natural language acquisition environments. Beginners particularly benefit from multimodal cues such as audio and visual elements to understand language patterns. Thus, corpus linguistics faces the challenge of integrating more context-rich, multimodal input to replicate the naturalistic conditions under which languages are typically learned (Pérez-Paredes & Ordoñana-Guillamón, 2025). It is expected that the integration of AI tools will facilitate the annotation of multimodal communication in ways that can bring multimodality to corpus compilation and eventually to DDL.

Corpus linguistics and ethical research practice

Although anonymity and informed consent have been regularly carried out and obtained in learner corpus research since the early days, other issues need our attention. From a methodological perspective, it is necessary that researchers present objective findings that do not necessarily align with their hypotheses or previous literature. This is an important methodological caveat of CL. As discussed in Chapter 7, researchers need to offer a transparent account of the corpus data analysed as full accountability in reporting and analysis is critical to uphold ethical standards (McEnery & Hardie 2012; McEnery & Brezina, 2022). The goal is to avoid introducing bias by using only favourable evidence. According to McEnery and Hardie (2012), this principle aligns corpus linguistics with scientific methods by promoting comprehensive data usage, enabling findings to be replicable and falsifiable. This requires that corpus data is transparent not only to the researchers and readers of the published paper or chapter, but also to the research community that may wish to replicate the study or use the same data. Total accountability helps maintain scientific rigour, as it guards against confirmation bias by ensuring that the entire dataset relevant to a research question is utilized. Although a corpus represents a limited sample of language, adhering to this principle within that dataset allows for more objective and reliable analyses. Designing a robust corpus is therefore paramount.

One of the challenges is how corpus data is distributed and made accessible to other researchers ethically. While some countries may offer powerful and convenient repositories to share research data, other countries or institutions do not offer such opportunities to host data. An example of the former is the UK Data Service,[32] which offers different access levels, ranging from open datasets to safeguarded data that requires registration and acceptance of an end user license. Controlled datasets that are too sensitive or confidential to be shared online can be used in a secure lab provided to researchers. The Common Language Resources and Technology Infrastructure (CLARIN)[33] offers digital infrastruc-

---

32. URL: https://ukdataservice.ac.uk/
33. URL: https://www.clarin.eu/content/depositing-services

ture for language resources to be archived and made available to researchers. In CLARIN the tools and data from different research centres are designed to be interoperable, enabling the integration of various data collections and the combination of tools from multiple sources. Another digital repository where corpus data can be freely uploaded and shared is IRIS.[34] We would like to see corpus data becoming more widely available to researchers.

Other ethical considerations of relevance to language learning researchers interested in corpus linguistics include legal and copyrights issues in collecting data for a corpus and the nature of the texts included. The former affects the accessibility and openness of the research, while the latter forces researchers to think about whether the texts collected are public or private, and how sharing them impacts their digital footprints, particularly if they are multimodal and contain audio or video. The collection of learner corpus data has often been carried out without the learners, so it may be a good idea to engage with the language learners and unpack the reasons for collecting a corpus and the opportunities it offers to understand language learning and adapt teaching and learning practices accordingly (McEnery & Brookes, 2025).

The future

Never have so many people been engaged in L2 learning across a variety of contexts, including, among many others, digital learning (Chun et al., 2016), informal learning (Conole & Pérez-Paredes, 2017), virtual exchanges (O'Dowd, 2021) and multilingual practices (Ortega, 2019). Given the digital nature of communication nowadays and the increasing computational capacities for capturing and processing language data, corpus linguistics research methods can play an important role in understanding how language learning insights can be enriched through analyses, descriptions, and hypothesis testing research designs that emphasise the analysis of the language used by learners across a variety of contexts. These scenarios create a wealth of opportunities for corpus researchers to design and devise new corpus data and new corpus collection methods that encompass new forms of communication and interaction in digital societies.

As Granger (2024) has recently suggested, the future of learner corpus research will be shaped by the increased diversity of the types of data collected, the increased interdisciplinarity of research teams, involving second language researchers and educators as well as Natural Language Processing (NLP) experts and, by increased automation for tasks such as error analysis, proficiency assess-

---

34. URL: https://www.iris-database.org

ment or annotation. To this, we add the opportunity for AI applications to be streamlined into researchers' toolkit in a way that facilitate the computation and treatment of complex data, from data cleaning to data analysis, whether this implies the generation of code or the testing of scripts for the application of advanced statistical tests.

Professor Michael McCarthy writes in the Foreword to this volume that corpus linguistics and the study of learner corpora are broad churches. This book has tried, using his words, to bring together a vastly diverse disciplinary landscape of research practices and foci. We have tried to offer a well-informed account of the main research CL methods to investigate language learning, looking at both learning and teaching camps.

The book offers a practical, yet comprehensive, overview of the methods that guide the analysis of learner language across words, phraseology, and patterning. The book showcases how corpus methods can be used to bring corpora to language teaching. In the next decade, we will see major growth in the use of learner corpus research. However, at its core will remain the need for ethical, principled, and systematic research methods and practices (Tracy-Ventura, Paquot & Myles, 2021). The more these align with the norms of the field of SLA, the more the synergy between the CL and SLA will thrive.

References

Aarts, J., & Meijs, W. (1984). *Corpus linguistics: Recent developments in the use of computer corpora in English language research.* Brill.

Ackermann, K., & Chen, Y-H. (2013). Developing the academic collocation list (ACL) — A corpus-driven and expert-judged approach. *Journal of English for Academic Purposes, 12*(4), 235–247.

Ädel, A. (2021). Corpus compilation. In A. Ädel (Ed.), *A practical handbook of corpus linguistics* (pp. 3–24). Springer.

Aijmer, K. (2004). Pragmatic markers in spoken interlanguage. *Nordic Journal of English Studies, 3*(1), 173–90.

Aijmer, K. (2011). Well I'm not sure I think… The use of well by non-native speakers. *International Journal of Corpus Linguistics, 16*(2), 231–254.

Aijmer, K. (2015). Corpus pragmatics: From form to function. In A. H. Jucker, K. P. Schneider, & W. Bublitz (Eds.), *Methods in pragmatics* (pp. 555–585). Mouton de Gruyter.

Alexopoulou, T., Geertzen, J., Korhonen, A., & Meurers, D. (2015). Exploring big educational learner corpora for SLA research: Perspectives on relative clauses. *International Journal of Learner Corpus Research, 1*(1), 96–129.

Altenberg, B., & Tapper, M. (1998). The use of adverbial connectors in advanced Swedish learners' written English. In S. Granger (Ed.), *Learner English on computer* (pp. 80–93). Routledge.

Anthony, L. (2022a). *AntConc* (Version 4.1.4) [Computer Software]. Waseda University. Available from https://www.laurenceanthony.net/software

Anthony, L. (2022b). What can software do? In A. O'Keeffe, & M. J. McCarthy (Eds.), *Routledge handbook of corpus linguistics* (2nd ed., pp. 103–25). Routledge.

Arnaudet, M. L., & Barret, M. E. (1990). *Paragraph development* (2nd ed.). Prentice Hall Regents.

Asención-Delaney, Y., Collentine, J. G., Collentine, K., Colmenares, J., & Plonsky, L. (2015). El potencial de la enseñanza del vocabulario basada en corpus: Optimismo con precaución. *Journal of Spanish Language Teaching, 2*(2), 140–151.

Aston, G. (2008). It's only human… In A. Martelli & V. Pulcini (Eds.), *Investigating English with corpora: Studies in honour of Maria Teresa Prat. Monza* (pp. 343–354). Polimetrica International.

Atkins, S., Clear, J., & Ostler, N. (1992). Corpus design criteria. *Literary and Linguistic Computing, 7*(1), 1–16.

Atwell, E. S. (1996). Comparative evaluation of grammatical annotation models. *Industrial Parsing of Software Manuals, 17*(25).

Bailey, D., & Lee, A. R. (2020). An exploratory study of Grammarly in the language learning context: An analysis of test-based, textbook-based and Facebook corpora. *TESOL International Journal, 15*(2), 4–27.

Baisa, V. (2016). Byte level language models (Unpublished doctoral dissertation). Masaryk University. https://is.muni.cz/th/en6ay/thesis_Archive.pdf

Baker, P. (2006). *Using corpora in discourse analysis*. Continuum.

Barfield, A. W. (2006). An exploration of second language collocation knowledge and development (Unpublished doctoral dissertation). Swansea University. https://www .proquest.com/docview/2024598214/fulltextPDF/

Bell, P., & Payant, C. (2021). Designing learner corpora: Collection, transcription, and annotation. In N. Tracy-Ventura & M. Paquot (Eds.), *The Routledge handbook of second language acquisition and corpora* (pp. 53–67). Routledge.

Biber, D. (1988). *Variation across speech and writing*. Cambridge University Press.

Biber, D. (2019). Text-linguistic approaches to register variation. *Register Studies, 1*(1), 42–75.

Biber, D., & Conrad, S. (2009). *Register, genre, and style*. Cambridge University Press.

Biber, D., & Gray, B. (2011). Grammatical change in the noun phrase: The influence of written language use. *English Language and Linguistics, 15*(2), 223–250.

Biber, D., & Gray, B. (2016). *Grammatical complexity in academic English: Linguistic change in writing*. Cambridge University Press.

Biber, D., Gray, B., & Poonpon, K. (2011). Should we use characteristics of conversation to measure grammatical complexity in L2 writing development? *TESOL Quarterly, 45*(1), 5–35.

Biber, D., Reppen, R., Staples, S., & Egbert, J. (2020). Exploring the longitudinal development of grammatical complexity in the disciplinary writing of L2-English university students. *International Journal of Learner Corpus Research, 6*(1), 38–71.

Biber, D., Gray, B., Staples, S., & Egbert, J. (2021). *The register-functional approach to grammatical complexity: Theoretical foundation, descriptive research findings, application*. Routledge.

Biber, D., Johansson, S., Leech, G., Conrad, S., Finegan, E., & Quirk, R. (1999). *Longman grammar of spoken and written English*. Longman.

Bikelienė, L. (2016). Evaluative adjectives in Lithuanian and native students' English writing. *Kalba ir Kontekstai, 7*(1), 197–206.

Bley-Vroman, R. (1983). The comparative fallacy in interlanguage studies: The case of systematicity 1. *Language learning, 33*(1), 1–17.

Bod, R., Hay, J., & Jannedy, S. (Eds.) (2003). *Probabilistic linguistics*. The MIT Press.

Boulton, A. (2009). Data-driven learning: Reasonable fears and rational reassurance. *Indian Journal of Applied Linguistics, 35*(1), 81–106.

Boulton, A. (2012). Hands-on/hands-off: Alternative approaches to data-driven learning. In J. Thomas & A. Boulton (Eds.), *Input, process, and product: Developments in teaching and language corpora* (pp. 152–168). Masaryk University Press.

Boulton, A. (2017). Corpora in language teaching and learning. *Language Teaching, 50*(4), 483–506.

Boulton, A., & Cobb, T. (2017). Corpus use in language learning: A meta-analysis. *Language Learning, 67*(2), 348–393.

Boulton, A. & Pérez-Paredes, P. (2024). Data-driven language learning. In R. Hampel & U. Stickler (Eds.), *Bloomsbury handbook of language learning and technology* (pp. 212–225). Bloomsbury.

Boulton, A., & Vyatkina, N. (2021). Thirty years of data-driven learning: Taking stock and charting new directions over time. *Language Learning & Technology*, 25(3), 66–89.

Brezina, V. (2021). Classical monofactorial (parametric and non-parametric) tests. In M. Paquot & S. T. Gries (Eds.), *A practical handbook of corpus linguistics* (pp. 473–503). Springer.

Brown, R. (1973). *A first language: The early stages*. Harvard University.

Burnard, L. (Ed.) (1995). Users' reference guide for the British National Corpus (Version 1.0). Oxford University Computing Services.

Bybee, J. (2007). *Frequency of use and the organization of language*. Oxford University Press.

Bybee, J., & Hopper, P. (2001). Introduction. In J. Bybee & P. Hopper (Eds.), *Frequency and the emergence of linguistic structure* (pp. 1–26). John Benjamins.

Callies, M. (2015). Learner corpus methodology. In S. Granger, G. Gilquin, & F. Meunier (Eds.), *The Cambridge handbook of learner corpus research* (pp. 35–55). Cambridge University Press.

Capel, A. (2015). The English vocabulary profile. In J. Harrison & F. Barker (Eds.), *English profile in practice* (pp. 9–27). Cambridge University Press.

Carreras, X., Chao, I., Padró, L., & Padró, M. (2004). FreeLing: An open-source suite of language analyzers. In M. T. Lino, M. F. Xavier, F. Ferreira, R. Costa, & R. Silva (Eds.), *Proceedings of the Fourth International Conference on Language Resources and Evaluation (LREC'04)* (pp. 239–242). Lisbon.

Carter, R. A., McCarthy, M. J., Mark, G., & O'Keeffe, A. (2011). *English grammar today*. Cambridge University Press.

Carter, R., & McCarthy, M. (2004). Talking, creating: Interactional language, creativity, and context. *Applied Linguistics*, 25(1), 62–88.

Centre for English Corpus Linguistics. (2023). *Learner corpora around the world*. Louvain-la-Neuve: Université Catholique de Louvain. Retrieved on 30 May 2023 from https://uclouvain.be/en/research-institutes/ilc/cecl/learner-corpora-around-the-world.html

Chambers, A. (2019). Towards the corpus revolution? Bridging the research — practice gap. *Language Teaching*, 52(4), 460–475.

Chang, J.-Y. (2015). A comparison of the first-person pronoun in NS and Korean NNS corpora of English argumentative writing. *English Teaching*, 70(2), 83–106.

Chang, P. (2012). Using a stance corpus to learn about effective authorial stance-taking: A textlinguistic approach. *ReCALL*, 24(2), 209–236.

Chau, M. H. (2003). Contextualising language learning: The role of a topic- and genre-specific pedagogical corpus. *TESL Reporter*, 36(2), 42–54.

Choi, W. (2019). A corpus-based study on 'delexical verb+ noun' collocations made by Korean learners of English. *Journal of Asia TEFL*, 16(1), 279.

Chun, D., Kern, R., & Smith, B. (2016). Technology in language use, language teaching, and language learning. *The Modern Language Journal*, 100(S1), 64–80.

Cobb, T. (1997). Is there any measurable learning from hands-on concordancing? *System*, 25(3), 301–315.

Cobb, T. (1999). Breadth and depth of lexical acquisition with hands-on concordancing. *Computer Assisted Language Learning*, 12(4), 345–360.

Cobb, T. (2005). Constructivism, applied linguistics, and language education. *Encyclopedia of language and linguistics* (Vol. 3, 2nd. ed., pp. 5–88). Elsevier.

Cobb, T., & Boulton, A. (2015). Classroom applications of corpus analysis. In D. Biber, & R. Reppen (Eds.), *Cambridge handbook of English corpus linguistics* (pp. 478–497). Cambridge University Press.

Collentine, J. (2000). Insights into the construction of grammatical knowledge provided by user-behaviour tracking technologies. *Language Learning & Technology*, 3(2), 46–60.

Conole, G., & Pérez-Paredes, P. (2017). Adult language learning in informal settings and the role of mobile learning. In S. Yu, M. Ally, & A. Tsinakos (Eds.), *Mobile and ubiquitous learning. An international handbook.* (pp. 45–58). Springer.

Conrad, S. (2019). Register in English for academic purposes and English for specific purposes. *Register Studies*, 1(1), 168–198.

Cotos, E. (2014). Enhancing writing pedagogy with learner corpus data. *ReCALL*, 26(2), 202–224.

Cotos, E. (2017). Language for specific purposes and corpus-based pedagogy. In C.A. Chapelle & S. Sauro (Eds.), *The handbook of technology and second language teaching and learning* (pp. 248–264). Wiley.

Council of Europe (2001). *Common European Framework of Reference for Languages: Learning, teaching, assessment.* Council of Europe. Retrieved on 26 November 2024 from https://www.coe.int/en/web/common-european-framework-reference-languages

Cowie, A.P. (1994). Phraseology. In J.M.Y. Simpson & R.E. Asher (Eds.), *The encyclopedia of language and linguistics* (Vol. 6). Pergamon.

Crawford, W. (2008). Place and time adverbials in native and non-native English student writing. In A. Ädel & R. Reppen (Eds.), *Corpora and discourse: The challenges of different settings* (pp. 267–289). John Benjamins.

Crosthwaite, P., Wong, L.L.C., & Cheung, J. (2019). Characterising postgraduate students' corpus query and usage patterns for disciplinary data-driven learning. *ReCALL*, 31(3), 255–275.

Curry, N., & Pérez-Paredes, P. (2023). Using corpus linguistics and grounded theory to explore interview and focus groups of EMI stakeholders. In S. Curle & J. Pun (Eds.), *Qualitative research methods in English medium instruction for emerging researchers* (pp. 45–61). Routledge.

Curry, N., Mark, G., Lee, H., McEnery, T., Burton, G., Clark, T., & Shin, D. (2025). Applying corpus research indirectly to language teaching materials and assessment development. In G. Brookes, N. Curry, & R. Love (Eds.), *Applications of corpus linguistics: Established and emergent contexts.* Cambridge University Press.

Dang, T. (2019). Corpus-based word lists in second language vocabulary research, learning, and teaching. In S. Webb (Ed.), *The Routledge handbook of vocabulary studies* (pp. 288–303). Routledge.

Daskalovska, N. (2015). Corpus-based versus traditional learning of collocations. *Computer Assisted Language Learning*, 28(2), 130–144.

Davies, M. (2008–). *The corpus of contemporary American English (COCA).* https://www.english-corpora.org/coca/

De Cock, S. (2003). Recurrent sequences of words in native speaker and advanced learner spoken and written English: A corpus-driven approach (Unpublished doctoral dissertation). UCL-Université Catholique de Louvain.

De Cock, S. (2011). Preferred patterns of use of positive and negative evaluative adjectives in native and learner speech: An ELT perspective. In A. Frankenberg-Garcia, F. Lynne, & A. Guy (Eds.), *New trends in corpora and language learning* (pp. 198–212). Continuum. https://dial.uclouvain.be/pr/boreal/en/object/boreal%3A75959

De Haan, P. (2000). Tagging non-native English with the TOSCA-ICLE tagger. In C. Mair & M. Hundt (Eds.), *Corpus linguistics and linguistic theory* (pp. 69–79). Rodopi.

De Haan, P. (2015). Nouns and noun phrases in advanced Dutch EFL writing: From quantitative to qualitative longitudinal data analysis. In E. Castello, K. Ackerley, & F. Coccetta (Eds.), *Studies in learner corpus linguistics: Research and applications for foreign language teaching and assessment* (pp. 127–142). Peter Lang. http://repository.ubn .ru.nl/handle/2066/155647

De Marneffe, M.C., Dozat, T., Silveira, N., Haverinen, K., Ginter, F., Nivre, J., & Manning, C.D. (2014). Universal Stanford dependencies: A cross-linguistic typology. In *LREC* (Vol. 14, pp. 4585–4592).

Deshors, S.C., & Gries, S.T. (2021). Comparing learner corpora. In N. Tracy-Ventura & M. Paquot (Eds.), *The Routledge handbook of second language acquisition and corpora* (pp. 105–118). Routledge.

Díez-Bedmar, M.B., & Pérez-Paredes, P. (2020). Noun phrase complexity in young Spanish EFL learners' writing: Complementing syntactic complexity indices with corpus-driven analyses. *International Journal of Corpus Linguistics, 25*(1), 1–33.

Dong, O.L., & Lee, J.-Q. (2017). Exploring the use of general adverbs in Korean pre-university learners' L2 writing. *Studies in Linguistics, 42*, 419–439.

Dörnyei, Z. (2007). *Research methods in applied linguistics*. Oxford University Press.

Douglas Fir Group. (2016). A transdisciplinary framework for SLA in a multilingual world. *The Modern Language Journal, 100*(S1), 19–47.

Durrant, P., & Schmitt, N. (2009). To what extent do native and non-native writers make use of collocations? *International Review of Applied Linguistics in Language Teaching, 47*(2), 157–177.

Ellis, N.C. (2006). Meta-analysis, human cognition, and language learning. In J.M. Norris & L. Ortega (Eds.), *Synthesizing research on language learning and teaching* (pp. 301–322). John Benjamins.

Ellis, N.C. (2017). Cognition, corpora, and computing: Triangulating research in usage-based language learning. *Language Learning, 67*(S1), 40–65.

Ellis, N.C., & Ferreira-Junior, F. (2009). Constructions and their acquisition: Islands and the distinctiveness of their occupancy. *Annual Review of Cognitive Linguistics, 7*(1), 188–221.

Ellis, N.C., Römer, U., & O'Donnell, M.B. (2016). Constructions and usage-based approaches to language acquisition. *Language Learning, 66*, 23–44.

Ellis, N.C. (2008). Phraseology: The periphery and the heart of language. In S. Granger & F. Meunier (Eds.), *Phraseology in foreign language learning and teaching* (pp. 1–14). John Benjamins.

Firth, J.R. (1957a). *Modes of meaning, papers in linguistics*. Oxford University Press.

Firth, J.R. (1957b). *Studies in linguistic analysis*. Wiley-Blackwell.

doi Fitriana, K., & Nurazni, L. (2022). Exploring English department students' perceptions on using grammarly to check the grammar in their writing. *Journal of English Teaching, 8*(1), 15–25.

Fligelstone, S., Pacey, M., & Rayson, P. (1997). How to generalise the task of annotation. In R. Garside, G. N. Leech, & A. M. McEnery (Eds.), *Corpus annotation: Linguistic information from computer text corpora* (pp. 122–136). Longman.

doi Flowerdew, J. (2006). Use of signalling nouns in a learner corpus. *International Journal of Corpus Linguistics, 11*(3), 345–362.

doi Flowerdew, J. (2010). Use of signalling nouns across L1 and L2 writer corpora. *International Journal of Corpus Linguistics, 15*(1), 36–55.

doi Flowerdew, L. (2015). Data-driven learning and language learning theories: Whither the twain shall meet. In A. Leńko-Szymańska & A. Boulton (Eds.), *Multiple affordances of language corpora for data-driven learning* (pp. 16–36). John Benjamins.

doi Forti, L. (2023). *Corpus use in Italian language pedagogy: Exploring the effects of data-driven learning.* Routledge.

Francis, G., Hunston, S., & Manning, E. (Eds.). (1996). *Collins COBUILD grammar patterns 1: Verbs.* Harper Collins.

doi Gabel, S. (2001). Over-indulgence and under-representation in interlanguage: Reflections on the utilization of concordances in self-directed foreign language learning. *Computer-Assisted Language Learning, 14*, 269–288.

doi Gablasova, D., Brezina, V., & McEnery, T. (2017). Collocations in corpus-based language learning research: Identifying, comparing, and interpreting the evidence. *Language learning, 67*(S1), 130–154.

doi Gablasova, D., Brezina, V., & McEnery, T. (2019). The Trinity Lancaster Corpus: Development, description and application. *International Journal of Learner Corpus Research, 5*(2), 126–158.

Gabrielatos, C. (2005). Corpora and language teaching: Just a fling or wedding bells? *Teaching English as a Second or Foreign Language, 8*(4), 1–34.

doi Gaskell, D., & Cobb, T. (2004). Can learners use concordance feedback for writing errors? *System, 32*(3), 301–319.

doi Gillings, M., Mautner, G., & Baker, P. (2023). *Corpus-assisted discourse studies.* Cambridge University Press.

doi Gilmore, A., & Millar, N. (2018). The language of civil engineering research articles: A corpus-based approach. *English for Specific Purposes, 51*, 1–17.

doi Gilquin, G. (2015). From design to collection of learner corpora. In S. Granger, G. Gilquin, & F. Meunier (Eds.), *The Cambridge handbook of learner corpus research* (pp. 9–34). Cambridge University Press.

doi Gilquin, G. (2015). The use of phrasal verbs by French-speaking EFL learners. A constructional and collostructional corpus-based approach. *Corpus Linguistics and Linguistic Theory, 11*(1), 51–88.

doi Gilquin, G. (2018). Exploring the spoken learner English construction: A corpus-driven approach. In R. Alonso (Ed.), *Speaking in a second language* (pp. 127–152). John Benjamins.

doi Gilquin, G., & Paquot, M. (2008). Too chatty: Learner academic writing and register variation. *English Text Construction, 1*(1), 41–61.

Gilquin, G., De Cock, S., & Granger, S. (2010). *The Louvain International Database of Spoken English Interlanguage.* Handbook and CD-ROM.

Gilquin, G., Papp, S., & Díez-Bedmar, M. B. (Eds.). (2008). *Linking up contrastive and learner corpus research.* Rodopi.

Goldberg, A. E. (2006). *Constructions at work: The nature of generalization in language.* Oxford University Press.

Götz, S. (2021). Analyzing a learner corpus with a concordancer. In N. Tracy-Ventura & M. Paquot (Eds.), *The Routledge handbook of second language acquisition and corpora* (pp. 69–89). Routledge.

Granger, S. (1994). The learner corpus: A revolution in applied linguistics. *English Today, 10*(3), 25–33.

Granger, S. (1996). From CA to CIA and back: An integrated approach to computerized bilingual and learner corpora. In K. Aijmer, B. Altenberg, & M. Johansson (Eds.), *Languages in contrast. Text-based cross-linguistic studies* (pp. 37–51). Lund University Press.

Granger, S. (2002). A bird's-eye view of learner corpus research. In S. Granger, S. Petch-Tyson, & J. Hung (Eds.), *Computer learner corpora, second language acquisition and foreign language teaching* (pp. 3–36). John Benjamins.

Granger, S. (2003). The international corpus of learner English: A new resource for foreign language learning and teaching and second language acquisition research. *TESOL Quarterly, 37*(3), 538–546.

Granger, S. (2009). The contribution of learner corpora to second language acquisition and foreign language teaching: A critical evaluation. In K. Aijmer (Ed.), *Corpora and language teaching* (pp. 13–32). John Benjamins.

Granger, S. (2015). Contrastive interlanguage analysis: A reappraisal. *International Journal of Learner Corpus Research, 1*(1), 7–24.

Granger, S. (2021). Commentary: Have learner corpus research and second language acquisition finally met? In B. Le Bruyn & M. Paquot (Eds.), *Learner corpus research meets second language acquisition* (pp. 243–257). Cambridge University Press.

Granger, S. (2024). From early to future learner corpus research. *International Journal of Learner Corpus Research, 10*(2), 247–279.

Granger, S., & Meunier, F. (2008). Introduction. In S. Granger & F. Meunier (Eds.), *Phraseology in foreign language learning and teaching* (pp. 15–20). John Benjamins.

Granger, S., & Rayson, P. (1998). Automatic profiling of learner texts. In S. Granger (Ed.). *Learner English on computer* (pp. 119–131). Routledge.

Granger, S., Dagneaux, E., Meunier, F., & Paquot, M. (2002). *The International Corpus of Learner English, (ICLE).* Presses Universitaires de Louvain.

Granger, S., Dupont, M., Meunier, F., Naets, H., & Paquot, M. (2020). *The International Corpus of Learner English* (Version 3). Presses universitaires de Louvain. https://dial.uclouvain.be/pr/boreal/object/boreal:229877

Gray, B. (2022). What can a corpus tell us about registers and genres? In A. O'Keeffe & M. J. McCarthy (Eds.), *Routledge handbook of corpus linguistic,* (2nd ed., pp. 235–249). Routledge.

Gray, B., & Biber, D. (2015). Phraseology. In D. Biber & R. Reppen (Eds.), *Cambridge handbook of corpus linguistics* (pp. 125–145). Cambridge University Press.

Gray, D. E. (2018). *Doing research in the real world*. Sage.

Greaves, C., & Warren, M. (2022). What can a corpus tell us about multi-word units? In A. O'Keeffe & M. J. McCarthy (Eds.), *Routledge handbook of corpus linguistics* (2nd ed., pp. 204–220). Routledge.

Green, A. (2012). *Language functions revisited: Theoretical and empirical bases for language construct definition across the ability range*. Cambridge University Press.

Gries, S. T. (2013). 50-something years of work on collocations: What is or should be next. *International Journal of Corpus Linguistics, 18*(1), 137–166.

Gries, S. T., & Stefanowitsch, A. (2004a). Extending collostructional analysis: A corpus-based perspective on alternations. *International Journal of Corpus Linguistics, 9*(1), 97–129.

Gries, S. T., & Stefanowitsch, A. (2004b). Co-varying collexemes in the into-causative. In M. Achard & S. Kemmer (Eds.), *Language, culture, and mind* (pp. 225–236). CSLI.

Gries, S. T. (2018). Operationalizations of domain-general mechanisms cognitive linguists often rely on: A perspective from quantitative corpus linguistics. In S. Engelberg, H. Lobin, K. Steyer, & S. Wolfer (Eds.), *Wortschätze: Dynamik, Muster, Komplexität* (pp. 75–90). Berlin: De Gruyter.

Gries, S. T. (2017). *Quantitative corpus linguistics with R. A practical introduction* (2nd ed.). Routledge.

Gries, St. T. (2022). How to use statistics in quantitative corpus analysis. In A. O'Keeffe & M. J. McCarthy (Eds.), *Routledge handbook of corpus linguistics* (2nd ed., pp. 168–181). Routledge.

Gui, S., & Yang, H. (2002). *Chinese Learner English Corpus*. Shanghai Foreign Language Education Press.

Hackstein, O., & Sandell, R. (2023). The rise of colligations: English can't stand and German nicht ausstehen können. *International Journal of Corpus Linguistics, 28*(1), 60–90.

Han, Z.-H., & R. Finneran. (2013). Re-engaging the interface debate: Strong, weak, none, or all? *International Journal of Applied Linguistics, 24*(3), 370–389.

Hancock, V., & Sanell, A. (2009). The acquisition of four adverbs in a learner corpus of L2 French. *Discours. Revue de Linguistique Psycholinguistique et Informatique, 5*.

Harrison, J., & Barker, F. (2015). *English profile in practice*. Cambridge University Press.

Hasselgård, H. (2015). Lexicogrammatical features of adverbs in advanced learner English. *ITL International Journal of Applied Linguistics, 166*(1), 163–189.

Hawkins, J. A., & Buttery, P. (2009). Using learner language from corpora to profile levels of proficiency: Insights from the English Profile programme. In L. Taylor & C. J. Weir (Eds.), *Language testing matters: Investigating the wider social and educational impact of assessment* (pp. 158–175). Cambridge University Press.

Hawkins, J. A., & Buttery, P. (2010). Criterial features in learner corpora: Theory and illustrations. *English Profile Journal, 1*(1), 1–23.

Hawkins, J., & Filipović, L. (2012). *Criterial features in L2 English: Specifying the reference levels of the Common European Framework*. Cambridge University Press.

Hernandez, T. A. (2018). Input flooding. In J. I. Liontas (Ed.), *The TESOL encyclopedia of English language teaching* (pp. 1–7). John Wiley & Sons.

Heuboeck, A., Holmes, J., & Nesi, H. (2008). *The BAWE corpus manual*. University of Reading.

Hilpert, M. (2014). Collostructional analysis. In D. Glynn & J. Robinson (Eds.), *Corpus methods for semantics. Quantitative studies in polysemy and synonymy* (pp. 391–405). John Benjamins.

Hilpert, M., & Blasi, D.E. (2021). Fixed-effects regression modeling. In M. Paquot & S.T. Gries, (Eds.), *A practical handbook of corpus linguistics* (pp. 505–533). Springer.

Hoey, M. (1991). *Patterns of lexis in text*. Oxford University Press.

Hoey, M. (2005). *Lexical priming: A new theory of words and language*. Routledge.

Hornby, A.S. (1974). *Oxford advanced learner's dictionary of current English*. Oxford University Press.

Huang, L.-S. (2011). Corpus-aided language learning. *ELT Journal, 65*, 481–484.

Huang, Z. (2014). The effect of paper-based DDL on the acquisition of lexico-grammatical patterns in L2 writing. *ReCALL, 26*(2), 163–183.

Hunston, S. (2002). Pattern grammar, language teaching, and linguistic variation. In R. Reppen, S.M. Fitzmaurice, & D. Biber (Eds.), *Using corpora to explore linguistic variation* (pp. 167–183). John Benjamins.

Hunston, S. (2022). *Corpora in applied linguistics*. Cambridge University Press.

Hunston, S. (2022). How can a corpus be used to explore patterns? In M. McCarthy & A. O´Keeffe (Eds.), *The Routledge handbook of corpus linguistics* (2nd ed., pp. 140–154). Routledge.

Hunston, S. (2019). Patterns, constructions, and applied linguistics. *International Journal of Corpus Linguistics, 24*(3), 324–353.

Hunston, S., & Sinclair, J. McH. (2000). A local grammar of evaluation. In S. Hunston & G. Thompson (Eds.), *Evaluation in text: Authorial stance and the construction of discourse* (pp. 74–101). Oxford University Press.

Hunt, K.W. (1965). *Grammatical structures written at three grade levels*. National Council of Teachers of English.

Ishii, Y., & Tono, Y. (2018). Investigating Japanese EFL learners' overuse/underuse of English grammar categories and their relevance to CEFR levels. In *Proceedings of the 4th Asia Pacific Corpus Linguistics Conference 2018* (pp. 160–165). Retrieved on 29 September 2021 from http://www.tufs.ac.jp/ts/personal/corpuskun/pdf/2018/Ishii&Tono2018.pdf

Johansson, S. (2009). Some thoughts on corpora and second-language acquisition. In K. Aijmer (Ed.), *Corpora and language teaching* (pp. 33–44). John Benjamins.

Johns, T. (1990). From printout to handout: Grammar and vocabulary teaching in the context of data-driven learning. *CALL Austria, 10*, 14–34.

Johns, T. (1994). From printout to handout: Grammar and vocabulary teaching in the context of data-driven learning. In T. Odlin (Ed.), *Perspectives on pedagogical grammar* (pp. 293–313). Cambridge University Press.

Jones, N., & Saville, N. (2009). European language policy: Assessment, learning, and the CEFR. *Annual Review of Applied Linguistics, 29*, 51–63.

Kilgarriff, A., Baisa, V., Bušta, J., Jakubíček, M., Kovář, V., Michelfeit, J., Rychlý, P., & Suchomel, V. (2014). The Sketch Engine: Ten years on. *Lexicography, 1*, 7–36.

King, N., Horrocks, C., & Brooks, J. (2019). *Interviews in qualitative research* (2nd ed.). Sage.

doi   Knight, D., & Adolphs, S. (2022). Building a spoken corpus: What are the basics? In A. O'Keeffe & M. McCarthy (Eds.), *The Routledge handbook of corpus linguistics* (2nd ed., pp. 21–34). Routledge.

doi   Knight, D., O'Keeffe, A., Mark, G., Fitzgerald, C., McNamara, J., Palmer-Fahey, T., Farr, F., Peraldi, S., Adolphs, S., Clark, L. & Cowan, B. (2024). Indicating engagement in online workplace meetings: The role of backchannelling head nods, *International Journal of Corpus Linguistics*, 29(3), 389–416.

Kobayashi, T. (2008). Usage of countable and uncountable nouns by Japanese learners of English: Two studies using the ICLE error-tagged Japanese sub-corpus. *Gakuen*, 816(10), 73–82.

doi   Kreyer, R. (2021). Collocations in learner English. In P. Pérez-Paredes & G. Mark (Eds.), *Beyond concordance lines: Corpora in language education* (pp. 97–120). John Benjamins.

Krishnamurthy, R. (2000). Collocation: From silly ass to lexical sets. In C. Heffer, H. Saunston, & G. Fox (Eds.), *Words in context: A tribute to John Sinclair on his retirement* (pp. 31–47). University of Birmingham.

Kyle, K. (2016). Measuring syntactic development in L2 writing: Fine grained indices of syntactic complexity and usage-based indices of syntactic sophistication (Unpublished doctoral dissertation). Georgia State University. http://scholarworks.gsu.edu/alesl_diss/35

doi   Kyle, K., & Crossley, S.A. (2015). Automatically assessing lexical sophistication: Indices, tools, findings, and application. *TESOL Quarterly* 49(4), 757–786.

doi   Kyle, K., & Crossley, S.A. (2018). Measuring syntactic complexity in L2 writing using finegrained clausal and phrasal indices. *Modern Language Journal*, 102(2), 333–349.

doi   Kyle, K., Crossley, S.A., & Berger, C. (2018). The tool for the analysis of lexical sophistication (TAALES) (Version 2.0). *Behavior Research Methods*, 50, 1030–1046.

doi   Lai, C., & Zhao, Y. (2006). Noticing and text-based chat. *Language Learning & Technology*, 10(3), 1094–3501.

doi   Laufer, B., & Hulstijn, J.H. (2001). Incidental vocabulary acquisition in a second language. The construct of task-induced involvement. *Applied Linguistics*, 22(1), 1–26.

doi   Laufer, B., & Nation, P. (1999). A vocabulary-size test of controlled productive ability. *Language Testing*, 16, 33–51.

doi   Leal Méndez, T., & Slabakova, R. (2014). The Interpretability Hypothesis again: A partial replication of Tsimpli and Dimitrakopoulou (2007). *International Journal of Bilingualism*, 18(6), 537–557.

doi   Lee, D., & Swales, J. (2006). A corpus-based EAP course for NNS doctoral students: Moving from available specialized corpora to self-compiled corpora. *English for Specific Purposes*, 25(1), 56–75.

doi   Lee, H., Warschauer, M., & Lee, J.H. (2019). The effects of corpus use on second language vocabulary learning: A multilevel meta-analysis. *Applied Linguistics*, 40, 721–753.

Leech, G. (1997). Teaching and language corpora: A convergence. In A. Wichmann, S. Fligelstone, T. McEnery, & G. Knowles (Eds.), *Teaching and language corpora* (pp. 1–24). Longman.

doi   Leech, G. (2015). Descriptive grammar. In D. Biber & R. Reppen (Eds.), *The Cambridge handbook of English corpus linguistics* (pp. 146–176). Cambridge University Press.

Leedham, M., & Fernandez-Parra, M. (2017). Recounting and reflecting: The use of first person pronouns in Chinese, Greek and British students' assignments in engineering. *Journal of English for Academic Purposes, 26*, 66–77.

Leńko-Szymańska, A., & Boulton, A. (2015). Introduction: Data-driven learning in language pedagogy. In A. Leńko-Szymańska & A. Boulton (Eds.), *Multiple affordances of language corpora for data-driven learning* (pp. 1–14). John Benjamins.

Leow, R. P. (2015a). Deconstructing the construct of learning. In R. P. Leow, *Explicit learning in the L2 classroom* (pp. 141–153). Routledge.

Leow, R. P. (2015b). *Explicit learning in the L2 classroom: A student-centered approach.* Routledge.

Lin, Y., Michel, J. B., Lieberman, E. A., Orwant, J., Brockman, W., & Petrov, S. (2012, July). Syntactic annotations for the google books ngram corpus. In Min Zhang (Ed.), *Proceedings of the ACL 2012 system demonstrations* (pp. 169–174). ACL. Retrieved on 4 December 2024 from https://aclanthology.org/P12-3000

Liu, D., & Jiang, P. (2009). Using a corpus-based lexicogrammatical approach to grammar instruction in EFL and ESL contexts. *Modern Language Journal, 93*(1), 61–78.

Loewen, S., & Plonsky, L. (2016). *An A–Z of applied linguistics research methods.* Bloomsbury.

Lorenz, G. (1998). Overstatement in advanced learners' writing: Stylistic aspects of adjective intensification. In S. Granger (Ed.), *Learner English on computer* (pp. 53–66). Addison Wesley Longman.

Love, R. (2020). *Overcoming challenges in corpus construction: The spoken British National Corpus 2014.* Routledge.

Lozano, C. (2022). CEDEL2: Design, compilation and web interface of an online corpus for L2 Spanish acquisition research. *Second Language Research, 38*(4), 965–983.

Lu, X. (2010). What can corpus software reveal about language development? In A. O'Keeffe & M. McCarthy (Eds.), *The Routledge handbook of corpus linguistics* (pp. 184–193). Routledge.

Lu, X. (2022). *Corpus linguistics and second language acquisition: Perspectives, issues, and findings.* Routledge.

Lundell, F. F. (2021). Formulaicity. In N. Tracy-Ventura & M. Paquot (Eds.), *The Routledge handbook of second language acquisition and corpora* (pp. 370–381). Routledge.

Luo, Q. (2016). The effects of data-driven learning activities on EFL learners' writing development. *SpringerPlus, 5*(1), 12–35.

Mackey, A., & Gass, S. M. (2022). *Second language research: Methodology and design* (3rd ed.). Routledge.

Mackey, A., & Gass, S. M. (Eds.). (2023). *Current approaches in second language acquisition research: A practical guide.* Wiley.

Martinez, R., & Schmitt, N. (2012). A phrasal expressions list. *Applied Linguistics, 33*(3), 299–320.

McCarthy, M. (1998). *Spoken language and applied linguistics.* Cambridge University Press.

McCarthy, M. J., & O'Keeffe, A. (2010). Historical perspective: What are corpora and how have they evolved? In A. O'Keeffe, & M. J. McCarthy (Eds.), *The Routledge handbook of corpus linguistics* (pp. 3–13). Routledge.

McCarthy, M. J., O'Keeffe, A., & Walsh, S. (2010). *The vocabulary matrix: Understanding, learning, teaching.* Cengage.

McEnery, T., & Brezina, V. (2023). *Fundamental principles of corpus linguistics.* Cambridge University Press.

McEnery, T., & Brookes, G. (2025). Corpus linguistics and ethics. In P. I. De Costa, A. Rabie-Ahmed, & C. Cinaglia (Eds.), *Ethical issues in applied linguistics scholarship* (pp. 28–44). John Benjamins.

McEnery, T., & Hardie, A. (2012). *Corpus linguistics: Method, theory and practice.* Cambridge University Press.

McEnery, T., Brezina, V., Gablasova, D., & Banerjee, J. (2019). Corpus linguistics, learner corpora, and SLA: Employing technology to analyze language use. *Annual Review of Applied Linguistics, 39,* 74–92.

McEnery, T., Xiao, R., & Tono, Y. (2006). *Corpus-based language studies: An advanced resource book.* Routledge.

McKay, S. (1980). Teaching the syntactic, semantic and pragmatic dimensions of verbs. *TESOL Quarterly, 14*(1), 17–26.

McNamara, J. (2020). Take him to the cleaners and make him do your homework: A corpus-based analysis of lexical structure used by English language learners (Unpublished doctoral dissertation). University of Limerick.

Meunier, F. (2011). Corpus linguistics and second/foreign language learning: Exploring multiple paths. *Revista Brasileira de Linguística Aplicada, 11*(2), 459–477.

Mishan, F. (2004). Authenticating corpora for language learning: A problem and its resolution. *ELT journal, 58*(3), 219–227.

Mitchell, R. (2020). Corpora and instructed second language acquisition. In N. Tracy-Ventura & M. Paquot (Eds.), *The Routledge handbook of second language acquisition and corpora* (pp. 252–264). Routledge.

Mitkovska, L., & Bužarovska, E. (2018). Subject pronoun (non)realization in the English learner language of Macedonian speakers. *Second Language Research, 34*(4), 463–485.

Murakami, A., & Alexopoulou, T. (2016). L1 influence on the acquisition order of English grammatical morphemes: A learner corpus study. *Studies in Second Language Acquisition, 38*(3), 365–401.

Myles, F. (2015). Second language acquisition theory and learner corpus research. In S. Granger, G. Gilquin, & F. Meunier (Eds.) *The Cambridge handbook of learner corpus research* (pp. 309–332). Cambridge University Press.

Myles, F. (2021). Commentary: An SLA perspective on learner corpus research. In B. Le Bryn & M. Paquot (Eds.), *Learner corpus research meets second language acquisition* (pp. 258–270). Cambridge University Press

Myles, F. (2005). Interlanguage corpora and second language acquisition research. *Second Language Research, 21*(4), 373–391.

Nation, I., & Hunston, S. (2013). Finding and learning multiword units. In *Learning vocabulary in another language* (pp. 479–513). Cambridge University Press.

Nation, I. S. P. (1990). *Teaching and learning vocabulary.* Newbury House.

Nation, P., & Beglar, D. (2007). A vocabulary size test. *The Language Teacher, 31*(7), 9–13.

Nesi, H., Gardner, S., Thompson, P., & Wickens, P. (2008). *British Academic Written English Corpus*. Oxford Text Archive. http://hdl.handle.net/20.500.12024/2539

Nesselhauf, N. (2005). *Collocations in a learner corpus*. John Benjamins.

Newman, J. & Cox, C. (2020). Corpus Annotation. In M. Paquot & S. T. Gries (Eds.), *A Practical handbook of corpus linguistics* (pp. 25–48). Springer.

O'Dowd, R. (2021). Virtual exchange: Moving forward into the next decade. *Computer Assisted Language Learning, 34*(3), 209–224.

O'Keeffe, A. (2021a). Data-driven learning: A call for a broader research gaze. *Language Teaching, 54*(2), 259–272.

O'Keeffe, A. (2021b). Data-driven learning, theories of learning and second language acquisition: In search of intersections. In P. Pérez-Paredes & G. Mark (Eds.), *Beyond concordance lines: Corpora in language education* (pp. 35–55). John Benjamins.

O'Keeffe, A., & Mark, G. (2017). The English Grammar Profile of learner competence: Methodology and key findings. *International Journal of Corpus Linguistics, 22*(4), 457–89.

O'Keeffe, A., & McCarthy, M. (Eds.). (2022). *The Routledge handbook of corpus linguistics* (2nd ed.). Routledge.

O'Keeffe, A., & McCarthy, M. J. (2022). Of what is past, or passing, or to come: Corpus linguistics, changes and challenges. In A. O'Keeffe & M. J. McCarthy (Eds.), *The Routledge handbook of corpus linguistics* (2nd ed., pp. 1–9). Routledge.

O'Keeffe, A., McCarthy, M. J., & Carter, R. (2007). *From corpus to classroom: Language use and language teaching*. Cambridge University Press.

Ortega, L. (2013). SLA for the 21st century: Disciplinary progress, transdisciplinary relevance, and the bi/multilingual turn. *Language learning, 63*, 1–24.

Ortega, L. (2019). SLA and the study of equitable multilingualism. *The Modern Language Journal, 103*, 23–38.

Osborne, J. (2008). Adverb placement in post-intermediate learner English: A contrastive study of learner corpora. In G. Gilquin, S. Papp, & M. B. Díez-Bedmar (Eds.), *Linking up contrastive and learner corpus research* (pp. 127–146). Rodopi.

Osborne, J. (2015). Transfer and learner corpus research. In S. Granger, G. Gilquin, & F. Meunier (Eds.), *The Cambridge handbook of learner corpus research* (pp. 333–356). Cambridge University Press.

Papp, S. (2007). Inductive learning and self-correction with the use of learner and reference corpora. In E. Hilgado, L. Quereda, & J. Santana (Eds.), *Corpora in the foreign language classroom* (pp. 207–220). Rodopi.

Paquot, M., & Gries, S. T. (Eds.), (2021). *A practical handbook of corpus linguistics*. Springer.

Paquot, M., & Granger, S. (2012). Formulaic language in learner corpora. *Annual Review of Applied Linguistics, 32*, 130–149.

Paquot, M., & Tracy-Ventura, N. (2023). Using foreign and second language learner corpora. In A. Mackey & S. Gass (Eds.), *Current approaches in second language acquisition research: A practical guide* (pp. 96–119). Wiley-Blackwelll.

Paquot, M., König, A., Stemle, E., & J.-C. Frey. (2023). *Core metadata schema for learner corpora*. UCLouvain.

Park, H. (2017). Noun phrases in Korean students' written English. *The Journal of Linguistics Science, 81*, 109–131.

Pérez-Paredes, P. (2010). The death of the adverb revisited: Attested uses of adverbs in native and non-native comparable corpora of spoken English. In M. Moreno Jaén, F. Serrano Valverde, & M. Calzada Pérez (Eds.), *Exploring new paths in language pedagogy. Lexis and corpus-based language teaching* (pp. 157–172). Equinox.

Pérez-Paredes, P. (2020). *Corpus linguistics for education: A guide for research.* Routledge.

Pérez-Paredes, P. (2022). A systematic review of the uses and spread of corpora and data-driven learning in CALL research during 2011–2015. *Computer Assisted Language Learning, 35*, 1–2, 36–61.

Pérez-Paredes, P. (2024). Frequency and keyness: What are they and how can they be used to explore representation? In C. Taylor & F. Heritage (Eds.), *An introduction to corpus and discourse studies: Analyzing representation* (pp. 43–65). Routledge.

Pérez-Paredes, P., & Curry, N. (2023). Exploring the internationalization and glocalization constructs in EMEMUS lecturers' interviews and focus groups. In E. Dafouz & U. Smit (Eds.), *Researching English-medium higher education: Diverse applications and critical evaluations of the ROAD-MAPPING framework* (1st ed., pp. 92–116). Routledge.

Pérez-Paredes, P. & Curry, N. (2025). Corpus linguistics in Languages for Specific Purposes (LSP). In T. Roelcke, R. Breeze & J. Engberg (Eds.), *Handbook of Specialized Communication*, pp. 407–432. De Gruyter.

Pérez-Paredes, P. & Curry, N. (2024). Epistemologies of corpus linguistics across disciplines. *Research Methods in Applied Linguistics, 3*(3).

Pérez-Paredes, P., & Díez-Bedmar, M. B. (2019). Researching learner language through POS keyword and syntactic complexity analyses. In S. Götz & J. Mukherjee (Eds.), *Learner corpora and language teaching* (pp. 101–127). John Benjamins.

Pérez-Paredes, P., & Mark, G. (2022). What can corpora tell us about language learning? In M. McCarthy & A. O´Keeffe (Eds.), *The Routledge handbook of corpus linguistics*, (2nd ed., pp. 313–327). Routledge.

Pérez-Paredes, P., & Ordoñana-Guillamón, C. (2025). Future challenges and opportunities for data-driven learning. In L. McCallum & D. Tafazoli (Eds.), *The Palgrave encyclopedia of computer-assisted language learning.* Springer.

Pérez-Paredes, P., & Sánchez-Tornel, M. (2014). Adverb use and language proficiency in young learners' writing. *International Journal of Corpus Linguistics, 19*(2), 178–200.

Pérez-Paredes, P., Sánchez-Tornel, M., & Alcaraz Calero, J. M. (2012). Learners' search patterns during corpus-based focus-on-form activities. *International Journal of Corpus Linguistics, 17*(4), 483–516.

Philip, G. (2008). Adverb use in EFL student writing: From learner dictionary to text production. In E. Bernal & J. DeCesaris (Eds.), *Proceedings of the XIII Euralex International Congress.* Universitat Pompeu Fabra. Istitut universitari de lingüística aplicada. Retrieved on 4 December 2024 from https://www.academia.edu/1090356/Adverb_use_in_EFL_student_writing_from_learner_dictionary_to_text_production

Plonsky, L., & Oswald, F. L. (2014). How big is "big"? Interpreting effect sizes in L 2 research. *Language Learning, 64*, 878–912.

Poole, R. (2018). *A guide to using corpora for English language learners.* Edinburgh University Press.

Quirk, R., Greenbaum, S., Leech, G., & Svartvik, J. (1972). *A grammar of contemporary English.* Longman.

Quirk, R., Greenbaum, S., Leech, G., & Svartvik, J. (1985). *A comprehensive grammar of the English language.* Longman.

Read, J. (1998). Validating a test to measure depth of vocabulary knowledge. In A. Kunnan (Ed.), *Validation in language assessment* (pp. 41–60). Lawrence Erlbaum Associates.

Rees, G. (2022). Using corpora to write dictionaries. In A. O'Keeffe & M. J. McCarthy (Eds.), *The Routledge handbook of corpus linguistics* (2nd ed., pp. 387–404). Routledge.

Reppen, R. (2010). *Using corpora in the language classroom.* Cambridge University Press.

Römer, U. (2011). Observations on the phraseology of academic writing: Local patterns — local meanings. In T. Herbst, S. Faulhaber, & P. Uhrig (Eds.), *The phraseological view of language: A tribute to John Sinclair.* Walter de Gruyter, 211–227.

Römer, U. (2019). A corpus perspective on the development of verb constructions in second language learners. *International Journal of Corpus Linguistics, 24*(3), 268–290.

Römer, U., & Berger, C. M. (2019). Observing the emergence of constructional knowledge: Verb patterns in German and Spanish learners of English at different proficiency levels. *Studies in Second Language Acquisition, 41*(5), 1089–1110.

Römer, U., O'Donnell, M. B., & Ellis, N. C. (2014). Second language learner knowledge of verb — argument constructions: Effects of language transfer and typology. *The Modern Language Journal, 98*(4), 952–975.

Römer, U., O'Donnell, M. B., & Ellis, N. C. (2015). Using COBUILD grammar patterns for a large-scale analysis of verb-argument constructions. In N. Groom, M. Charles, & S. John (Eds.), *Corpora, grammar and discourse: In honour of Susan Hunston* (pp. 43–72). John Benjamins.

Saeedakhtar, A., Bagerin, M., & Abdi, R. (2020). The effect of hands-on and hands-off data-driven learning on low-intermediate learners' verb-preposition collocations. *System, 91.*

Şahin Kızıl, A. (2023). Data-driven learning: English as a foreign language writing and complexity, accuracy and fluency measures. *Journal of Computer Assisted Language Learning, 39*(4), 1382–1395.

Samoudi, N., & Modirkhamene, S. (2020). Concordancing in writing pedagogy and CAF measures of writing. *International Review of Applied Linguistics in Language Teaching, 60,* 699–722.

Schäfer, R. (2021). Mixed-effects regression modeling. In M. Paquot & S. T. Gries (Eds.), *A practical handbook of corpus linguistics* (pp. 535–561). Springer.

Schmidt, R. (1990). The role of consciousness in second language learning. *Applied Linguistics, 11*(2), 129–158.

Schmidt, R. W. (2001). Attention. In P. Robinson (Ed.), *Cognition and second language instruction* (pp. 3–32). Cambridge University Press.

Schmitt, N., & Celce-Murcia, M. (2020). An overview of applied linguistics. In N. Schmitt & M. P. H. Rodgers (Eds.), *An introduction to applied linguistics* (3rd ed., pp. 1–15). Routledge.

Schmitt, N., & Rodgers, M. P. H. (Eds.), (2020). *An introduction to applied linguistics* (3rd ed.) Routledge.

Schmitt, N., Schmitt, D., & Clapham, C. (2001). Developing and exploring the behaviour of two new versions of the vocabulary levels test. *Language Testing, 18*(1), 55–88.

Schweinberger, M. (2020). How learner corpus research can inform language learning and teaching: An analysis of adjective amplification among L1 and L2 English speakers. *Australian Review of Applied Linguistics, 43*(2), 196–218.

Scott, M. (2008). Developing wordsmith. *International Journal of English Studies, 8*(1), 95-106.

Schwieter, J. W., & Benati, A. (2019). Introduction. In J. W. Schwieter & A. Benati (Eds.), *The Cambridge handbook of language learning* (pp. 1–10). Cambridge University Press.

Scott, M., & Tribble, C. (2006). *Textual patterns: Key words and corpus analysis in language education.* John Benjamins.

Sharwood Smith, M. (1981). Consciousness-raising and the second language learner. *Applied Linguistics, 2*, 159–68.

Shea, M. (2009). A corpus-based study of adverbial connectors in learner text. https://api.semanticscholar.org/CorpusID:60824289

Sinclair, J. (1991). *Corpus, concordance, collocation.* Oxford University Press.

Sinclair, J. (2004). *Trust the text: Language, corpus and discourse.* Routledge.

Sinclair, J. (2003). *Reading concordances.* Pearson.

Sripicharn, P. (2002). Evaluating data-driven learning: The use of classroom concordancing by Thai learners of English (Unpublished doctoral dissertation). University of Birmingham.

Staples, S., Egbert, J., Biber, D., & Gray, B. (2016). Academic writing development at the university level: Phrasal and clausal complexity across level of study, discipline, and genre. *Written Communication, 33*(2), 149–183.

Stefanowitsch, A., & Gries, S. T. (2003). Collostructions: Investigating the interaction of words and constructions. *International Journal of Corpus Linguistics, 8*(2), 209–243.

Stockwell, G. (2022). *Mobile assisted language learning: Concepts, contexts and challenges.* Cambridge University Press.

Stoll, S., & Schikowski, R. (2021). Child-language corpora. In M. Paquot & S. T. Gries (Eds.), *A practical handbook of corpus linguistics* (pp. 305–327). Springer.

Stormbom, C. (2018). Epicene pronouns in intermediate to advanced EFL writing. *International Journal of Learner Corpus Research, 4*(1), 1–22.

Stubbs, M. (2007). On texts, corpora and models of language. In M. Hoey, M. Mahlberg, M. Stubbs, & W. Teubert (Eds.), *Text, discourse and corpora: Theory and analysis* (pp. 127–161). Continuum.

Swain, M. (2006). Languaging, agency and collaboration in advanced second language proficiency. In H. Byrnes (Ed.), *Advanced language learning: The contribution of Halliday and Vygotsky* (pp. 95–108). Continuum.

Swales, J. M. (1990). *Genre analysis: English in academic and research settings.* Cambridge University Press.

Szudarski, P. (2017). *Corpus linguistics for vocabulary: A guide for research.* Routledge.

Szudarski, P. (2023). *Collocations, corpora and language learning.* Cambridge University Press.

Tan, M. (2005). Authentic language or language errors? Lessons from a learner corpus. *ELT Journal, 59*(2), 126–134.

Text Inspector. (2018). Online lexis analysis tool at textinspector.com. Retrieved on 29 September 2021 from textinspector.com

Therova, D. (2020). Review of academic word lists. *TESL-EJ, 24*(1). Retrievd on 4 December 2024 from https://tesl-ej.org/wordpress/issues/volume24/ej93/ej93a5/

Thewissen, J. (2013). Capturing L2 accuracy developmental patterns: Insights from an error-tagged EFL learner corpus. *The Modern Language Journal, 97*(S1), 77–101.

Todd, R. W. (2001). Induction from self-selected concordances and self-correction. *System, 29*(1), 91–102.

Tognini-Bonelli, E. (2010). Theoretical overview of the evolution of corpus linguistics. In A. O'Keeffe & M. J. McCarthy (Eds.), *The Routledge handbook of corpus linguistics* (pp. 14–28). Routledge.

Tomasello, M. (2003). *Constructing a language: A usage-based theory of language acquisition.* Harvard University Press.

Tono, Y. (2012). International Corpus of Crosslinguistic Interlanguage: Project overview and a case study on the acquisition of new verb co-occurrence patterns. In Y. Tono, M. Minegishi, & Y. Kawaguchi (Eds.), *Developmental and crosslinguistic perspectives in learner corpus research* (pp. 27–46). John Benjamins.

Tono, Y., & Díez-Bedmar, M. B. (2014). Focus on learner writing at the beginning and intermediate stages: The ICCI corpus. *International Journal of Corpus Linguistics, 19*(2), 163–177.

Tracy-Ventura, N., & Paquot, M. (2021). Second language acquisition and corpora: An overview. In N. Tracy-Ventura & M. Paquot (Eds.), *The Routledge handbook of second language acquisition and corpora* (pp. 1–8). Routledge.

Tracy-Ventura, N., Paquot, M., & Myles, F. (2021). The future of corpora in SLA. In N. Tracy-Ventura & M. Paquot (Eds.), *The Routledge handbook of second language acquisition and corpora* (pp. 409–424). Routledge.

Van Rooy, B., & Schäfer, L. (2002). The effect of learner errors on POS tag errors during automatic POS tagging. *Southern African Linguistics and Applied Language Studies, 20*(4), 325–335.

VanPatten, B. (1993). Grammar teaching for the acquisition-rich classroom. *Foreign Language Annals, 26*(4), 435–450.

VanPatten, B., & Benati, A. (2010). *Key terms in second language acquisition.* Continuum.

Vyatkina, N. (2013). Specific syntactic complexity: Developmental profiling of individuals based on an annotated learner corpus. *The Modern Language Journal, 97*(S1), 11–30.

Vyatkina, N. (2016). Data-driven learning of collocations: Learner performance, proficiency, and perceptions. *Language Learning & Technology, 20*(3), 159–179.

Vyatkina, N. (2023). *Corpus applications in language teaching and research: The case of data-driven learning of German.* Routledge.

Wang, Y. (2016). *The Idiom Principle and L1 influence. A contrastive learner-corpus study of delexical verb + noun collocations.* John Benjamins.

Widdowson, H. G. (1998). Context, community, and authentic language. *TESOL Quarterly, 32*(4), 705–716.

Wigglesworth, G., & Storch, N. (2009). Pair versus individual writing: Effects on fluency, complexity and accuracy. *Language Testing, 26*(3), 445–466.

Wong, W. (2005). *Input enhancement: From theory and research to the classroom.* McGraw-Hill.

Wulff, S. (2021). Usage-based approaches. In N. Tracy-Ventura & M. Paquot (Eds.), *The Routledge handbook of second language acquisition and corpora* (pp. 175–188). Routledge.

doi Xu, Q. (2015). Lexical priming effects of textbooks on EFL learners' use of 'give'. *English Language Teaching, 8*(10), 123–132.

doi Yilmaz, M. (2017). The effect of data-driven learning on EFL students' acquisition of lexicogrammatical patterns in EFL writing. *Eurasian Journal of Applied Linguistics, 3*(2), 75–88.

doi Yoon, H., & Hirvela, A. (2004). ESL student attitudes toward corpus use in L2 writing. *Journal of second language writing, 13*(4), 257–283.

doi Zalbidea, J. (2021). On the scope of output in SLA: Task modality, salience, L2 grammar noticing, and development. *Studies in Second Language Acquisition, 43*(1), 50–82.

doi Zare, J., & Aqajani Delavar, K. (2023). A data-driven learning focus on form approach to academic english lecture comprehension. *Applied Linguistics, 44*(3), 485–504.

doi Zhang, Z. (2022). Noticing in second language acquisition. *BCP Education & Psychology, 7*, 184–190.

Index

A

aboutness 145–146
Academic Collocations List (ACL) 135–136
academic language 12, 45, 125, 126
Academic Phrasal Lexicon 135, 136, 137
Academic Word List (AWL) 132, 135
academic writing 45, 72, 116, 120, 127–128
ACE corpus 49–51
ACL *see* Academic Collocations List
annotation 26, 31, 50, 51, 52, 53, 56, 57, 64, 69, 75, 104, 158, 161, 180, 182, 183, 184, 186
AntConc 2, 15, 16, 17, 18, 21, 23, 25, 26, 27, 80, 82, 92, 104, 108, 145
ArabCC (Learner Corpus of English Essays) 127–129 17, 128, 129
association measures 87, 89, 90, 92, 94, 95, 113, 119
automated speech recognition 50–51
automatic analysis 130, 140, 144
AWL *see* Academic Word List

B

BASE *see* British Academic Spoken English Corpus
BAWE *see* British Academic Written English Corpus
BNC *see* British National Corpus

British Academic Spoken English Corpus (BASE) 135
British Academic Written English Corpus (BAWE) 45, 125, 127, 128
British National Corpus (BNC) 11, 19, 20, 21, 22, 26, 29, 30, 42,

77, 79, 93, 94, 103, 107, 111, 112, 113, 122, 123, 125, 132, 133, 134, 135, 140, 141, 142, 168

C

CAF (Complexity, Accuracy Fluency) measures 154, 158, 159, 162, 163, 164, 172, 174
CALL (Computer Assisted Language Learning) 148–178
Cambridge Learner Corpus (CLC) 35, 37, 38, 42, 65, 77, 90, 91, 92, 104, 105, 111, 125, 128, 131, 139, 140
CCLE *see* Corpus of Chinese Learner English
CEDEL2 *see* Corpus Escrito del Español como L2
Chinese Learner English Corpus (CLEC) 106
CIA (Contrastive Interlanguage Analysis) 37, 38–41 42, 43, 45, 47, 49, 58, 61, 66, 76
CLARIN (Common Language Resources and Technology Infrastructure) 184, 185
CLAWS tagger 61, 64, 68, 77
CLC *see* Cambridge Learner Corpus
CLEC *see* Chinese Learner English Corpus
COCA *see* Corpus of Contemporary American English
collexeme analysis 100, 107, 108, 109, 110
Compleat Lexical Tutor see Lextutor
complexity analysis 13, 14, 42, 44, 79, 130, 159, 161–165
concordance 25, 26, 45, 77, 90, 98, 107, 108, 122, 123, 146, 150, 151, 154, 160, 173, 178
constructivism 171–172

conversation 9, 10, 12, 51, 77, 87, 124, 126
Corpus and Repository of Writing (CROW) 35
Corpus Escrito del Español como L2 (CEDEL2) 36, 65
Corpus of American Soap Operas 8, 150, 151
Corpus of American Soap Operas 150, 151
Corpus of Chinese Learner English (CCLE) 97
Corpus of Contemporary American English (COCA) 124, 125, 126, 128, 130, 132, 138 152, 160, 168
CQL (Corpus Query Language) 65, 104, 105, 108, 122
cross-sectional design 13, 14, 32, 33, 34, 36, 39, 40, 42, 43, 58, 91, 93
CROW *see* Corpus and Repository of Writing

D

developmental analysis 14, 42, 43, 44, 53, 72, 103, 178, 183
dictionary making 117, 118, 119, 120
dispersion 9, 23, 27, 100

E

EF-Cambridge Open Language Database (EFCAMDAT) 35, 43, 111
effect size 166–169
EGP *see* English Grammar Profile
English Grammar Profile (EGP) 131, 137, 138, 139, 140
English Vocabulary Profile (EVP) 31, 137, 138, 142
enTenTen corpus 118
ethical research 184–185

F

FLOB see Freiburg-LOB Corpus of British English

formulaic language see phraseology 85, 86, 87, 94, 120

Freiburg-BROWN Corpus of American English (FROWN) 97

Freiburg-LOB Corpus of British English (FLOB) 97

FROWN see Freiburg-BROWN Corpus of American English

G

GLCLC see Guangwai-Lancaster Chinese Learner Corpus

Grammaticality Judgment Correction Task (GJCT) 76, 80

Guangwai-Lancaster Chinese Learner Corpus (GLCLC) 36

I

ICCI see International Corpus of Crosslinguistic Interlanguage

ICE-GB see International Corpus of English

ICLE see International Corpus of Learner English

ICNALE see International Corpus Network of Asian Learners of English

idiom principle 86

International Corpus Network of Asian Learners of English (ICNALE) 35

International Corpus of Crosslinguistic Interlanguage (ICCI) 44

International Corpus of English (ICE-GB) 108

International Corpus of Learner English (ICLE) 34, 36, 39, 40, 43, 57, 58, 59, 61, 62, 68, 69, 70, 71, 72, 73, 83, 85, 97, 103

interpretability hypothesis 76, 80

IRIS 185

K

keyness 29, 30

keyword analysis 2, 29–30, 117, 145–147, 175

L

Learner Corpus of English Essays see ArabCC

Lexical Tutorsee Lextutor

Lextutor 131–136

LINDSEI see Louvain International Database of Learner English

LOCCLI see Longitudinal Corpus of Chinese Learners of Italian

LOCNEC see Louvain Corpus of Native English Conversations

LOCNESS see Louvain Corpus of Native English Essays

log-likelihood 88, 114, 145

logDice 89–92, 119

LONGDALE see LONGitudinal Database of Learner English

Longitudinal Corpus of Chinese Learners of Italian (LOCCLI) 36

LONGitudinal Database of Learner English (LONGDALE) 35

longitudinal design 13, 14, 32, 33, 35, 36, 42, 43, 44, 49, 72, 91, 93, 94, 95, 174, 180

Louvain Corpus of Native English Conversations (LOCNEC) 41, 70, 72

Louvain Corpus of Native English Essays (LOCNESS) 39, 40, 61, 62, 70, 72, 74, 75, 76, 103

Louvain International Database of Learner English (LINDSEI) 34, 39, 40, 41, 52, 70, 72

M

Macedonian English Learner Corpus (MELC) 76, 79

manual analysis 12, 44, 51, 57

MELC see Macedonian English Learner Corpus

MI see mutual information

MI score 90–93

Michigan Corpus of Upper-Level Student Papers (MICUSP) 125, 126, 128, 130, 160

MICUSP see Michigan Corpus of Upper-Level Student Papers

Movie Corpus 8, 14

multi-word units (MWUs) 16, 21, 23, 24, 27, 28, 30, 49, 51, 86, 113, 119, 120, 125, 127, 138, 181

mutual information (MI) 89–93, 112–113, 119

MWUs see multi-word units

N

n-grams 21, 23, 92, 114, 119, 127, 135, 144

Natural Language Processing (NLP) 43, 64, 68, 82, 185

NAWL see New Academic Word List

New Academic Word List (NAWL) 146

O

OCAE see Oxford Corpus of Academic English

Open Cambridge Learner Corpus 35, 37, 38, 65, 77, 90, 91, 92, 104, 105, 125, 128

open-choice principle 86

overuse (see also underuse) 39, 62, 70, 71, 72, 73, 87, 126, 181

Oxford Academic Phrasal Lexicon 135, 136, 137

Oxford Corpus of Academic English (OCAE) 135

P

PHRASal Expressions List (PHRASE List) 134, 135, 137

PHRASE List see PHRASal Expressions List

phraseology 40, 85–99, 103, 186

pragmatic analysis 3, 10, 15, 40, 41, 43, 87, 182, 183

principle of total accountability 121, 123

proficiency 13, 16, 30, 32, 33- 38, 42–45, 46, 48–50, 59, 72, 111, 130, 131, 140, 143, 144, 145, 165, 168, 176, 177, 178, 181, 183, 185

pseudo-longitudinal design   32,
   33

R
reference corpus   29, 30, 36, 71,
   145, 146
representativeness   4, 8, 9, 11, 12,
   14, 16, 32, 40, 46, 48, 53, 120,
   145, 180, 183
research design   3, 31, 32, 48, 58,
   71, 84, 85, 86, 88, 91, 92, 93, 94,
   149, 172, 175, 185
research questions and corpus
   design   1, 36, 40, 46, 52, 53, 63,
   75, 80, 127, 149, 155, 159, 163,
   174, 175, 176, 177, 178, 179, 181

S
Second Language Acquisition
   (SLA)   4, 10, 11, 13, 31, 42–46,
   53, 58–59, 149, 170–178, 180–182
Sentence Transitions List   135,
   137
SKELC   74
SKELL   152, 153
Sketch Engine   2, 8, 64, 65, 66, 67,
   68, 77, 80, 82, 83, 87, 88, 89, 90,

92, 104,105, 119, 120, 127, 128,
   145, 152
Sociocultural theory   172–174

T
T-score   89–94
TAALES *see* Tool for the
   Automatic Analysis of Lexical
   Sophistication
TAASSC *see* Tool for the
   Automatic Analysis of
   Syntactic Sophistication and
   Complexity
TagAnt   80, 81
taggers   61, 63, 65, 66, 68, 69, 77
teacher mediation   172, 173, 174,
   176
Text inspector   131, 138. 140–144
TLC *see* Trinity Lancaster
   Corpus
tokenisation   63
*Tool for the Automatic Analysis of
   Lexical Sophistication*
   (TAALES)   131, 144, 145, 147
*Tool for the Automatic Analysis of
   Syntactic Sophistication and
   Complexity* (TAASSC)   44

transcription   31, 46, 50, 51, 52, 66
Trinity Lancaster Corpus
   (TLC)   34

U
underuse (*see also* overuse)   39,
   41,62, 70, 71, 72, 73, 87, 126, 181
Uppsala Student English Corpus
   (USE)   97
usage-based theory   42, 92, 94,
   111, 174, 177, 178, 179, 181, 182,
   183
USE *see* Uppsala Student English
   Corpus

V
verb-argument constructions
   (VACs)   44, 100, 107, 110

W
WordSmith Tools   45

Z
zipfian distribution   111